"The book, a blend of stand-up-and-cheer triumphs and bittersweet cautionary tales, is a revelation, and it is a must-read for anyone curious about not just women's soccer, but the beautiful game."
The Globe and Mail

"A big, stunning masterpiece"
Allison Lee, *The Equalizer*

"A startlingly good book. These are moving, uplifting stories from around the world – what top soccer is like when there's no money or fame in it and you just do it for love."
Simon Kuper, author of *Soccernomics*

"Gwendolyn is the master at finding incredible soccer stories – stories that need to be heard – and telling them in a way that leaves you begging for more."
Julie Foudy, ESPN, former USWNT captain

"Oxenham is one of my favorite soccer writers; she connects on a deeply human level with the people who are the soul of the global game."
Grant Wahl, *Sports Illustrated* senior writer, Fox Sports TV

"A terrific collection of stories of the adventures undertaken and the struggles faced by players around the world."
Guardian, 'The best books on sport, 2017'

"What a fine thing that a superb writer has found these 'untold stories' … and remedied that situation."
The Boston Globe, 'The best books of 2017'

"Oxenham understands a good sports story must work as a mirror to reflect the world around it. And, like *Friday Night Lights* or *Seabiscuit*, *Under the Lights and In the Dark* does just that ... This work is truly a testament to women's soccer and women in sports."
Washington Independent Review of Books

"You think major challenges exist for female players here? Wait until you read what it's like in the rest of the world in this eye-opening account by a former player and well-traveled writer."
Washington Post

"An eye-opening, cohesive collection of fascinating stories that will help bring women's soccer to the next level."
Library Journal

"One of the most compelling sports books I have ever read."
Female Coaching Network

"The twelve-year-old girl reading this as part of her English homework will be as engrossed as the 60-year-old who never dreamt that these things could happen to a female soccer player. That's a fantastic skill to have as a writer."
Gorey Guardian

UNDER
THE LIGHTS
AND IN
THE DARK

UNDER THE LIGHTS AND IN THE DARK

Untold Stories of Women's Soccer

GWENDOLYN OXENHAM

ICON

First published in the UK in 2017
by Icon Books Ltd, Omnibus Business Centre,
39–41 North Road, London N7 9DP
email: info@iconbooks.com
www.iconbooks.com

This edition published in the UK in 2018 by Icon Books Ltd

Sold in the UK, Europe and Asia
by Faber & Faber Ltd, Bloomsbury House,
74–77 Great Russell Street,
London WC1B 3DA or their agents

Distributed in the UK, Europe and Asia
by Grantham Book Services, Trent Road, Grantham NG31 7XQ

Distributed in the USA
by Publishers Group West,
1700 Fourth Street, Berkeley, CA 94710

Distributed in Australia and New Zealand
by Allen & Unwin Pty Ltd,
PO Box 8500, 83 Alexander Street,
Crows Nest, NSW 2065

Distributed in South Africa
by Jonathan Ball, Office B4, The District,
41 Sir Lowry Road, Woodstock 7925

Distributed in India by Penguin Books India,
7th Floor, Infinity Tower – C, DLF Cyber City,
Gurgaon 122002, Haryana

Distributed in Canada by Publishers Group Canada,
76 Stafford Street, Unit 300
Toronto, Ontario M6J 2S1

ISBN 978-178578-319-7

Text copyright © 2017 Gwendolyn Oxenham

The author has asserted her moral rights.

Every effort has been made to contact the copyright holders of the material
reproduced in this book. If any have been inadvertently overlooked, the
publisher will be pleased to make acknowledgment on future editions if notified.

No part of this book may be reproduced in any form, or by any
means, without prior permission in writing from the publisher.

Typeset in Chaparral by Marie Doherty

Printed and bound in the UK
by Clays Ltd, St Ives plc

To the players: the heroes of the past who made the stories of this generation possible; and the heroes of the present who shape the game for tomorrow

Contents

ABOUT THE AUTHOR

Gwendolyn Oxenham is the author of *Finding the Game: Three Years, Twenty-five Countries and the Search for Pickup Soccer* (St Martin's Press) and the director of *Pelada*, a documentary centered on the global game. She has written for *The Atlantic*, *Sports Illustrated*, and *Slate*. A Duke University soccer alum, she received her MFA in creative writing from the University of Notre Dame. She lives in Dana Point, California with her husband and two sons.

Introduction

IN JULY OF 2004, I stood with my teammate on the side of a dirt road in Itanhaém, Brazil, holding out my thumb, attempting to hitchhike to professional *futebol* practice. We played for Santos FC, the most storied club in Brazil, and this was our daily routine: Karen batted at my thumb and mumbled at me in Portuguese, never satisfied with my technique. A two-toned car with missing hubcaps slowed down and honked (you learn quickly that the nice cars pass you by, but the sketchier ones are always willing to stop). We took off after the car, running and laughing, yelling, "*Obrigada!*", having saved ourselves the 45-minute walk to the field. Karen sat in the front seat with her elbows propped on her knees and kept up continuous chatter with the driver, stopping only to wave victoriously as we passed teammates still on foot. I had learned that if I kept my mouth shut I could pass for Brazilian. When the driver looked questioningly into the rear-view mirror at the mute girl in the back, Karen slung her thumb at me and said, matter-of-factly, "*Americana*." As Karen went back to chatting, I sat on the animal-fur-covered backseat and considered my summer.

One year earlier, I had graduated from college, the same year the US professional league folded. I went to grad school and found a new life. But on a snowy morning in South Bend, Indiana, I received an email with the subject line: PROFESSIONAL BRAZILIAN TEAM LOOKING FOR AMERICAN GOALSCORER. I opened it and stared at the text – live in a bungalow on the beach, play for Santos Futebol Clube – and then I typed, "I'm a forward," even though I was a retired outside mid who almost never scored goals. One month later I was on a plane to São Paulo. I wouldn't get paid – few did. I didn't care. All my life I'd grown up on Brazilian *futebol* folklore. There was no way I could pass up the chance to play for Santos, home of Pelé himself.

I spoke no Portuguese; my teammates spoke no English. My summer was an incredible, wordless haze: we trained twice a day, six to seven hours. Sometimes a horse grazed on the grass at midfield. My teammates could juggle the ball on their shins. We often trained barefoot on the beach, running plyometrics over cardboard hurdles. When the Brazilian winters dumped too much rain on the field and there were high tides at the beach, we ran sprints on the main highway, occupying one lane, passing cars dousing us with water. After training we walked home slowly. When it was warm enough, we jumped in the ocean – even Cris, our six-foot-tall keeper who did not know how to swim and who once had to be rescued but who kept going in anyway. Back in our dorms, we ate rice and beans for dinner. In the alley behind our rooms, we washed our jerseys by hand in the concrete basins as my teammates tried to teach me to samba. At night, on our bunk beds, we passed back and forth my Portuguese–English dictionary. I learned about their lives. They came from all over Brazil, from the highlands of the Northeast to a tiny island without cars. They had all learned to play on the street with the boys, and most had a familiar dream: to one day make the national team.

THIS GLIMPSE INTO the life of a Brazilian *futebol* player lasted for only one season, but it made me wonder what the women's game looked like in the rest of the world. When I watched the Women's World Cup on television, I knew nothing about the majority of the teams taking part. What were their lives like? You hear a lot about "inequality" in women's soccer – what are the stories that grow out of that broad term?

I wanted to find out what it means to be a top women's player, not just in the United States, where I live, but everywhere, from Nigeria to Russia. I often tried to web my way around the world via teammates of my former teammates, which means that many of the stories I found have an American tie (a tie that often runs through Portland, the heartbeat of women's soccer in the United States). Dozens of players across the world shared their stories and their time. Whether from Liverpool or Lagos, Tokyo or Kabul, Kingston or Paris, here's one thing that was always true: at an early age, they found the game and held on, driven neither by money nor fame – only the desire to be great. Here are their stories.

La Gringa

FEBRUARY 2016, AT 8.15 on a Friday night in a rented high school gym in Queens, New York, two teams of Latino men get ready to play futsal – a fast-paced, small-sided version of soccer. The fans lean against the wall, empanadas in hand, eyes on the court, eyes on the white girl – *la gringa* – who warms up alongside the men.

Though Allie Long gives off no signs of being anything but at ease, as a spectator, you can't help be nervous for her – just by nature of sheer contrast: the men warming up are burly and brutish, all hairy legs and tattooed forearms. Some have their hands tucked beneath the waistbands of their shorts, like at any second they will reach down and jostle their balls. Their stretches are choppy and brusque, aggressive bursts of toe touching. And though the game has not yet started, they already smell like sweat.

Then there's Long: the gym lights glint off her blonde ponytail. She arrives at the court wearing a zip-up, cowl-neck hoodie. A forest green infinity scarf is slung over the top, looking effortlessly glamorous. She has on black Lycra leggings and Nike sneakers with neon yellow mesh. She strips off several top layers until she is down to a t-shirt, an oversized men's v-neck that somehow makes her seem all the more feminine.

When the referee catches sight of her, he does a double-take, head whipping back in her direction. Incredulous, he says, "Are *you* going to play?" When she nods, he pushes for further clarification:

"With *them*?" he asks, gesturing to the men surrounding him. Again, Long nods.

In high school gyms across Queens, the Bronx, Brooklyn, and Manhattan, immigrant men from all over the world play for money in cutthroat futsal leagues, games often stretching until three in the morning. In most of those gyms, Long is a familiar face, having played in these leagues for the past four years. But P.S. 130 is one of the few gyms and leagues she has not yet played in. Her usual Friday night team is currently in Vegas, playing for a $36,000 pot (which they will win). Long, in training, always in training, needed a game, and her friend Diego invited her to play with his team of Argentines.

Long briefly exits the gym, presumably to change out of her leggings. The group of Ecuadorians she'll be playing against stand in a huddle and talk about her in Spanish, every sentence peppered with *gringa* or *rubia* ("blonde girl").

When Long returns, she is wearing Paris Saint-Germain soccer shorts. While it's common practice for players to don the shorts of the professional team they support, often bought in gift shops or ordered on the internet, Allie's shorts are *actual* Paris Saint-Germain shorts. In 2014, she was the starting center midfielder for the women's side.

Long hurriedly pulls on crew socks, tiny shinguards, and turf shoes. She tugs her team's Argentine jersey over the top of her t-shirt. She then removes the t-shirt, slipping it out of the head hole – a deft move she's clearly done thousands of times.

Allie doesn't start, instead stretching along the sideline as the game begins. The game falls into its rhythm: it is fast-paced and blunt, heavy bodies lurching on the basketball court, nearly clumsy-looking, were it not for the grace with which they ping the ball: it's almost all one-touch, zipping from one player to the next, each player attuned to the others.

Five minutes into the game, the spectators are chanting, "*Cambio Rubia, Cambio Rubia*" – sub in the blonde girl, sub in the blonde girl.

Their wish is granted: Allie subs in, woven into the fabric of the game – bodies moving in, moving away, constantly in flux. She shows no signs of being intimidated – she doesn't let herself hide, doesn't drift to the side or fade into the background. She's constantly pushing to make herself available. Within ten minutes, she scores two goals and sets up three others.

The audience response isn't gaudy – they don't scream and laugh, although that does frequently happen. It is only a collective intake of breath, small sounds of appreciation and approval – the same noise they make when any other player does something beautiful.

When the whistle blows, Long gathers her stuff and heads out, holding her bag in one hand, a napkin-wrapped empanada in the other. She climbs into a silver Lexus – off to her next game.

• • •

ALLIE LONG IS a professional soccer player for the Portland Thorns. She is a contender for the United States national team. Four times, she had worn the United States national team jersey and represented her country – but she had never done it when it mattered; she had never played in the World Cup or the Olympics or in any international tournament with stakes. That is what she wants more than anything else – and to do that, to get there, she plays in underground men's leagues across New York, sometimes playing four or five games a night during the offseason. "It is hands down the best training I get," says Long as she starts her car and inches out of her curbside parking spot. "Anybody can train – but these games are different – I wanted to do something I knew no one else was doing."

Nothing about these games is light-hearted. There's both prize money and pride on the line. Teams are run by community kingpins who own restaurants or construction companies or some other undisclosed operation. Each team owner wants to have the best team in the neighborhood – so they're willing to shell out cash for the best players. In no way is Long the only one to have played pro; many of the men have played in different tiers of professional leagues all around the world. Team managers put in calls to the ringers: "I'll give you $100 to play for my team on Thursday night." By moving from game to game, a good player can make up to $800 a night – which is more than they make in their day jobs as construction workers and dishwashers. (The fans, too, stand to make money – come play-off time, there is rampant betting – money passed from hand to hand in the crowds that surround the court.) In the 2015 National Women's Soccer League (NWSL), for the six-month season, the starting salary was $6,842. An NYC men's league ringer can make more than that in two weeks.

Long, as a star of the NWSL, makes more toward the top of the salary range – $37,800. For her, the money is not the prime draw of the NY leagues – it's the intensity level the money brings with it. "I love the pressure. I love that I have to perform," says Long.

In France, the league was very unbalanced – two or three teams significantly better than the rest – and her Paris side would win games by six goals. Long sometimes wouldn't break a sweat. That doesn't happen here. Here, when it's four against four, plus keepers, you can't get lost. Every touch counts. You lose the ball or get stripped or play the ball poorly, and someone's scoring against your team, and there's no question whose fault it is. When you're the girl – when the whole gym is looking at you to see whether you stack up, you can't let that happen. And you know – always

• 4 •

you know – what they'll say if your team loses: that it's because of the girl.

• • •

REWIND TO SUMMER 2008. Allie Long was a University of North Carolina soccer player. To train for her senior season, her long-time coach Adrian Gaitan invited her to train with his men's semi-pro team. Her first day out, they played small-sided games. Allie's team lost three games in a row. As her team stood in line, one guy said, "Why the hell do we keep losing?" A guy from the other team – the winning team – jogged by and called out, "It's because you've got the girl on your team."

Allie stood there, pissed, mind-blowingly pissed – it was *not* because of her. She stared at the back of the kid's buzzed head, thinking, *That mother-fer. I hate that kid. I really hate that kid.* He turned back toward her and grinned. He winked, like, *I don't mean that. I'm just saying that to get you worked up.* But the wink didn't make it better. *Does he think this is a joke?* Long thought. *This is not a fucking joke.*

The guy taunting her was Jose Batista, known to most as Bati. Half-Colombian, half-Brazilian, he's always joking, always smiling. He's funny, and with every practice Allie became more aware of that. She'd tell herself, "Don't laugh at him. You hate him." But he broke her down, joke by joke, play by play. He wasn't the machismo-brimming asshole she thought he was, even if she still got angry when thinking about that first joke. He was the first one to tease – to say the one thing he knew would piss her off the most – but he was also the first to recognize her contributions. And beyond a smile that was impossible not to notice, he was so smooth on the ball, graceful and calm. He could break down a defense with one pass, and he was the type who had the audacity to chip a penalty kick up the middle no matter how much was at stake. It was undeniably attractive.

They gravitated toward one another: one night Bati and his friend Gustavo, "Goo," came out to Long Island to see her – "The Jungle" they called it, so different from the Queens neighborhood where Bati grew up. ("I'm a city boy – I remember looking around – all the nice houses, the open space, the fact that you had to have a car – and being like, what is this place?" says Bati.) Then Allie and Bati started training together outside of practice, hitting long balls, doing one-v-ones, talking shit, learning each other's tendencies. They understood each other and played off of one another – on the field and off of it.

When Long left for her senior year at UNC, Bati and Goo regularly made the eight-hour drive down to see her. He understood what a big part of her UNC was. He knew about the UNC obsession she'd had as a kid – how she'd owned the UNC *Dynasty* DVD box set, how she'd read long-time UNC coach Anson Dorrance's book, *The Vision of a Champion*. He knew the only reason why she'd gone to Penn State her freshman year was because she didn't think she could possibly be good enough for UNC, and that her transfer to UNC her junior year was the best decision she'd ever made. So, he and Goo made the trek to Fetzer Field, two of the 6,000 powder-blue wearing fans rooting for Allie.

And whenever Long was back in New York, she came to Bati's futsal games – which were as big a part of Bati as UNC was a part of her. His father, a Brazilian, had played in these leagues 30 years earlier. Bati had been coming to these games since he was born; he and his brother grew up chasing a ball through the school hallways. When he was sixteen, his dad decided he was ready to play with the men.

Allie's first time out to watch, she got sucked in – wowed by the pace, the intensity. Bati's "crew," as Long refers to them, was unreal: there was Mohammad Mashriqi, who plays for the Afghanistan national team. And Alan, who would eventually play his way onto the US national futsal team. There was Bati's child-hood friend, Mike Palacio, who played a year for the New York Red Bulls. They played the kind of soccer that made you better just by witnessing it – Allie went to every game she could. But it was an odd feeling to sit there in street clothes – to be the one blonde girl in the stands, to have nobody know that she too could play. It wasn't long before she started imagining herself out there. The game was so fast – kind of terrifyingly fast – and she wasn't sure she could keep up. But as soon as that question was in her mind, that was it: playing out there was all she could think about.

For two seasons, Bati fended Allie off. "Not that he's the boss of me or anything," Allie clarifies. But with thousands of dollars at stake, fights break out every night and the play gets dirty. "These guys have nothing to lose. Allie's got everything to lose," said Bati.

But while she was training for her first season as a profes-sional soccer player, drafted to the Washington Spirit, Allie played in Bati's pickup games – games without anything on the line. Always, she played well. The guys out there started saying it: "Dude, you should bring her out." Finally Bati and his pickup friends made a new futsal team and Allie was on the roster. Bati was nervous about it. It wasn't just the fear of injury – "He wanted to know I could handle myself," says Long. He never quite said that directly, but as they climbed out of the car at their first game, he just looked at her and said, "You know you have to play sick right?"

That first game, she was nervous, shy – so determined to prove she could hang. At the beginning, she one-timed every ball. And then, once her credibility and confidence built up, occasionally, she allowed herself to take a risk. Initially defenders took her too lightly – a patronizing half-smile on their face – like, *is this serious?*

It was only after she burned them that they started to play for real. That first night, the gym went wild for her – throwing things onto the court, yelling "*La Gringa, La Gringa.*"

Soon Bati's phone kept ringing for Allie. The first time a team manager called and offered to pay her $80 to come out, Allie and Bati assumed he must be calling for her to play in one of the few women's leagues. But when they got out there, it was all men; like any other ringer, they'd pay her to play. Not only was she good, she also filled the gyms in a way that other players hadn't: fans pay a $4 admission and on nights she played, people just kept streaming in the door, wanting to see *la rubia, la blanquita.*

It wasn't immediate acceptance from everyone – especially from the guys she beat. "Nobody wants to get embarrassed," says one of the guys she plays against, "and almost always, that's exactly what happens." One guy got in her face, yelled, "*Ir a jugar con sus muñecas!*" and then, to make sure she got it, he sputtered it out in English, "Go play with your dolls!" And, sure, there are sometimes jokes. There was the one night when she fell hard into the crowd of men and they drunkenly yelled in español, "Touch her ass! Touch her ass!" (When she responded in Spanish – "I know what you are saying," they erupted in chastened laughter.) But more than jokes, there is acceptance, inclusion – a palpable, wholesale, gym-wide shift in attitude.

Like any women's player, Long has seen the internet comments, how every article about women's soccer ends with anonymous comments that become a cesspool of hate – how it's boring, how the women's pro league will never survive because there is no audience, no one cares, no one wants to watch. But Long exists in two worlds where that's not true – in Portland, where the Thorns attract more fans than some men's MLS teams, and here – where these men from machismo-rich cultures are glad to have her.

"They love her," says Bati. "Now, when I come out to games, people don't even say hi to me. They just ask me, 'Where's my *gringa*?'"

• • •

LIKE BATI, ALLIE inherited the game – her great uncle, Croatian, is a football diehard, yet another player who, according to family folklore, got close to making the national team. He started the first girls club in Long Island, and Barb, Allie's mom, grew up playing for it. This was no rudimentary bumble ball, and this wasn't a flash-in-the-pan chapter of Barb's life: Barb has played her entire life. To Allie, this meant her mother was cooler than the other moms. Mother and daughter played together on the strip of road in front of Allie's childhood home – at age six, at age fifteen, at every age, sending balls back and forth, counting, always keeping track. Even now, they play together. Two days before I followed Allie around Queens, Allie and her mom played in a Long Island pickup game. Barb was never the talent that her daughter is, but she's the kind of player you can trust – today, at 52, she's still an orchestrator who finds and sets up her teammates. According to Allie's father, his daughter's intuitive awareness of the game, which she's had since she was a kid, comes from her mother. "And her looks – she got her mom's beauty," he adds, Long Island accent thick. "But her ferocity, her competitiveness, her stubbornness – she got that from me."

Mr. Long is 6'2" and 250 pounds. His forehead looks like that of Frankenstein's monster thanks to the scars from 60 plus stitches. His nose has been busted too many times to remember. He's had multiple knee operations, and he's fresh off of shoulder cuff surgery. So far, no injury has kept him away from the game he loves – competitive men's rugby. "I'm a rough and tumble kind of guy; I like to mix it up," he says. "The first time I caught sight of it – [American] football practice without the pads – I thought, That's for me, I like to kick ass." He's plays on competitive club teams and has traveled all over the world for rugby. He's never made any money from it. He just does it because he loves to compete. At 60, he's still going and will continue to play as long as his body holds up. (And Mr. Long seems to have different standards than most on what "holding up" consists of.) Like his daughter, he does not quit.

• • •

EN ROUTE TO her next game, Allie drives past laundromats, liquor stores, and grocery stores with pictures of giant guinea pigs in the windows. It is not easy driving. She weaves through Queens traffic, makes cross-traffic turns, merges into small spaces on busy streets, all the while speaking steadily and passionately with her Long Island accent, not quite as heavy as her father's. She wants me to know about everybody – she tells me about the best player she's ever played with, a kid dubbed "Messi," a tiny teenager who disappeared for a couple years when he got sent to juvie. "There are so many guys who are just incredible – *incredible*," she says, "and they never make it! I want to, like, start a club, a program or nonprofit or something, for all these guys. I don't know what I would call it, like, 'Guys Who Don't Get a Shot – Now You Do,'" she says.

Bati is one guy who did get a shot – in and out of US national teams, he was clearly talented. His father told him, "Go to Brazil." The mecca of *futebol*, the country where the game will exist forever in our imagination as the game at its most beautiful. When he was eighteen, he went for it: he tried out for Atlético Mineiro in Belo Horizonte and he landed a year-long contract. The American who grew up in Queens entered an entirely different world. Gone were the first-world niceties and the easy city life. Now he was living in a six-by-six-foot room in 100-degree weather, with no air conditioning, no cable, no internet – nothing but his Nokia cellphone.

The older Brazilians didn't go easy on the new American kid. No one spoke to him – not a word, not in the cafeteria, not in the locker room, nowhere. They'd throw all his clothes in the shower; they'd cut through the leather on his cleats. On the Nokia, he'd call his Colombian mother. "Mom, I can't do this, I can't make it here. Mom, send me new cleats." He thought it was just freshman hazing – he told himself he just had to get through it but eventually he broke. When his Colombian mother arrived in Brazil, she wanted to take her baby home. It's not hard to imagine her scooping him up in her arms.

It is his biggest regret in life. His father didn't talk to him for two years.

Some decisions seem smaller over time – less impactful on a life's eventual trajectory – but this decision wasn't like that. Having played professionally, however briefly, Bati was no longer eligible to play Division 1 soccer in the States. He played Division 3 and earned All-American honors, but nobody cared. "He just completely fell off the map," says Long.

Allie, who relays the story, shakes her head as she looks over her shoulder, merging into the next lane. She hurts for him. "I want to go back in time, I want to make him stay. I never would've let him go home." It's hard for her to imagine that he will never get another shot.

• • •

WE ARRIVE AT Lawrence High School on the other side of Queens. The gym is packed and loud, hundreds sitting in the bleachers behind the netted court. Growing up in a nearly all-white town in Long Island, this world that blooms up around the court is a big part of what Allie loves. Latin rap music blares out of the speaker.

Men chant and play drums. The smell of ground beef emanates from the pop-up kitchen/card table in the back of the gym, where tacos and enchiladas cook on portable burners. Families sit court-side, little boys propped up on their fathers' shoulders, little girls playing with Barbies and braiding hair, and, occasionally, taking note of Allie.

As we walk through the crowd, Long points people out. In whichever gym you enter, there are players whose whispered reputations follow them: that guy got a tryout with the Seattle Sounders. That guy played for Colombia in the '94 World Cup. Long stops to hug a guy she identifies to me as "Fat Ronaldo" – he is not *the* Fat Ronaldo, but when video footage of him nutmegging a player got uploaded to YouTube, that's who everyone mistook him for. "Fat Ronaldo's still Got it" ran one caption. The clip got over one million views.

Fat Ronaldo, also called Il Fenomeno, is one of the ringers who bounces from game to game. On any given week, he makes $600–700 a night.

"I'm a paid whore," he says, grinning, as Allie and I stand next to him.

Fat Ronaldo turns to Allie, redirects the subject back to her: "What's the deal? Why aren't you in camp?"

Allie's first invite to the national team came in 2010, when she was 23. First day of camp, she tweaked her MCL and the dream turned nightmare. Stubborn, unwilling to get that close and then have to sit on the sideline, she tried to play through it. It didn't work: she was there, she could taste it, she rubbed shoulders with her heroes – but it was yanked away. She didn't get invited back for four years.

In May of 2014, Allie again got the call-up. This time she played in her first national team game and did well, getting her first assist in her third appearance, against France. She stayed on the national team radar – in January of 2015, ahead of the Canada World Cup, she again got called in. She was in the hunt, she was so close.

At the end of camp, head coach Jill Ellis told Long that she was no longer considering her for the World Cup. Long cried the whole plane ride home.

A year later, Ellis called in 26 players to the first residency camp of 2016, to compete for one of eighteen spots for the Olympic team. Since the US won the 2015 World Cup, there had been unexpected pregnancies, unexpected retirements, unexpected injuries – and the roster that once looked on lockdown seemed wide open. Of the 26 players called into camp, there were ten new faces. Allie wasn't one of them. Bati was the one who broke the news to Allie, quietly, directly: "The roster was announced. You weren't on it."

Long stands next to Fat Ronaldo and her response has no bitter undertones. She is positive, upbeat, and understanding. "Jill needs to get a look at some of the younger girls – you know, gotta give them a shot, gotta see what they can do."

There's Mallory Pugh – seventeen-year-old high school sensation. And there's Lindsey Horan, the twenty-year-old who was the first US women's player to skip college and go straight to the pros, signing for Paris Saint-Germain for a reported six-figure salary. Horan plays the same position as Long.

"Does this mean you're out of the Olympic picture?" Ronaldo asks.

"Not for sure," Allie says. Allie got an email from the team general manager, telling her to make sure all her paperwork was filled out for her Brazilian visa – just in case. She knows that she can't hang her hat on that – a good 30 or so players probably got that email. She knows that if she had a good shot, she'd be in camp. But that email meant it wasn't impossible.

Ronaldo nods sagely. "Well, you'll get your chance. And when you get in there, you gotta pull out all the stops – do a roundhouse or a couple of rainbows if you have to. Do whatever you need to do."

Long smiles, shakes her head. "Nah, I'm a center midfielder – I just gotta keep it simple. Like Busquets." Sergio Busquets is defensive center midfielder for Barcelona, Long's favorite team.

"But Busquets is a hitter – you don't strike me as a hitter."

"Oh I can hit," she says, smiling, running her hand through her ponytail. "Hitter" refers to the hard-hitting tackles that mark both Busquets and Long's style of play. As defensive-mids, they snuff out attacks, bearing down upon anyone who tries to move through their midfield.

Many of the guys Allie plays with and against inquire about the national team – Allie is their girl and they want it for her. They follow her games for Portland, texting her when she scores, when she wins, when she loses. They know that she was only a hairs-breadth away from making the World Cup team. And they know that she played her 2015 pro season with something to prove: that she finished as the second leading scorer in the women's pro league, that she was named the Thorns MVP. When she didn't get called into the January 2016 camp, some were aghast and indignant, sure she'd been wronged. (One guy said, "Who ain't giving you a fair look? You need me to take out the coach?") Others, like Ronaldo, are just encouraging, administering advice: just keep at it, just keep doing what you're doing.

• • •

AT 10.30PM, ALLIE's next game begins. This time she's playing against women. While she has played with the best women in the world, that's not what tonight looks like. This league is composed of women who come from countries where females simply do not play. Now, in the United States – a country where women's soccer is a thing – they've picked up the game late in their lives and it shows: the level is significantly lower than that of the men.

Allie has too much class to say so directly, but this is one game she's not excited to play in. She's doing it because $100 for a 30-minute game is too good to say no to, and because she's not a snob – she's not going to be the girl who thinks she's too good to play with other girls. Plus, she knows she grew up with every opportunity; the rest of these women did not. She recognizes that there's something important in these games – these games are progress.

At this gym, each team wears replica jerseys of a pro team. The team Allie is playing for is wearing Orlando Pride jerseys, the new NWSL team. She has me snap a picture of her holding out the Orlando emblem and raising her eyebrow, to send to Alex Morgan, US national team star forward. Morgan, Long's best friend and future maid of honor, played with Allie in Portland, but will play the 2016 season for Orlando. While Allie is caught up in the irony of the front of her jersey, I'm drawn to the back, where REAL LATINAS is bannered in all-caps across her shoulders, her blonde ponytail bouncing across the letters.

As the game starts, again what you notice is the contrast. Beyond the juxtaposition of Allie's fair features with every-one else's dark ones, it's the body types: Allie is a machine; the other players aren't. Their bodies are normal-looking, some twiggy, some curvy, none subjected to the two-a-day, sometimes three-a-day workouts that Allie's is. She's in the best shape of her life. It's fitness and speed training in the morning, games at night – that week, Allie played in two games on Tuesday night, three games on Wednesday, two on Thursday and two tonight. "If that phone call comes, I'm going to be ready," says Long.

In this game, Allie's face looks different than in the last – not as charged, not as alive. Allie's team goes down 2–0 in the first five minutes. Allie's face is 100 per cent expressionless. Long doesn't like to lose, and she definitely doesn't like to lose to players who are nowhere near as good as she is.

Thirty seconds later, Long nutmegs a player, and it's a nasty one – with her sole, she rolls it clean through the middle of the charging defender's legs. The entire, packed gym responds: groans, whistles, thigh slaps. That's the moment the other team develops a vendetta against Allie. They don't like her – this blonde girl who isn't around half the time but then comes in and tries to steal the win that would otherwise be theirs. One girl is shoving Long and getting in her face, elbowing her, and muttering in Spanish about taking her down. I wonder if Allie will respond – will take a cue from her ass-kicking father and prove that she's the "hitter" she says she is – but she doesn't. She just mounts a utilitarian-style comeback, making one simple pass and hard tackle after another.

Not every player is a beginner – there's a girl on her team who played at Notre Dame, and the other team has a keeper who played in Ecuador and a midfielder who played in Brazil. But the game is still largely marked by ugly moments that suggest an over-all lack of skill – toe balls, players split too easily, wide gaps in the defense. Allie tries to figure out how she can still get something out of the game. While the men's games are exercises in quick thinking and release, this women's futsal game demands Allie take her team on her shoulders. And she does that – she is the force in the center, the orchestrator who runs the passing game, slipping balls to the Notre Dame girl as the team comes from behind and wins. But when the game ends, Allie just looks relieved it's over. This game didn't make her a better player, and she knows it. She is here, and her best friends are at national camp.

At the end of the game, a little girl and her mother come up to Allie – would it be okay if they take a picture with her? "Yeah, yeah, of course, of course," Allie responds.

In Portland, this is par for the course; little girls always want autographs. But in this gym, filled with families from countries where girls and women do not play, it's not as common. These one or two starry-eyed girls who bite their lips and can't quite look her in the eye – too starstruck, too in awe – matter more than anything else to Long. Even more so than the women's game she just played in, these girls are signs of change – change she can have a part in. She takes this part seriously: she crouches down, eye-level with the girl, who's probably ten or eleven, and puts her face right alongside the kid's. She remembers being a kid, she remembers when her Grandpa took her all the way to Florida during the Olympics so that she could see the national team, she remembers how just like that, she knew what her dream was – to one day be them.

• • •

WHEN ALLIE WAS ten, her parents drove her six hours to watch the women's national team play a friendly against Australia in Connecticut. Mia Hamm was Allie's hero – "Hamm was her frigging star of the universe," says Long's father. Allie had seen the team play in the Olympics, but at this game, there would be a chance to get autographs – and Allie had eyes only for Hamm.

Post-game, throngs of kids huddled at the edge of the bleachers, leaning over the railing with a Sharpie, holding out jerseys and soccer balls and cleats and posters, waiting for autographs. But Long took stock of the players and noticed that Hamm wasn't one of them.

Mr. Long, who was trying to keep his daughter in his field of vision, suddenly lost her. "You got an eye on her? You see her?" he called, frowning, to his wife. Allie was there, in the mess of kids, and then she was nowhere – just gone.

Minutes later, Mr. Long saw a streak of blonde racing across the field. Long had crawled through the other kids' legs, climbed under the fence, dropped down to the field, bolted past security, climbed over yet another fence, and, on the sprint, gone to find Hamm – who she figured must be on the other side of the field.

Mr. Long chased after her, explaining to security that his ten-year-old was on the loose. He was ready to give Allie hell, to ground her for months, but when he found her, triumphant and exuberant on the outskirts of the field, signed Mia Hamm poster in hand, the anger and parental fear were overpowered by other feelings. He stared at his daughter's smudged red-white-and-blue face in wonder – the whole time starting to get an inkling of what's coming, of the lengths his daughter will go to, of just how similar she is to him. "She won't take no for an answer," says Long.

• • •

THAT MOMENT SHE shoved her poster in Mia's face wasn't Allie's last Hamm encounter. A few years ago, for an entire summer in Los Angeles, Hamm trained a handful of hopefuls – among them, Tobin Heath, Alex Morgan, Kelley O'Hara, and Long. (Because that's the kind of person Hamm is, training the next generation, helping them get there – no money involved, just grace.)

Did Long tell Mia Hamm that she once scaled two fences and sprinted across the field to hunt her down? "Mention I was a crazy, psycho stalker? No, I did not," laughs Long. "I played it cool."

Hamm has a killer dry wit. (When Gary Smith wrote his *Sports Illustrated* profile on her, she deadpanned *The Jerk*: "Are you going to start with 'She grew up a poor, black, child ...'?") She's also kind, generous, encouraging. And, of course, relentless. When Mia Hamm is shouting at you to push harder, you do it – you find that last drop of energy to burst forward.

At the Home Depot training center, Morgan, Heath, Long,

and O'Hara stood across from Hamm, heaving in and out, smiling at her, acting nonchalant – like they were all just friends, just mutual tellers-of-jokes, sprinters-of-sprints, kickers-of-balls. But to Allie, to all of them, Mia Hamm is still *Mia Hamm*.

The title of that UNC book Allie had as a kid – *Vision of a Champion* – was based around Hamm. Coach Anson Dorrance caught sight of Hamm running cones and sprints in an empty park. He wrote her a note: "The vision of a champion is someone who is bent over, drenched in sweat, at the point of exhaustion, when nobody else is watching." For many women's soccer players, it may be the defining quote of their lives – and in more ways than they ever imagined.

• • •

WE LEAVE THE GYM at around 11.45pm. As we sit in traffic, Allie pulls up a picture on her cell phone. Earlier that morning, Long went wedding dress shopping with her mother and found one. It's no puffy, princess style for Long. Her dress is straight Audrey Hepburn – ivory and silk, long-sleeved, form-fitting, and classic, a plunging, v-neck back. It's stunning.

In October, Allie and Bati will get married, and Tobin and Alex are two of her three maids of honor. There are seven bridesmaids total. "I know, I know," she says sheepishly.

She glances over at me, gestures toward my belly – I am six months pregnant during my visit with Allie – and says, "Bati and I want to have kids so bad." Her original idea was to make the 2015 World Cup team and the 2016 Olympic team, and then have kids after that. Now, having to face the fact that she hasn't been invited to the camp of Olympic hopefuls, she's having to retool the dream. "Maybe I'll freeze my eggs," she says, lobbing out the comment, seemingly unsure of whether or not she is joking. What she does know: there's no way she's giving up now. If her dreams didn't come true in 2015 and 2016, then she's gunning for 2019 and 2020. By 2019, she'll be 32 – the same age at which Mia Hamm retired. It would be her last shot to break in to the US national team. "I'll have hope until the last second. I'll always be ready for when that call comes," says Long.

• • •

THREE DAYS LATER, she's in Houston, staying in Bati's family's new home, spending the remaining days before preseason training with a personal trainer who's putting her through exercises that are different from anything she's ever tried. Ironically, the US national team happens to be in Texas playing an Olympic qualifying match against Costa Rica. Allie goes to the game. Alex Morgan had put her and Bati on the guest list. That morning, she surprises Tobin at the hotel – they go for coffee and Tobin gives her one of her game jerseys. She wears that to the game – HEATH bannered across her shoulders. She is rooting for her friends. She is all fan. But not quite – because people keep recognizing her, keep asking to take her picture.

When the game starts, she sits back, watching from her spot in the stands. Which, you know, hurts. She vacillates on whether or not this is good for her. "She tries not to watch, but she always does. I tape the games for her," says her mom. She studies the game – looking for what's missing – so that she knows what she needs to be able to offer.

• • •

ONE MONTH LATER, she reports to Portland for preseason. Portland is the best women's soccer city in the world. Last season her grandmother flew out to watch her play – although she never went to one of her daughter's games, at age 84, she's a convert, willing to trek across the country to watch her granddaughter.

Barb sat beside her, choked up and proud, watching her daughter play in front of 20,000.

There is no better place for Long to prove her worth. The Thorns roster is the female equivalent in talent to Barcelona, stocked with international superstars. Last season, Long's MVP accolades didn't get her the call-up. This season there are new additions to the roster including: Horan, the PSG twenty-year-old who skipped college, and Amandine Henry, who won the Silver Ball – the runner-up award for best player – at the women's World Cup the previous year. Both play Long's position.

Equalizer Soccer, the most in-depth source for NWSL soccer news, publishes an article: "The Amandine Henry signing and what it means." Under the bolded header, "Who Will Lose Playing Time?" it says: "... the name to watch is Allie Long. A fixture in the Thorns midfield since day one, Long can play the top or bottom of the midfield though not necessarily out wide. With Lindsey Horan in the team and battling for an Olympic spot, Long would seem to be the odd woman out among those three."

In Long's mind it is the perfect test.

• • •

IN PRESEASON SHE is playing some of the best football of her life. There are four US national pool players on the team – Meghan Klingenberg, Tobin Heath, Lindsey Horan, Emily Sonnett – and Long goes toe-to-toe with all of them. She plays well enough to warrant a phone call – Portland coach Mark Parsons tells Jill Ellis that Long is killing it, that he thinks she deserves to be called in.

They are on a team-bonding overnight trip to Bend, Oregon when she gets the news: Ellis wants her to report to national camp in April. The team gets out at various scenic spots – she climbs up rocks and walks between lush green trees, but it's hard to see any of it. At a gas station, she whispers the news to Tobin – Tobin bear hugs her and whisper-screams into her ear. They climb back in the team van, and Long sits there, trying not to cry, trying to play it cool.

Still, Long knows how far she has to go. It's late in the game – January, February, March – those were the camps to prove yourself. Coming in during April, only a couple months before the Olympic roster is set, her chances hover just above zero.

• • •

ON APRIL 6, THE United States play Colombia in a friendly, and Allie starts in the center of the midfield. Ellis tells her that she's got 45 minutes. She'll be subbed out at half-time.

In the stands, Allie's parents, Bati, as well as Diego and Allen from the NYC men's leagues, form the Allie fan club. It is freezing cold but they don't notice – too busy staring at Allie, at her runs, at her tackles, at every touch. Every once in a while, they turn to each other with wide, euphoric eyes, no words needed: Allie's doing it – she's conjuring Busquets. Her presence is undeniable: she orchestrates, keeps it simple, and strips the ball off the Colombians. She threads hard-to-see through-passes, never playing the ball laterally when there is an option to go forward.

And then, at the top of the eighteen-yard box, she hits a rocket – it swerves, beats the keeper, and clangs off the cross bar. In the stands, Diego, Allen, Bati, and her parents jump and scream – it was beautiful; it missed; it was, like her entire career, so close.

In the 32nd minute, Horan sends in a ball from the flanks, and Allie pivots while backpedaling and heads the ball clinically into the corner of the net: it's the United States' second goal, and Allie's first goal of her international career. The stone face is gone – her radiant smile, and her leap into Horan's arms, will be the cover photo on the *Sports Illustrated* website later that night.

In the stands, Diego, Allen, Bati, and her parents lose their minds.

Long's night, it turns out, isn't over. Ellis changes her mind and keeps Long in for the next half. In the 65th minute, Long scores again, another header. This time, she's more collected in her celebration – she is just doing her job, just finishing a ball like she would in any other game.

That night Bati is flooded with 102 texts and 300 comments on Facebook, most of them from the futsal guys: "So happy for her – but not surprised. We see it week in and week out"; "Dude, she's better than you"; "My boy Jose Batista's wifey doing it big"; "OMFG – send her to Rio!"

She plays in two more qualifying games against Japan, starting both of them and playing the entire game. Of course, this gets her hopes up – but she tries to talk herself down, telling herself it doesn't mean anything. Ellis is just trying to give her as much time to be seen as possible.

During the semi-final of the men's European Championship, she gets the call. She answers on the first ring. Ellis teases, "Waiting by the phone?" And then Long hears the words that seemed almost impossible just six months ago: "You're going to Rio. You earned this."

In Rio, she's a starter. Against France she is named "Player of the Game." Suddenly the media is interested in her. Everyone wants to talk to the player who kept getting turned down. She says again and again, "It's a dream come true, it's what I wanted and worked for my whole life." But nothing she says can quite capture how incredible it feels to spend more than a decade watching your best friends from the stands – and then to finally step on the stage and prove you belong.

She is aware of how differently this story could have turned out. As an elite athlete you have to believe that hard work and perseverance will get you there. But Allie is keenly aware that sometimes, that's not how it goes.

• • •

AT THE END of my night following Allie around Queens and Brooklyn, we pulled up alongside a curb in Brooklyn. Long was wolfing down a leftover cold empanada – tired and beat but still running on adrenaline, happy to keep talking, wanting to make sure I had a full sense of what these leagues were about, of just how much talent is out there. "Really, those guys are so, so good. You just can't believe they never made it." She revisited the idea she mentioned earlier: "I mean it, there's gotta be some kind of program to start, something that says, 'You missed me but I'm still here – and I can ball with the best of them.'"

Welcome to Russia

AT THE END of Dani Foxhoven's second day and fourth practice with the Russian side FC Energiya Voronezh, she sits down in the grass and takes off her cleats. A wiry, upbeat brunette with a big grin, she's feeling good – tired and good. The team is in Belek, Turkey for preseason and she has spent the past hour doing one-touch passes. She's untying her laces when Vasilich, her 64-year-old head coach, charges her, shouting in Russian. He leans down over her, his red face in hers. He grabs her by the ear-lobe and yanks her to her feet. He does not let go of her ear. With his other hand, he open-hand slaps her across the face.

The team translator, a 24-year-old named Tanya whom the club found in the language department at the local university, comes running over. "He wants you to stand up!" she says, fretting and apologetic. "He says, 'Women should not sit on the ground.'" She explains that sitting on the grass can affect a women's fertility, that the cold ground is not good for her organs.

Dani looks at Tanya, looks at Vasilich, and says, "Tell him to never lay a hand on me again."

That's the moment when the doubt creeps in, when she wonders if maybe it was a mistake to sign a five-month contract to play professional women's soccer in Russia.

• • •

ONE MONTH EARLIER, Dani Foxhoven graduated from the University of Portland one semester early so that she could play in the United States Women's Professional Soccer (WPS) league. She was drafted seventeenth overall to the Philadelphia Independence.

On January 30, 2012, two weeks before she was due to report for preseason, she woke up to a text message from her agent: "The US women's pro league has folded. You won't be going to Philly after all." Her agent got on the phone and tried to find her a new place to play. But the agents of all the other American players were also on the phone, also looking for interested teams. And Foxhoven was just a former college player untested in the professional realm. There was nowhere for her to play in Germany, nowhere in Sweden, nowhere in England. After many phone calls, her agent had no offers.

With no job prospects, she couldn't afford to keep living in Portland. Two weeks earlier she was on the brink of making her dreams come true; now she was calling home in tears, asking if she could move back into her parents' one-bedroom condo.

On a Tuesday, her father flew out to help her pack her life into her '91 Civic and make the drive down snow-blanketed interstates back to Colorado. She was driving across the white nothingness of Wyoming, contemplating life without soccer, when she got the call from her agent: if she was interested, there was a Russian team that would take her. They had qualified for the Champions League tournament – the top professional soccer competition in the world – for the past five years. They'd pay her $3,000 a month, which, by women's soccer standards, was good – very good. He told her it had to happen fast. She had a day to think it over.

When she hung up the phone, she looked over at her father and smiled. Already, she knew she was doing it: if she had to go all the way to Russia to be a professional soccer player, that's what she was going to do. "A door that had been closed was now open again, and I was going to do whatever it took to keep it open," says Foxhoven.

In the passenger's seat, her father pulled up the team on Wikipedia. They'd been around since 1989 and had won more championships than any other Russian team. Players from all over the world – from Italy to Equatorial Guinea – had played for Voronezh. Five Americans played there in 1996. Spanish star, Vero Boquete, one of the top players in the world, 2011's WPS Player of the Year, had played for them the previous season.

The next ten hours of slow driving along alternate routes, she and her dad imagined Dani in Russia. She had seen old movies about the USSR and she had vague understandings of communism and the Iron Curtain – it was odd to her that a country with a long history of repression was offering her the best chance to play women's soccer. But she had no idea what the current Russia was like and, in a way, that excited her more than if she were more familiar.

Her father, more of a listener than an advice-giver, said only, "It will probably be lonely. It will probably be hard. And if you're ready for that, do it."

That Saturday she boarded a plane.

• • •

SEVERAL DAYS AFTER her coach slapped her in the face, Dani has her guitar out. She has hauled it across the world because ever since she was a freshman in college, when twin sisters Megan and Rachael Rapinoe taught her how to play, she has relied on it. Already she is glad she has it.

Most of the players on the team are stand-offish. When she first introduced herself, she smiled and said, "Hi, I'm Dani." They looked at her and shook their fingers: "No, you are not Dani – *she* is Dani," they said, in Russian, pointing to another player, Elena

Danilova, the star of the Russian national team, a petite blonde with ice blue eyes. Foxhoven would just be called "*Amerikanskaya*."

The Russians have not spoken to her since. Except for the eighteen-year-old Asaya, whom she calls Baby, the youngest member of FC Energiya. Through gestures and pantomime, she tells Dani to learn to play "Waka Waka" by Shakira, her favorite song.

So now Dani is in the hotel hallway in Turkey, guitar in her lap. She's not thinking about how it felt to be picked up by the earlobe – she's focused only on learning chords, memorizing words.

The music acts like a homing call for the international players: the Jamaican, the Brazilian, the Swede, and the Cameroonians follow the music to the hallway.

Simone, the Brazilian who has played in two World Cups and two Olympics, mentions that Marta, international superstar and fellow Brazilian, is staying with her Swedish team a few hotels down the beach. Marta is *muita boa* at guitar – they should all go sit and play on the beach.

It is not yet tourist season and the beach is otherwise deserted. Surrounded by the skeletons of unassembled cabanas, they sit in white plastic patio chairs, bare feet in the sand, snow-capped mountains rising up directly behind teal water. Dani processes the scene: Marta – her footballing hero, the best woman ever to play the game, five-time FIFA World Player of the Year – has taken over her guitar. Vero Boquete, the Spanish star who now plays with Marta for Tyresö FF, is next to her, smiling and dancing. Marta is jamming out, singing first to *forró*, traditional Brazilian folk music, then to Shakira. And so is Baby. They are whisked from far corners of the world, all here for the chance to play football. Two Brazilians, one Spaniard, one Jamaican, two Cameroonians, one Swede, one American, one Russian – sitting on a beach in Turkey, singing a song about Africa. It is all decidedly cool. This isn't the kind of experience you walk out on – doesn't matter if your coach slapped you for sitting down in the grass. She has no idea what she's in for in the next five months, but she knows she isn't going home.

• • •

IN THEIR FINAL preseason game, FC Energiya plays Tyresö FF – often considered the top women's team in the world. Marta and Boquete make up their frontline. And now Foxhoven is on the same field with them. This is what she is after – the chance to play against the best in the world.

Thirty minutes in, the game takes on a menacing tone. Marta goes in for a cleats-up tackle – it is clean, she gets all ball, but Vasilich charges onto the field, screaming in Marta's face. Marta, in Portuguese, screams back. It devolves from there: players screaming at each other in several different languages. Then Vasilich gestures his hand and Foxhoven's team is walking off the field. Finally, she hears some English: "Well, that's it. Game over." FC Energiya climbs on the bus, with Tyresö, the best team in the world, still standing on the field.

It is antithetical to Dani's being to walk out on a game. Again, warning bells sound in her head.

• • •

ONE THREE-HOUR FLIGHT and an eight-hour bus ride later, the sunny guitar jam on a Turkish beach seems like a different universe. At 3.30am in the middle of a snowstorm, they arrive in Voronezh, Russia. "The Base," their new home, is a four-storey building surrounded by a ten-foot cement wall, guarded by a 24-hour watchman. The wall, presumably, is to protect them from the poverty of the surrounding area. But in the coming days it will also come to feel like it's designed to keep them in;

the players are told when they are allowed to go out and when they are not.

The next morning they stand on a snow-blanketed field, each player carrying a shovel. They huddle together, bundled and hunched, and go at the field in strips, tossing shovels of snow over a three-foot wall. The internationals shiver and make jokes – *Welcome to Russia.*

It is Omolyn Davis's first time shoveling snow. The Jamaican who describes herself as "all tomboy" is tattooed and thin, with short, shaved hair, pretty eyes, muscular arms, and an interest in street fashion. When she's not bundled in giant, puffy jackets, her typical look is a straight-brimmed baseball cap with the sticker still on, diamond studs, white v-neck, heavy gold chain, baggy shorts, and high tops. This tough boy image is in rather startling contrast to her voice, which is delicate, lilting, and melodic. This voice works in a strange juxtaposition to the world she describes: Omolyn grew up in a rough borough of Kingston. Certain times of year you couldn't leave the house after 7pm because of the gang wars. She learned to play football in cutthroat street games – the kind of games where every guy brings his knife. "There are always fallouts. First thing they're going to do is run for their knives," says Omolyn. Or, sometimes, they said, "I'm gonna go for my gun." They'd hop the fence and take off running, and that's when Omolyn knew to clear out. Many of the guys she grew up playing with are dead or in jail.

Her mom didn't like her being out there. Omolyn has nine siblings, including six older brothers, none of whom played – not seriously, not like Omolyn. So why this tomboy daughter of hers spent her days in a parking lot, playing rough with a ball, was pure mystery to her mother.

But all that ball kicking in the parking lot made Omolyn good – good enough to be the only girl on her school team. At the primary school championships, her mother took note of the full stands and the chatter about her daughter, coming from all around her, everyone saying: "Oh what? There's a girl starting? How did a *girl* make the team?"

Omolyn landed a scholarship to attend Excelsior High School, a private school with a reputation for sports. She was the only one from her neighborhood to go there. She has no doubt that football saved her life: "Anything the guys wanted to be doing, I probably would be doing too – the drugs, the violence. If it weren't for football, I probably wouldn't be here," says Davis. At Excelsior, she met a coach, Gilbert, who became her father figure, who pushed her forward. There, her whole world opened up: she made the Jamaican national team; got noticed by American college scouts; scored goals for George Mason University; and was drafted in the first round to play for Boca Raton-based magicJack – becoming the first Jamaican ever to play in a US women's pro league.

But one year in, the league folded and she was back at home. Then her agent called, telling her about the chance to play in Russia. She knew nothing about the country – not what language they spoke, where it was located on the map, or what the weather was like – and she didn't bother to look it up. "I was just too excited; I didn't care," says Davis.

Her first morning with the team, at breakfast, no one said "hi" to her. No one looked at her. When Omolyn said, "Good morning," no one said anything back. "I understand that no one speaks English, but I'm pretty sure they know what 'good morning' means."

They don't want to be friends, fine, thought Omolyn. She was here to play, and no amount of snow or unfriendliness was going to scare her off.

• • •

FOR THE CAMEROONIANS, Augustine Ejangue and Njoya Nkout, it is their second year with the team, their second round of snow shoveling. Their Russian-speaking agent had come to them with this high-paying opportunity and they'd taken it. When they first arrived, no one spoke French and they spoke no Russian or English. Until the team hired Tanya to translate, they could not communicate.

It was a difficult year: when Augustine and Njoya left for a week to play for the Cameroonian national team in an Olympic qualifying game, Augustine contracted malaria; back in Voronezh, she was sent to the local hospital. In her country, malaria was common and easily dealt with; in Russia, the hospital did not have the medicine or treatments to adequately deal with it. For three or four days, she was gravely, terrifyingly ill.

Every day Njoya and Tanya would visit her, but they couldn't live there, couldn't be with her around the clock. "It was hard to see her alone in that place," says Tanya. Augustine was unable to speak the language, unable to understand the nurses or the doctors. Sweating and trembling, delirious with fever, she ached for family, for familiarity, for home.

But she made it through the worst of it, and once she stabilized, they moved her into a new ward of mostly older women, *babushkas*. There, she developed a friendship with one babushka in the bed next to her. The Cameroonian culture places great value on their elders – they are never left alone in a hospital. Augustine would hold the old woman's hand, bring her lunch, make sure she had enough blankets and pillows, and the old woman doted on her back, checking on her, teaching her Russian, making her feel less alone in this lonely place.

Within a month, she was back with the team. For both Njoya and Augustine, it is their first time as professionals, and they have no standard for comparison. There are parts they dislike, but they have each other, and they have the game that brought them here.

• • •

"THE CLUB WAS not a story of democracy and business cooperation, but a story of a king in his kingdom, a tsar in his country. The main coach is the founder of the club. He has always been there. He hires people, no one hired him. His position is very stable and his power is almost unlimited," reflects Tanya.

Ivan Vasilievich Saenko, referred to as Vasilich, is the coach. His two sons act as assistant coach and general manager. His wife, Nadezhda Bosikova, former star of the Russian league, has played on the team for twenty years. Now 39, she is nowhere near as good as the other players and she hates playing, but Vasilich insists she continues and threatens her when she tries not to play. "She is the master of soccer," he'd say to Dani via Tanya. "And I am the master of everything – I know everything there is to know about soccer. I'm the king of science. I am team doctor, team coach, team strength and conditioner."

Every day the schedule – field training, weight training, mealtimes – is posted on the wall. There is one curious entry – beside lunch, the schedule reads "vitamins." In the meal room, the players quickly discover why. Beside lunch plates – one piece of chicken or liver, cucumber and tomato salad, one piece of bread, which is also what they get for dinner – there is a paper cup with multi-colored pills. The internationals laugh with each other and finger the assortment – surely they're not supposed to take all of them. Vasilich appears over them and when they ask what they are, he just says, "Vitamins." Uncomfortable with taking unidentified pills, they ask to see a label, a name, anything. Vasilich refuses. The first few days, they don't take them, pocketing the pills. But Vasilich catches on quick. At mealtime, he appears by their side and stands over them until they swallow the pills. Every day they take around twenty pills.

On the field, it often feels more like training for the Russian military than training for a football team: they heave large bricks, crawl through sand pits, climb over wooden trestles, zigzag through randomly-placed obstacles. They do no tactics, no scrimmages, no walk-throughs, no small-sided games. After one training session spent running down the field while swinging a heavy ball and chain in circles, Foxhoven writes in her blog, "I will be able to beat a Rossiyanka player in hand-to-hand combat come Monday."

Vasilich, of course, lords over all of it. While the internationals have encountered coaches who are yellers, coaches who might toss Gatorade cups, sneer, or make you feel small, none of them has encountered anything like him. They don't have to speak the language to get the gist of what he's shouting. There are certain words that reappear – words they look up later when they get to their rooms. *Blyad* is a favorite. Literally it translates as "whore," and that's often how he uses it. It can also mean "damn" or "fuck- ing" – and Vasilich liberally employs this use as well, tossing it in every third word.

• • •

TANYA, THE TRANSLATOR, is as nice as they come. Dani describes her as the only Russian hippy she's ever met. When Tanya's pro- fessor recommended her for the job, she thought it would be interesting, a great start to a career in translating. And in many ways it is wonderful – in the two seasons she's there, 2011 and 2012, she meets players from all over the world and loves getting to learn more about their countries and their cultures, and also to help them understand Russia.

"I played a role of an airbag in foreigners' transit to Russian cultural environment. I hope my presence there made someone's life a little easier," says Tanya. During the 2011 season, she took the Italian, Pamela Conti, to the supermarket to find mozzarella for her pizza; she took Dani to art museums; she took the Cameroonians to the bank and helped them transfer money to their families at home.

But when she eagerly accepted the position, she had never imagined what it would be like to stand next to Vasilich, to be the go-between, and to be forced to interpret what he was screaming. "During trainings, matches, and breaks he could explode with the worst words of my native language," says Tanya.

Tanya tries to strip it down – to just relay the bits of constructive instruction. Vasilich demands that she translate everything. She often refuses. But the players too want to know – want to confirm what they already can feel.

So, at their pressing, Tanya stutters out translations: "He says you'd make better whores than you do soccer players." And, "It would be a better sport if you all played naked."

• • •

BEFORE PRACTICE, THEY report to oxygen-deprivation training in the lunch room, where each player puts on a resistance breathing device that resembles a gas mask. A huge accordion-like oxygen regulator is attached to a tube. The masks are designed to limit oxygen; breathing under resistance, the idea is that athletes thereby strengthen lung capacity and build the diaphragm.

For 30 to 40 minutes, the masked players sit at tables covered with lacey, doily-style tablecloths, sucking for air, listening to Vasilich, king of science, master of everything, lecture in Russian as classical music plays in the background. More than once, he walks to the other side of the cafeteria and removes an eight-by-twelve photo from the wall and brings it over to discuss. He points at one man and says several times, "*Mafiya*." Then he happily continues talking. Augustine, who can by now understand Russian, translates in broken English for Dani. "That man the head mobster in Voronezh. He help our team be successful."

The mafia: it's hard to know what that even means. Dani's seen *The Godfather*, some episodes of *The Sopranos* – that's about where her knowledge of the mafia ends. Organized crime. Cover-ups. What would that have to do with a women's soccer team?

• • •

IN 1996, ONLY five years after the fall of the USSR, the first group of Americans came to play in Russia. When American Wynne McIntosh looked around at all the poverty and wondered how there was money for women's pro soccer, the then translator was matter of fact with her: "The government is run by the mob. The mob gets to decide if they're going to put money into schools and streets – or fund pro sports."

The US State Department's secret diplomatic cables leaked in 2010 second the translator's assessment, declaring Russia "a virtual mafia state." The *Guardian*'s Luke Harding summarized the documents:

> The gangsters enjoy secret support and protection and in effect work 'as a complement to state structures.' [...] Arms trafficking, money laundering, personal enrichment, protection for gangsters, extortion and kickbacks, suitcases full of money and secret offshore bank accounts in Cyprus: the cables paint a bleak picture of a political system in which bribery alone totals an estimated $300 billion a year, and in which it is often hard to distinguish between the activities of the government and organised crime.[1]

The international players don't know how or if the "mafia" factors into the Russian women's game, or if Vasilich just employs the word to instill fear, his predominant mode of coaching.

But there's no denying that the whole set-up is odd: there are huge budgets – in 2009, WFC Rossiyanka, the top team, had a reported budget of €9 million,[2] which is unheard of in the women's game anywhere in the world. Yet the stands are almost always empty. No one in Russia pays attention to women's soccer, making it the perfect setting for massive money laundering and kickbacks.

The players go off only what they can see – Vasilich's nine luxury cars, the mansion he brags is worth $24 million, the two giant bodyguards that accompany Vasilich everywhere. Vero Boquete recalls a game in Bristol in the 2011 Champion's League season: it was pouring rain and the bodyguard held the umbrella over Vasilich while he himself got soaked. That seemed like something straight out of the movies. "I'd never seen anything like that in my life," comments Boquete. And there's the time the team attends a men's professional game: a man was smoking a cigarette close to the team and Vasilich didn't like that. So he instructed his men to go deal with him; they physically picked him up and threw him out. "You don't do stuff like that unless you're important," says Davis. "You've got to be some kind of boss to get away with something like that."

• • •

DURING WEIGHT TRAINING, Vasilich singles out one player at a time and, along with the trainer, takes her upstairs to his office. Eventually, Vasilich summons Foxhoven. On the way up to the fourth floor, he explains through gestures that he has something that will help her strained hamstring. His last idea involved kneading her leg with a meat pulverizer – "a medieval-looking torture device – a lint roller with rows and rows of attached dog collar spikes," describes Dani. Her red-welt covered leg was then slathered with something that smelled like Icy Hot but which felt like "trolls setting her leg on fire." After the third application, she hobbled outside and buried her leg in the snow.

So she's a bit apprehensive of what Vasilich's next idea will be.

In his office, he has her lie down on her stomach on the training table. Dani glances over her shoulder and sees the trainer preparing a needle and syringe. She balks, sits up: "No, I'm not comfortable with this. I want my translator here," she says. But they just say, "*Eta normalne, eta normalne* ... vitamins" and tell her to lie back down on the table. The trainer pulls down one side of her shorts and gives her an injection in her butt cheek.

In college, players with chronic pain sometimes got cortisone shots to get through the season. She wants to think it is just a cortisone shot. But cortisone shots are localized, delivered directly to the problem area. They aren't administered into your bare butt. As she walks back to weight training, she has no idea what has just been injected into her.

In the previous season, during Boquete's time there, the injections also happened. When Vasilich first approached Boquete, she said no and waited first to talk with the trainer, a nice woman whom she trusted. She also talked with Danilova and Terekhova, who knew Boquete from playing against her in national team games. Everyone assured her that the shots were just vitamins. Vasilich just preferred to administer them this way because it kicked in faster. So Boquete, like Foxhoven, like the rest of the team, got the injections.

Omolyn Davis is one player who refuses. Vasilich enlists Tanya to help talk her into it. Tanya, miserable-looking, looks down and says, "He's trying to say it's in your contract." But Davis's contract is in English. "Does he think I can't read?" she asks. Vasilich tells Foxhoven and Augustine Ejangue that it is for injuries, for sickness, and Davis isn't sick, isn't injured. She's not getting the shots.

• • •

EVEN WITH TWO-A-DAY training sessions, there is so much time, unbelievable amounts of time, spent in their rooms – time to question everything, time to wish they could go back home. Dani has her methods of distraction. To get her mind right, she plucks on her guitar; listens to music with lyrics she can cling to; reads Harry Potter; learns Russian and Spanish; and soaks up everything she can about Russia, trying to understand this country she's in. She's slowly coming to a beginner's understanding of the fall of the USSR and the ensuing shotgun capitalism implemented by Yeltsin: how Yeltsin declared it was time for the free market test and public resources were snapped up by rich oligarchs – all the power in the hands of a corrupt few. In no time, millions went from being middle class to having nothing.

On the team's off-days, when they are allowed to leave The Base, Dani takes off, wanting to see the Russia beyond the ten-foot walls. Sometimes Ximel, her Swedish roommate, comes with her, sometimes she goes alone, walking the neighboring streets, taking in colorful, ramshackle houses that are half brick, half corrugated tin. Some are painted down the middle – half blue, half green, the equatorial line indicating the two-room split of the house. With her camera, Dani seeks out beauty: painted glass bottles turned into garden hedges, pastel towers of tires, memorable graffiti – a *Finding Nemo* fish, scrawled Russian characters, the face of a very unhappy old man. Most days it is eerily quiet – just the barking of stray dogs and the sound of her own feet crunching on snow.

When she comes back to The Base, she feels re-oriented, life put back into perspective, coaches and teams and soccer cut down to size.

• • •

ON SUNDAY, APRIL 8, they take a nine-hour bus ride to Moscow to play their first game of the Russian Championships. Everyone is ready to get started, ready to remember why they are here.

When they arrive in Moscow, it is 1°C. During warm-up, the rain and sleet begin. Ten minutes in, their rain jackets and gloves feel more like weights than warmth-providers. But this is nothing new to Dani, who has spent the past five years in rainy Portland.

Most everything else is different. In Portland, she played in front of the best fans in women's college soccer: every game packed with a sea of purple. Villa, one of the men's dorms, formed a drum squad; no matter how cold it was, they came out shirtless, in kilts, and chanted the entire game. In Moscow, the stands are almost empty.

As the game nears its start, Dani hears the Russian national anthem for the first time. In 2000, President Putin restored the old Soviet anthem. Some, like Communist Party leader Gennady Zyuganov, viewed it as a restoration of "the great music of victory" from World War II. For others, the song invokes the violence and fear of Stalin's rule. For the international players, the six-minute anthem, which sounds like a military march, is mainly just long. They look out at the empty stands, hopping around, mentally willing themselves toward warmth.

As a forward, Foxhoven stands at the edge of the center circle as the whistle blows, adrenaline overpowering the cold. This is her first game as a professional and, in her mind, everything is on the line. This is her chance to prove herself, to show that she is meant to play.

The tempo of the game is fast; the style is, well, Russian – aggressive and physical, as though all of the other teams also train by running through sand pits and heaving around metal balls. While one part of Foxhoven's mind catalogues the differences – the lack of short passes, the way players just boot the ball forward

– the rest of her is on instinct mode. After Njoya Nkout challenges the keeper for a ball in the air and the ball bounces toward goal, Foxhoven is there to finish, scoring her first professional goal.

Always, since she was a kid playing in Colorado, she's found that once she scores her first, goalscoring feels simple – and that apparently holds true in Russia. Not long after her first goal, Danilova – the Russian Dani, the "real" Dani – loops a ball in, and *Americanskaya* volleys it home.

Danilova – the player who has been unwaveringly cold to her, the player who frequently screams at her teammates for not finding her or for failing to finish what she sets up – runs towards American Dani and high-fives her. Dani grins at her. Danilova doesn't smile back but that's okay with Dani – she'll take the high-five.

After the game, the Russian players, for the first time, acknowledge Dani with affirming handshakes and cheek kisses as they all head into the locker room, freezing, trembling, happy.

In the shower, the players fumble for the knobs, anxious for the warm water to return feeling to their limbs. But there is no hot water. The Russians smile wanly, the only type of smile Dani has seen in Russia. Again, the players laugh and gasp and say, "Welcome to Russia." It's like bathing in snow.

Dani puts on every layer in her bag and gets on the bus for the nine-hour drive home. She sits down in a seat, but the Russian players stop her. "No," they say, gesturing toward the aisle. The team bus does not have enough seats; the Cameroonians share one seat, and she and Ximel sit on the floor for the next nine hours.

• • •

BACK AT THE BASE, Dani does treatment on her hamstring and heads to mandatory sauna time – or *banya* as they call it in Russia.

Dani has never quite understood saunas and the desire to voluntarily place oneself in 120-degree temperatures and inhale other people's sweat. She strips down to her sports bra and shorts and enters The Base sauna gingerly. Two men who work at The Base are already in the sauna, and, judging from the amount of sweat that slings onto her as they come in for a cheek kiss, have been for a very long time. She slips on a white, wool beanie and tries to casually position herself on the floor. After her hours on the bus floor, it's become something of a comfort, and, more importantly, it seems like the position furthest away from the men and their sweat.

One of the men speaks to her in Russian – she makes out nothing except "*Amerikanskaya*." He appears to be asking her a question. Because she is indeed the *Amerikanskaya*, she replies, "Yes? *Da?*"

He then grabs her towel from the floor, spreads it out on a top bench, grabs Dani's hand, and pats that bench, as though to say, *Hop on up!* Realizing that her "*Da*" must have committed her to something she did not intend to commit to, she hastily retreats: "*Nyet, nyet*." But the men say, "*Da, da!*" So Dani lies down, with no idea of what's coming. The big man exits the sauna and returns with two bundles of leafy oak branches, tied together to make two brooms.

In her blog, "A Bottle from a Glass," she writes about what happens next:

> I am not exaggerating one bit when I say he just slapped/beat my entire body with the leaf branches. My legs, my feet, my back, everything. It fanned all of the hot air onto my body and I seriously felt like I was burning up and getting no air.
>
> Then after about two minutes of slapping he flipped me over. By this I mean that he actually flipped me ... one second

I was looking at the ground, the next I was looking at the ceiling. I didn't know what was going on, I was still trying to breathe and figure out why I was getting hit with leaves, then all of a sudden I was on my back and he was again slapping the front side of my body. He even slapped my face. It knocked my hat off and so someone put it back on and it was covering my eyes, not like they were open anyways (I was getting slapped in the face, after all). Then when my hat was over my eyes, he apparently got a bucket of snow and dumped it all over my body. It completely took my breath away, not like I had any air in my lungs anyways.[3]

He grabs her hand, takes her out of the sauna and into a shower stall that resembles a sink on the ground, and hoses her off with freezing water. He brings her back in, asks, "*Eta normalne?*"

She shoves her hat up out of her eyes and responds, "Yes, *sí, da.*"

He laughs at her, and instantly Dani decides she likes this man. Because laughter isn't easy to come by in Russia. She misses being funny, misses people laughing at her jokes. Even if this joke is her own wild bewilderment, she is glad for it. She leaves the sauna happy, feeling like it was a giant metaphor for her entire Russian experience:

I have been slapped by a lot of branches and experienced things I never knew existed, almost (and actually have) passed out several times, had my eyes covered, asked to do things I have never been asked before ... but I have come away from all of them smiling and laughing at what just happened!

In the comments section of her blog, her grandpa, whose username is "Popsie," writes,

I saw that on a Samantha Brown show on the travel channel. They would sit in a hot spa, get beat on by branches and then run out into the snow. Supposed to be really good for you! haha. Probably really expensive too! Funny!

• • •

WYNNE MCINTOSH, ONE OF the Americans who came to Russia in 1996, also has memories of saunas and getting hit with branches – like Dani's grandpa, she understood that this sauna practice isn't too far outside of the realm of normal, that there are similar practices across Europe. But what felt less normal was that it was usually Vasilich himself hitting the half-dressed players.

Most of the players were young – nineteen- and twenty-year-olds from all over Russia, including Vasilich's current wife, Nadezhda Bosikova. She was the leading scorer in the Russian league in 1994, 1995, 1996, 1997, 1998, and 2000 – until her career was interrupted when she gave birth to Vasilich's son, Matthew. According to the local Voronezh news station, at the end of the 2004 season, there was a "mass player exodus" – Bosikova the only one left on the roster. When asked by the local reporter if she too thought about signing with another team, she said that, after the birth of her son, that was not an option.[4]

• • •

BY EASTER IN 2013, the snow has melted and families walk down the muddy dirt roads surrounding The Base, wearing their finest clothes, carrying bread and bouquets of synthetic flowers.

With most of the team having gone home to their families for the holiday, Tanya takes Dani into the city center to see the Easter festival. There is one main road to the city center. Normally packed with buses, cars, trash, and stray dogs, on holidays, it is closed off and emptied of cars. Every block there is a stage set up for traditional Russian dancers, singers, and flamethrowers. Russian babushkas sell *pirogi*, dumplings stuffed with stewed cabbage, and *kvass*, a drink made from stale rye bread that tastes like a mixture of flat Pepsi and non-alcoholic beer. Dani and Tanya eat pirogi, drink the kvass, and talk about where each of them comes from. Dani asks Tanya about her family background and Tanya just looks at her: "Only an American would ask that. I am Russian. Everyone is Russian – for thousands of years, our families have lived only here."

At Lenin Square, Tanya and Dani stand outside the grand white columns of the Voronezh State Opera, built in 1890, where for more than a hundred years ballerinas have performed Tchaikovsky's *Swan Lake*. Outside of the largest Orthodox Church in Voronezh, they see the line of women who wrap around it, waiting to have the holy men bless their homemade Easter bread. They take pictures with dancing women wearing French braids and military fatigues. In front of the Voronezh Sea, they walk the sidewalk and Dani watches the wind whip across the icy water as it begins to unthaw, grateful for today – grateful to witness the Russia that Tanya wants her to see, the beauty in a country that can, to an outsider, too often feel like nothing but a nightmare.

On the city bus ride back to The Base, Dani tries to pry her bus fare out from her wallet as the bus starts to move – hitting potholes, braking. Dani lurches from one side to the other, stumbling and falling into Russians. After she accidentally sits on her third woman, she laughs and smiles apologetically at the woman. The woman does not smile back. No one laughs with her. Dani passes her coins forward and jokes half to herself, half to Tanya, "Rough crowd."

Tanya shrugs. "Here, you do not smile unless you truly have a reason to smile," she says. "People are not fake. We are not generous with our smiles." That much Dani has picked up on.

And she gets it. She understands that players like Danilova grew up in bleaker circumstances than she did, even if she doesn't know the particulars: that Danilova's father – the one who taught her how to play – walked out on the family. That Danilova's mother died four years later. That it's now up to her to provide for her four brothers and sisters.[5] And that football is the only thing that kept her from a worse fate. The longer American Dani spends in Russia, the more she understands the skepticism, the guardedness, and why they might feel affronted by her always-have-a-smile-on-my-face attitude and American tendency toward quick trust and easy friendship.

But Dani's still hopeful. There was the high-five, and there was the recent evolution of her nickname: she is no longer called *Amerikanskaya*. After coming down to the meal room one afternoon wearing glasses, one of Vasilich's sons called out, "Hillary! Hillary Clinton!" This mystified her – as she looks nothing like Hillary. The thought process appeared to be something along the lines of "Glasses make you look smart; Hillary is a smart American; you are like Hillary." The players had laughed, the name had stuck, and now it's grown on her – it is, at least, more personal than *Amerikanskaya*.

• • •

FOXHOVEN'S GOALSCORING CONTINUES, and the winning continues. For their first home game, during the Russian Cup, they finish regulation in a 2–2 tie. Russian Dani scores the first goal, a beautiful half-volley, and American Dani chases down a long ball, beats the last defender, and scores the second. All the Energiya players make their penalty kicks and FC Energiya wins.

Their next game is a nineteen-hour train ride away, in Krasnodar, on the other side of Russia. Dani and Simone, the Brazilian, are travel partners – they share a compartment with two babushkas. Their train car, which they will discover is true of most Russian train cars, smells like body odor, whisky and cigarette smoke. They take turns sticking their head out the train window, wind in their face as they stare at the countryside.

In Krasnodar, they win 3–0. Foxhoven scores all three goals.

When the game is over, they climb on the rented team bus but they don't go anywhere – traffic is so bad that in 30 minutes, they only cover two blocks. Carrying their gear, they climb off the bus to take the local street car, a USSR relic. It is packed – so packed that for the first time Dani can understand how people get crushed to death. But it is also fun – she is sandwiched between locals. And even the Russians, the never-smile Russians, are laughing and incredulous as one more body climbs on.

When you are winning, it's easy to classify almost everything under "adventure." But even with the winning, there are things that are harder for her to laugh at – details Dani leaves off her blog because she doesn't want her family to worry. She doesn't tell them about the shots, or about the particulars of what Vasilich yells. She doesn't tell them about the game where she didn't play at all, didn't even dress because, Vasilich explained, "The game has already been decided."

And then of course there's the fact that she only got paid one-third of what she was supposed to the first month, and that no one has been paid since then.

• • •

OMOLYN DAVIS ISN'T okay with that. Her contract stipulates that she is to get paid on the 25th of every month. When that didn't happen the first month, she thought, *Okay, maybe they forgot*. But three months in without salary is not a mistake.

The international players tell Tanya they want to meet with Vasilich. He refuses, says he'll only meet with them individually.

Davis thinks they should strike. The internationals talk about refusing to go to practice until they get paid.

But that's not an easy decision to make: they are players who have spent their entire lives following a coach's instructions, showing up at a designated spot and doing whatever is asked of them. And they are here in Russia so that they have the chance to continue to play – so not playing, not showing up to practice runs counter to the logic that has dominated their existences. Come practice time, Davis is the only one who doesn't show up.

Davis's last professional experience probably factors in. She played for magicJack, for another infamous owner/coach, Dan Borislow – a man who requested that the players refer to him as "Daddy," a man who single-handedly brought down the second iteration of the US pro league. Borislow and Vasilich have a lot in common: they both had millions to burn; they both made sexual comments about players and routinely swore at and belittled them; they both did whatever they wanted. In 2011, the magic-Jack players voted to file a grievance to the players' union. On October 25, the WPSL governors voted to terminate the franchise.

So maybe Davis is more fed up than the other players, more unwilling to just go along with it and hope to get paid eventually. She's not here for the amazing experience. There's the way people look at her. The kids on the bus who have never seen a black person – kids who stare and whisper, who recoil or hide their faces or literally run. There's the security guard who followed her throughout the store, even though she was only shopping like everyone else. There's the giant pills she's forced to take, Vasilich standing over her. There's the insults Vasilich hurls at her and the memory of the game where he called her over right before she took her penalty kick and said, via Tanya, "If you don't score this, you're done – off the team." She had scored, they'd won, and he'd tried to laugh, but she hadn't laughed with him. She could handle Vasilich, she could handle this alternate world – but not for nothing, not out of the goodness of her heart. She wants to get paid.

With her agent's help, she gets a lawyer. When FC Energiya finds out, they are aggrieved. They tell her they're going to pay her, that she's going to get her money, that there was no need to get a lawyer. They ask her for her passport. Her agent had specifically told her, "Whatever you do, don't give them your passport." She refuses to hand it over. Her agent tells her not to let anyone into her apartment. And she doesn't – she locks herself in.

She doesn't know what's true and what's not. Vasilich is the kind of man who likes to boast. In the meeting in his office, adorned with trophies, photos, and a giant poster of his face, he had pointed at that picture and talked about "the mafia." Omolyn figured that the mafia talk was supposed to intimidate her. But she was unimpressed. *I'm from Jamaica, you cannot scare me*, she'd thought to herself.

But she is scared now. She calls the Jamaican Embassy; she calls her mother. Her mother was always a protector. Once, after twelve-year-old Omolyn nutmegged a guy – a "salad" as they refer to the move in Jamaica – the guy drop-kicked her, both feet straight to her chest. Omolyn ran home and told her mother. When Omolyn came through that door crying, her mother grabbed the biggest kitchen knife she had and took off barefoot.

But there's not much she can do for Omolyn now. Like her agent, her mother tells her not to leave. She follows their advice: when Vasilich's sons buzz the door, she doesn't answer. For four days, they ring the buzzer and she ignores it. For four days, she doesn't eat. She won't come out until they buy her a ticket home.

Finally, they tell her they've got her money. She meets with Vasilich's son, the general manager, and he pulls out a briefcase full of cash and fills an envelope. He tells her she has a plane ticket for the following day.

She thinks they're giving her a ride to the airport, but the man drops her off at the bus stop. She has thousands of dollars in cash with her. Her mind is in hamster mode, whirling with what-ifs: *What if this is a set-up, if they gave her all this cash and now they're going to kill her?* For the three-hour bus-ride, she sits alert. Hours later, she boards the plane – she's out of there.

She is not the only international to leave FC Energiya early out of fear. The group of Americans who came in 1996 also left early.

Three weeks into their stay the translator stopped showing up, presumably fired, and it became a lot harder to know what was going on. One day Vasilich's sons showed up at the Americans' hotel rooms. But they only wanted Wynne McIntosh and goal-keeper Erin Fahey to come with them. They left the other three behind. Fahey and McIntosh climbed into a dark car and didn't know where they were going or why. After enough turns down dark roads and a descent into a dark room, they got scared. Led down a stairway into a basement, an unknown man was waiting for them. He directed them to sit down in a chair – and Fahey and McIntosh nervously joked that this was starting to feel a little too much like the movies they'd seen. "Uh, are our lives in danger?" McIntosh asked Fahey.

The man stood across from them and aimed not a gun but a camera. They later pieced together that it was for a roster or official player card – that the team had decided they wanted McIntosh and Fahey but not the others, and just hadn't bothered to let any of them know.

McIntosh decided she'd had enough "adventure"; she was done with basements, with feeling unsafe, with Vasilich shouting. The Americans called the Embassy and, days later, they were gone.

• • •

In EARLY MAY 2013, the losing starts. After another ten-hour night train to Moscow, they lose to Zorkiy, the third-placed team. The circumstances are bizarre. Foxhoven's not the type of player to complain about officiating, but these are the most bogus calls she's seen in her life – a steady stream of them that interrupts any kind of continuous play. They are tied 1–1 when Zorkiy is awarded a penalty kick for a hand ball in the box – although the ball did not so much as skim anyone's hand. Foxhoven, incredulous and pissed off, responds: in the 85th minute, she leaps above her defender and scores one of the better headers of her career. She is celebrating when she sees that the referee is calling back the goal. Foxhoven wasn't offside, and she did not come in contact with the player in front of her. She has no idea how the goal could get called back.

On the sidelines, Vasilich is losing his mind. Tanya explains to Dani later that, from what she can tell, he knew the game had been bought – that the other team was supposed to win – but that he had tried to win it anyway.

While Dani writes about the loss, and the maddeningly bad officiating, on her blog, she only vaguely alludes to predetermined outcomes:

> It is such a frustrating thing to have a game decided by a force outside of the two teams playing. Like two little kids playing together and sharing a toy and an adult coming in and taking away the toy from one of the kids and unfairly giving it to only one of the kids to use. It leaves the other kid feeling unfairly treated, cheated and incomplete.

Tanya reflects, "I believe that some of the matches in the Russian championship were bought. Sometimes it was evident … And it was the biggest disappointment for me personally. I asked myself many times what the sport was? Business? But no one knew anything, we could only guess."

For home games, men whom Vasilich points out as the local mafia show up at The Base. They look like you would imagine: slick black hair, Adidas track suits, gold bracelets and necklaces with cross pendants. They sit and drink and laugh with Vasilich and the referees. Dani never ventures near them, but the Russian national team players are sometimes summoned over to shake hands and chat.

Their next big home game – the biggest game of the season – is against Rossiyanka, the first-placed team. They too import players from all over the world.

In the 65th minute, Rossiyanka has a free kick and Foxhoven is marking the Brazilian center back, who has a good six inches on her. They go up for a header. Foxhoven loses it in the sun. It hits her in the chest and goes into goal. She has continued her scoring streak – this time scoring for the other team. FC Energiya loses 0–1.

Back in her room, sitting at the desk and looking out the window at the ten-foot cement wall enclosing The Base, Dani calls her grandma. Her grandma is as tough as they come. As a child, she and her parents lived homeless on the streets until Child Services stepped in and put her in an orphanage. She married her husband, Dani's grandpa, when she was sixteen and they have been happily married for more than half a century.

Dani doesn't tell her grandma any of the particulars, just indicates that it's been a bad few weeks.

She writes down what her grandma tells her over Skype: "Some people want to ride the roller coaster of life and some people want to ride the merry-go-round. Me? I'm happy staying on the merry-go-round. But you, Dani, are meant for the roller coasters."

• • •

THIS PART OF the ride is all downhill – they continue to lose games they aren't supposed to. Before games, there is no sense of passion or excitement to play – only fear. "Fear is driving this team, and it is steering us in the only direction it knows ... backwards," Dani writes in her blog.

On the sidelines, Vasilich, wearing a sharp gray blazer and purple dress shoes, is out of control. Dani records him: "And she chases all the passes – fucking player, you're fucking clumsy. Did you see that fucking fool? Fucking fool. Scums should receive nothing." He spews, in Tanya's words, "refined evilness." He continues, "Bitch, filthy pop-eyed bitch. Damn. Lena, why are you fucking do this? Damn. Why are you falling down, fucking whore? Run! Motherfucker, bastard. Get out of here, condom." Dani's three-minute recording of him ends with, "Bitches! Everyone is going back home! Fucking insidious spongers ... fuck you!"

Tanya notes that in America or Europe, coaches couldn't get away with speaking like that. "But in Russia, the players, the staff, the referee, think, *Oh, it's terrible, but it's not my business.* Longanimity and social passiveness are our national traits," says Tanya. "I also wasn't ready to fight against this evil avalanche. I felt so small against this, and those 90 minutes just overwhelmed me."

After each away game, the players climb onto the train, silent, subdued, and hungry. When they had won away games, they were treated to cognac and McDonalds before beginning the long journeys home; when they lose, they get nothing. So far Dani has lost twenty pounds she didn't have to lose.

During one ride back to Voronezh, Elena Terekhova, one of the Russian national team players, slips into Simone and Dani's cabin. She sits on the bed, there to hang out, to talk. "How is it going?" she asks in English.

Dani, dumbfounded, stares at her. "You speak English? All this time you've spoken English?"

She shrugs. "I just didn't want to speak with you. I didn't know if I would like you." Americans, in the Russians' eyes, were fake, fat, and stupid, she explains. "But you, Dani, are none of these things." Simone, Dani, and Elena spend the rest of the train ride watching football games, listening to music, and doing Vasilich impersonations.

• • •

WITH EVERY LOSS Vasilich grows sourer. Sometimes during practice, he stays in the kitchen and perches himself in the window overlooking the field. He eats pumpkin seeds and watches. Then, when something enrages him, the team watches as his body flies upward and then disappears from the window: within seconds, he is streaming across the field, bee-lining for one of them. There is a Russian word, "*bychit*", which means to behave like a bull. Tilt your head down, raise your eyebrows, open your eyes wide, and charge. This is Vasilich's technique.

When Dani gets charged, it's because of a short pass, which he has told her countless time is pointless – *just kick the ball forward*. But after years of habit, she can't cut it out, and these neat little passes summon Vasilich down from the window. He comes at her, grabs her by the foot, waves her leg around, screaming profanity-laced threats.

Dani wants to go ape-shit on him, to scream back. But this is Russia and she doesn't know the rules, the consequences. She only knows she cannot quit. One man isn't going to get in the way of her dream – even if she no longer has a clear sense of what that dream is. Like most kids, she wanted to play on the national team, to play professionally. But while she played on youth national teams growing up, that dream is seeming farther away. There is no professional league in her country anymore. But all her life she's climbed a ladder to the top, and, even if she no longer knows where she's climbing to, she's not stopping now.

Vasilich is a strong believer in the merits of karate. He hangs a punching bag in one goal. They do a series of flying karate kicks, then sprint to the other end of the field to do more flying karate kicks. They are in the midst of those kicks when he brings over a player who is sitting out, having broken her nose in a previous game. He uses her body to demonstrate how to block a player out. Then, out of nowhere, he turns around and punches her in the face with the outside of his fist. Blood explodes out of her nose.

They'd seen him rough players up – slaps to the face, water bottles thrown at the back of their heads. But they've never seen anything like this. "We just stood there – completely speechless," says Foxhoven.

Like Foxhoven, Vero Boquete was also stunned by Vasilich's treatment of his players: "For me the, worst part of being there was seeing the way he treated the Russian players. He knew he had the power."

There is one player from former Soviet state Georgia who sticks out in Vero's memory: she was in her late thirties; never played a minute; and endured the brunt of Vasilich's verbal assaults. After witnessing Vasilich break her down, Boquete asked Terekhova and Danilova why the Georgian put up with it. Boquete tried to tell the Russians that they didn't have to be treated that way.

Danilova and Terekova were matter of fact with her – where was the Georgian supposed to go? "She has no family, no job skills, no education. You don't understand all of the situation," they told Boquete. "You are here only to make money. As foreign players, you don't have to accept it. Always, you guys complain about the conditions – if you don't like it, you can leave. We can't. We have no other options."

The following day, Boquete caught sight of the Georgian on the far side of the complex, running alone, around and around an outer field. They made eye contact with one another and nodded. They were unable to speak, but in that moment, Boquete understood: this game was all she had.

BY THE END of June, the FC Energiya 2012 season is in dire straits. They play Rossiyanka again and it's a must win. In the first half, Foxhoven gets hit hard in the side of the head and blacks out. When she comes to, Natsya, the team captain, says to her, "*Doctor? Doctor?*"

Foxhoven responds in English, "Give me a second," which Nastya interprets as, *No, I do not need a doctor*. "*Davay! Davay!*" she says, helping Foxhoven up – let's go, let's go. She continues to play.

FC Energiya loses 2–0.

After the game, Vasilich is again in her face, screaming at the top of his lungs, but Dani's out of it, in a concussed daze: she just stares at him with glazed eyes.

Her headache won't go away, and she doesn't travel to their next game against Kubanochka FC. Were they to win, they'd still have a shot at finishing second and qualifying for Champion's League. The team loses 1–0. Their season is over.

• • •

VASILICH HAS AN end-of-season barbeque at his mansion. It's three stories; there's a spiral staircase and white marble floors, white marble everything. All of the rumors – about money-laundering, about Vasilich's tight connections with the Russian underground – are easy to believe. And his excess of wealth makes it harder to swallow when FC Energiya declares bankruptcy. In 2012, with the exception of Omolyn Davis, who got paid for the three months she was there, no one else gets paid.

The players fight it for a while. Foxhoven's agent files a complaint to the Russian Federation, then a complaint to FIFA. Vasilich tells her they will rip up her complaint, that it means nothing. He appears to be right – no one cares, no one responds.

This not-getting-paid problem is not exclusive to FC Energiya. While Rossiyanka is in France for a Champion's League match, a liaison from the French team pulls aside the international players – including Americans Kia McNeill, Yael Averbuch, and Leigh Anne Robinson – and asks if they've been paid. The Russian owner had told the French that the foreigners were treated like queens – given fur coats, showered with gifts. This is not true. They have received a per diem for food but there has been no paycheck. The Americans fly back to the States early, and two of the three are never paid.

The Rossiyanka experience is tamer than the Energiya experience (though Rossiyanka is the team that made international news in 2011 when Coach Tatiana Egorova decided to boost attendance rates by having the team play an exhibition game in their bikinis). But the Americans on that team still go home with their own set of colorful stories: how one of the players sits in the coach's lap at dinner, arms around his neck; how if the "Boss Man" wants you to drink vodka with him, you drink, whether or not you have practice later in the day; how toward the end of the season, the Americans are taken out on the town to a Russian Chip-n-Dale show, where a man wearing a bow tie and a bikini dances provocatively in front of them, crotch entirely too close to Yael Averbuch's face. Like so many of the other players who played in Russia, the Americans describe their days in Russia as a "life experience."

• • •

WHEN DANI GETS back to the United States, she will discover

that not getting paid is not the worst of her problems – that the imprint from FC Energiya is worse than she imagined. But before she returns, she first heads to London to watch her friends play in the Olympics, Simone playing for Brazil, Njoya Nkout and Augustine Ejangue playing for Cameroon.

All three players know what is at stake: play well here and get noticed – have the chance to play professionally somewhere else. Simone lands a contract with Paris Saint-Germain, where she plays for the next three years. The Cameroonians do not fare as well – they lose all three Olympic games and both players end up back in Russia in 2013, this time playing for Rossiyanka. But the following season, in 2014, Ejangue lands a contract with Tyresö, Marta's team, the top team in the world. Just before she is to report, the team suffers a financial implosion – one more team that goes bankrupt. She instead heads to Norway, playing for Amazon Grimstad.

Nkout spends 2014 at home in Cameroon, playing for the local ladies' team. In 2015, she goes to the States. Now, like Ejangue, she is playing in Scandinavia, both still following the game around the world.

Omolyn Davis also continues the adventure – this time heading to Kazakhstan. The level, her agent tells her directly, isn't great. But it's a chance to continue making money and to continue playing actively while they look for something else.

Of course, there's the fear that it will be like Russia, and some things are: the language, the surroundings, the nice facilities surrounded by poverty. And like FC Energiya, there are injections. Before the big games, the coach or the captain walks around the locker room and, without a glove, administers shots in the butt or arm. The coach would tell her, "It will make you strong, do it." The captain would chime in, "You can run, run, run."

"I am Jamaican, I can run, run, run anyway," Davis responds.

Still, Omolyn likes Kazakhstan more than Russia. The feeling in the air is different. The team is friendly – they hang out beyond the locker room, they go out together, they smile at her.

During a game against guys in Turkey, she injures her knee and heads home early. She attempts to play with the Jamaican national team with her injured knee, but the coach insists on surgery. Her knee doesn't recuperate well. "The physiology isn't like it is in the States," says Davis.

And, frankly, after her experiences with magicJack, after Russia, after Kazakhstan, some of the luster has worn off. She decides she'll give football a rest.

Back at home, she gets a job in customer service for Panasonic, which is based in Jamaica. ("You got a problem with your Panasonic TV, chances are you're talking to us.") Her dream is to go into fashion, to open up her own shop.

The street games she grew up playing in still go on, but she doesn't join in. The asphalt is too hard on her knees. But she often sees the guys around, and they say what they've always said, "We saw you on the TV, we heard your name on the radio – you're a big baller. Remember we taught you, that's why you were so rough, that's why you can play with anyone."

• • •

ON ARRIVING HOME, Dani gets herself tested to see just what substances she has in her. She tests positive for three different types of anabolic steroids.

The silver-linings, laugh-at-your-life approach she clung to in Russia eludes her now; she feels tired and sad and angry. Her body feels weird – she is nauseous, something is off. Russia has taken its toll.

But having played in Russia, she has now played professionally, which opens other doors for her. Her agent lands her a tryout in Germany. The first few days go well, but in a scrimmage against boys, she is invisible; it is one of those games where she just can't figure out how to make herself appear.

After the game, the coach tells her, "You're not what we're looking for." Maybe the hardest part is that she agrees – this person she is isn't what she's looking for either. Physically, mentally, she feels bad, and she can't figure out how to pull herself out of it.

She thinks it's depression – the fatigue, the sleeplessness, the nightmares, the ever-present knot in her stomach. But then there's blood in her stool. She gets more tests and is diagnosed with Crohn's disease, a chronic inflammatory bowel disease that causes fatigue, diarrhea, pain, and weight loss. Causes are unknown. It is thought that some people are genetically predisposed, and that it can be triggered by physical stress. Her doctors can't tell her for sure whether or not her time in Russia brought this on – it's definitely possible that the disease was prompted by the shots, the pills, and the constant strain. But it's also possible that she would have developed it no matter what.

What Dani's most concerned with is what it means for her now. Playing a professional sport with Crohn's won't be a cake walk, but it's not impossible. She still wants badly to be the player she knows she can be. She doesn't want her four months in Russia and her botched tryout in Germany to be the last taste in her mouth. She wants one more shot. And that's when, in her words, "by the grace of God, the women's US pro league comes back."

A couple of years out of college, Foxhoven's pretty much off the radar. She doesn't have any illusions of being drafted. But every team holds an open tryout – anyone is allowed to give it a shot. Unlike the two previous iterations of the league, WUSA and WPS, the National Women's Soccer League will have a team in Portland. Portland is her city, her stomping ground – it is the place that believed in her.

Attending an open tryout is humbling. There's the fear that you are grasping at straws, the possibility in your mind that you are somebody who doesn't actually belong. But Portland head coach Cindy Parlow Cone calls Foxhoven. "I know you had a lot of success at UP [the University of Portland] and that you've shown you can play at the professional level. Now I just need to see you play in person," says Cone.

Here, at open tryouts, short passes are allowed. And Foxhoven, who has been a goalscorer since her youth days playing for the Colorado Rush, continues to score goals. She tells no one about her diagnosis. There are times when she gets light-headed, when she needs a second to regroup, but she does it, she handles it. And at the end of the week, she gets the phone call: she will be signed as a Discovery Player; she will make $10,000 a year. That salary is the discussion of a lot of news articles. But to Dani it may as well be a million dollars. She sits down and cries, beyond grateful for the chance to play.

She will be a forward alongside Alex Morgan and Christine Sinclair – unbelievable talents, two of the most famous goal-scorers in the sport. Foxhoven makes a plan for herself: "Every practice, every game, I'm going to try and be as good as they are."

On opening day, 16,479 fans show up at Jeld-Wen Field, a new attendance record in women's professional soccer. The fan base established at the University of Portland migrates over; the Portland Timbers Army develops a Thorns contingent; and the environment – the stadium-wide chants, the smoke bombs, the giant billowing banners known as *tifos* – is unlike anything the women's professional soccer world has ever seen. As Foxhoven takes all of this in, goosebumps on her arms and the back of her legs, she thinks, *Every second in Russia was worth it – because it is what got me here. This is what it means to be a professional athlete.*

Foxhoven begins the season as a bench player, but not just any bench player: her teammates call her Super Sub. She scores three goals, two game winners, off the bench. By the end of the season, she is starting.

Her whole family – mom, dad, grandma, grandpa – travel to Portland to watch the games. As her grandma sits amid the shouting fans, watching Dani score the winner, fans erupting around her, her smile is huge. She thinks, *That's my Dani, that's my roller coaster rider*. For the 90 minutes that she sits in the stadium, she is there with her granddaughter, on top of the ride.

A Home on the Pitch

BECCA MUSHROW SHOWED up at her first women's shelter still dressed in her school uniform – purple checkered shirt, navy skirt and blazer, knee high socks. She walked down the narrow hallway; in the lounge on the left, women of all stripes stood looking at her, asking, "Who's that? Who's the new girl?" She sort of smiled and gave them a nod. She didn't let on that she was terrified. She headed back to her room and her plan was to keep to herself but that didn't go well; within an hour, people were knocking on her door, asking, "Are you OK? How old are you? *Sixteen?* Ahh, you're only a baby. We'll look after you."

Mushrow had never gotten to be the baby. Her father, bipolar and schizophrenic, had often been violent. Always, she tried to protect her mum. At six or seven years old, she took her first swing at him, crying out, "Stop hitting her! Get off her!" He'd stopped short, surprised by the small thing hurling herself at him and wailing on him. He gazed at her with awe and pride and said, "Don't ever be afraid of no one."

"I'm not afraid of nobody," she said.

"Not even me?"

"Leave my mum alone."

He broke down and cried and hugged both of them.

He killed himself when Becca was fourteen years old. Her mother had used drugs heavily since – which meant that Becca, as the oldest sibling, had to take care of her younger brother and sister. When she landed in the hostel (an all-ages homeless shelter), she was tired of trying to be a grown-up, was all for being the young one. She went wild. She started smoking weed, selling weed, doing coke. What she discovered was that if you act loud and crazy and confident, people believe you. The party was always in her room. She stopped going to school. It didn't feel like a tail-spin; it didn't feel like anything, which was exactly what she wanted. She got kicked out of every hostel in Liverpool for "antisocial behavior." ("I actually think it'd be more accurate to call it *over-social* behavior," she jokes.)

No matter how hard she partied, she couldn't escape those moments in the hostel when she was unbearably aware of being alone. She lay there in the basic bedroom and thought, *No one actually cares*.

• • •

AND THEN, OUT of nowhere, there was football. Paula, the friendly, motherly staff lady behind the desk at the hostel had printed out a flyer and stuck it on the wall: *Do you want the opportunity to represent England in Mexico in the Homeless World Cup? Come out and play football*. And Paula, whom Mushrow sometimes talked to, said, "Becca, go on and go – you like football." Which was true. She'd never played on an organized team, but she grew up rooting for Liverpool and kicking a ball around in the street with the guys.

On the morning of the posted practice, Mushrow decided everybody in the hostel was going with her. The bedroom doors were electronic but if you jiggled them and pushed and kicked them a bit, they opened right up. She went from room to room, everybody's wake-up call: "Come on, time to play football!" she chirped in her Scouse accent as everyone groaned and cursed. Of the 27 women in the hostel, she probably got fifteen to come out with her. They piled into the minivan and headed out to the Everton Professional training fields.

Some of the women were 50- and 60-year-olds; some were alcoholics and drug addicts. Most had never kicked a ball or stood on a field. So they were all kind of nervous and giddy, and Mushrow was the ringleader – cutting up, making jokes, tiptoeing on the perfect pitch, catcalling the coaches. One coach, Fara Williams, a brunette with steady brown eyes, just stood there, eyeing her, bemused. "Everybody else you could fool, but there was no fooling Fara," says Mushrow. "She was one of us."

• • •

SHE WAS ONE of us. On one level, Mushrow means that Williams is, like her, a smart ass. ("I was a cheeky kid – I always talked back," acknowledges Williams.) But on a deeper level, she's talking about Williams's past. Because Fara Williams, England's most capped player of all time, knows what it's like to be homeless.

Williams's childhood was normal enough – she grew up on a Battersea estate with her mother, uncle, and three brothers. Football was everything. When she describes to me her memories of going to Chelsea games, her voice becomes animated: "It was a fifteen-minute walk across the bridge to the stadium, a five-minute sprint back – and then we'd play right out in front, me and my little brother versus my older brother, pretending to be Dennis Wise, Mark Hughes." Every afternoon, with twenty or 30 boys who lived on the estate, they played in a caged field, ripping up the knees on their tracksuits.

"Our parents used to call us back in for dinner, and that was embarrassing for everybody – you're in the cage and then the next thing you could hear your name – Adam! Karl! Fara! They'd shout it out loud. Our uncle would call us, so it wasn't so bad for us – it was when people's mums called them in a really high-pitched kind of voice that it was really embarrassing. And if you didn't come, they'd come to fetch you in person. 'Come on, go home! Dinnertime!'"

Fast-forward a few years and mothers-calling-you-home-for-dinner would seem a universe away. A family fallout – the main cause of homelessness – drove her out. For six years, at the same time as she was suiting up for England's national team, she moved from hostel to hostel. Her teammates, for the most part, did not know. In the hostels, she didn't talk to anybody and held on to the one thing she had: football.

Williams doesn't often talk in detail about being homeless. Any time an interviewer presses her about it, she says some version of "Yeah, I mean, I never look back at that period – I always look forward." In the most in-depth interview she has given, with the *Guardian*'s Donald McRae, she describes her first night on the street in South London: "Like everyone else, I had a perception of what homelessness looks like. I'd see this homeless guy coming towards me and I'd think: *Bloody hell, I'm scared. He's mental. He's crazy.* I'm walking past people with cans – and even those without cans looked rough. I'm absolutely cacking myself."[6]

But she remembered something one guy told her – that homeless people only act crazy to protect themselves so that nobody will come near them. That night she took that as advice for herself: every hundred yards she'd spin around, turning as she walked, trying to make herself look mad. "I also started making loud noises if an intimidating group was near me – to make it look as if I was crazier than them." It's an unforgettable image: a teenaged Williams walking alone in the middle of the night, turning in circles and making sounds in the dark, petrified of the strangers on the street.

Williams understands fronts, understands defense mechanisms. And as she looked at Mushrow, this tough-talking, baby-faced sixteen-year-old with dark circles under her eyes, she could see herself.

• • •

THE WOMEN FROM the hostel came to the field for four hours on Thursdays – two hours in the classroom, talking about translatable skills like communication and teamwork; then two hours on the pitch. Run by the Liverpool Homeless FA, a community feeder program for the Street Football Association, the program aims to change lives through football.[7] The women were all distantly aware of the Mexico Homeless World Cup opportunity – that a squad would be chosen to represent England from a countrywide pool of homeless players – but nobody was focusing on that. They came out because it was fun. (And because Mushrow kept rattling their doors every morning.) "Everyone in the hostel, whether you liked football or not, had a laugh," says Mushrow.

On the field to warm up, they did reflex games: Fara partnered them up and had them stand back-to-back, a ball between the sets of shoulders. As she directed, *Head! Shoulders! Knees!* they patted body parts. And then: *Ball!* Each woman scrambled to grab it before her partner, wrestling and shouting and laughing. If reflexes were suspiciously slow, if it was taking someone entirely too long to pat shoulders or knees, Williams just smiled and adjusted accordingly. "If she could see you were stoned, she'd make it worse for you. After a few practices running, we figured, don't bother, it's just better not to."

Every practice ended with a game. "That's when Fara came the most alive," says Mushrow. "She's like a big kid. The one who is always saying, 'Can we play a game now? Can we play a game now? Can we play?' She was running around nutmegging everyone, thinking it was hilarious." Constantly, she gave Mushrow a hard time. She played keep away – "Come on Becca, come on," she'd say as she held the ball away, rolling it beneath her cleat, keeping it just out of Becca's reach, always darting away. Mushrow chased, shouting, "Fara I'm going to take you out when I catch up to ya!"

In the background, someone else shouted, "Don't kick Fara! She costs money!"

When Mushrow was bent over, sucking in air, having given up on the idea of ever getting the ball back, Fara returned, patted her on the back and said cheerily, "Better stop smoking then."

Fara was not the only one who could talk trash. They joked with her that she was "half-famous." And any time they did manage to pick the ball off her, they let her hear it. One day a tiny 50-year-old Greek lady called for the ball – "Fara! Pass it here!" – and when Fara's pass was a little too far out of her reach, she yelled, "You are shit superstar, you are shit!"

This – the playing, the laughing, the banter – is why Williams came out every week. She wanted them to know the same mindless happiness that she did. For her, football was something she was good at, and that – being good at something – was powerful. Lying in that hostel bed, she always thought that football was going to take her out of there. These women just "having a laugh" out on the field, might never quite feel that same intensity, but they could still experience the sense of belonging, of community, of having a home on the pitch.

• • •

FARA GOT THEM tickets to her Liverpool games, and they came in the cold, bundled up, sitting in a pack. The games were not crowded ("half-famous" and all), but the stands were right up against the field and the brisk air was festive. "We were on our best behavior – we knew we were representing Fara," says Mushrow. One of the women brought her daughter – a four- or five-year-old whom Mushrow claimed during the games. She sat on Mushrow's lap as they all cheered for Fara, watching her closely. Their superstar was not shit.

On Williams's forearm, she has a tattooed quote: "That which does not kill me makes me stronger." Those words, of course, don't have to be true. Sometimes every mistake and every hurt leads to a worse mistake and leaves you weaker. But watching Fara, all you see is the confidence – the grace – and it must be something to sit in the stands knowing that her past, similar to your own, is what's gotten her there, what's made her who she is: a half-famous footballer who still wants to spend time with the likes of you.

They cheered, "We love you Fara!"; they sang Alicia Keys' "This Girl Is on Fire"; and they belted out Liverpool's club anthem, "You'll Never Walk Alone."

• • •

AWAY FROM THE PITCH, Mushrow did not quite manage to stay out of trouble. After a bar fight where she stuck up for a friend, she was sentenced to house arrest. She wore an electric monitor around her ankle; from 7pm to 7am, she wasn't allowed to leave the hostel. During the day, she had community service at a soup kitchen. She was in the middle of assembling bags – loaf of bread, jar of jam, carton of milk – when she got a call. "What size kit are you?" a voice asked. "I need to know because you're going to Mexico."

Mushrow shouted "Fuck!" before she could help it. Then she started inquiring, "Really? No, really? I mean, do you mean it?"

"I didn't believe her at all," says Mushrow. Mushrow is not a football wizard, but, as the coaches kept trying to tell her, she is a leader. The same qualities that got her in trouble – the party-in-my-room mentality, the jokes that everyone laughs at, the way she can affect the feel of any given moment – could turn the whole tide of her life. So they were sending her to Mexico, and when the whistle blows for their first game, Mushrow will be captain.

• • •

EL ZOCALO IS THE main square in the heart of Mexico City. On the east side there's the presidential palace, a huge colonial fortress. On the north side is the majestic, sinking Metropolitan Cathedral – the oldest in Latin America, its architectural style part Mexican *churrigueresque*, part neoclassical, part baroque. Around the basilica, traditional Concheros dancers in loincloths and feathered headdresses chant, their drums sounding across the plaza. Government workers, tourists, and vendors criss-cross the square. There are also homeless people – Mushrow kept seeing them, mothers with young kids just sitting on the curb, no government support, no hostels. She gave a boy the hologram toy from her Cheetos bag and the way he grinned at her made her feel both happy and sad – already she felt changed from the person she was back in England.

This square, paved with the ruins of an Aztec temple, has held public gatherings for hundreds of years – concerts, demonstrations, marches, rallies, giant art tableaus, and now, in 2012, the Homeless World Cup. In the center of the square, they erected a turf field and surrounding grandstand – where 70 different nations competed. A coming together of cultures and lives, people from Kazakhstan to Brazil sharing stories that were both similar and incredibly different. In the stands, people cheered and chanted and waved the flag of their country. An escaped bundle of balloons took off into the sky. On the field, games were intense. Something was at stake. A player scored and pounded his chest. One of the players on the men's team, a barber in a former life, shaved ENG into the side of Mushrow's head. A small English flag was painted on both of her cheeks and she wore a jersey identical to the ones worn by the superstars. To play in front of a crowd, to have everyone watching, to represent her country – she had never felt anything like it.

They got clobbered. But that wasn't the point. When Fara

flew in two days after the opening game, coming to Mexico directly from national duty, she gathered them together for a morale-boosting powwow: *Hang in there, guys; keep your heads up; stay positive; keep fighting*; that sort of thing.

Then, when she was walking away with Mushrow, she said, "You guys aren't very good, huh?"

Mushrow laughed. "You go out there and try to play against those tiny fast girls!"

"I don't have to," said Fara as they walked.

The rest of the week she soaked up the atmosphere alongside Fara. "Even Fara said it felt like the real thing, like an Olympics," says Mushrow.

A production company was filming a short feature on Fara and they kept following her around, saying, "Hey, Fara, how 'bout an interview" and Fara, who doesn't love the spotlight, kept hiding, kept shaking them off. "Becca," she said. "why don't you go on and do the interviews for me?"

"Because they don't want me, Fara! They want you!"

With the rest of the England team, they visited the soccer Hall of Fame in Pachuca. All the homeless teams milled around, checking out the cool interactive displays – you could play giant human foosball or find out how the strength of your shot compared to the greats. There was a kids' table with cutout footballs to decorate and Fara and Mushrow stood there coloring.

"Most of the time, it was just normal, but every once in a while it would hit me – *Whoah, this is Fara Williams*. To be in Mexico, to be with Fara ... it was all incredibly overwhelming." She just stood next to Fara, bent over the table, scribbling with crayons.

• • •

BACK IN ENGLAND, back in her hostel, the whole world felt different. When her friends were doing drugs in their rooms, she passed. "That wasn't what I wanted anymore," she says. "In Mexico, I saw that there was more to life." Trading jerseys with people from all around the world, hearing their stories – wanderlust seeped in. She left Mexico with a desire to go places, to learn, to see new cultures.

She also wanted more football – more of whatever it was she had just experienced. One player on the England men's homeless team played on a Liverpool homeless futsal team, which got her thinking – *We need a women's team*. She went to a chair of the Street Football Association and said, "Make us a girls' team."

He boomeranged the demand: "*You* make a girls' team."

So, with Fara, she did: Fara took her from hostel to hostel but made Mushrow do the talking. At the emergency accommodation hostel, the roughest kind of hostel, Mushrow felt a bit intimidated by the group of girls standing there looking at them; she inched backwards, hoping the half-famous one would step up and do the talking, but Fara just stood behind her and nudged her forward. "There's Thursday football training, and now we're going to play games on Sundays. It's nothing serious, we just have a laugh," blurted out Mushrow.

Mushrow's new team of hostel girls played in the Wavertree Futsal League when the season kicked off, playing against teams that trained and competed a lot more regularly. "Even though we were absolute rubbish," says Mushrow, "we were still proud because Fara was our coach."

One Sunday night Fara brought a couple of her Liverpool teammates with her. "I begged 'em to put on a kit and play for us," says Mushrow. So Fara and the other professionals put on jerseys and hopped on Mushrow's team. "We were like, 'How do you like us *now*?'" It was fun to win, fun to have the ballers on their side – but they had just as much fun when they lost. "We'd get beat 10–2, but those two goals … we'd go crazy," says Mushrow. "We celebrated like we just won the World Cup. And the other teams would just be looking at us like we were nuts."

• • •

ONE DAY AT practice, she was helping Fara pick up cones when Fara asked her, "Would you like to help me with my coaching? Be my minion?"

Before Mushrow could respond, Fara added, "You'd have to be up early."

"What's early?"

"Half-past five."

It was still dark outside when Fara pulled up in her Mercedes. It was freezing cold and Mushrow got in as fast as she could, turning on the seat warmers. ("I loved those seat warmers," she says.) They drove an hour or two to the day's camp, listening to Alicia Keys.

Now, instead of hanging around the hostel getting into trouble, Mushrow was outside, working with kids. "She was basically working a full-time job without getting paid," says Williams.

Mushrow loved it – loved working with kids. She helped set up cones and fetched balls; partnered up with whichever kid was a bit of a troublemaker. "You get on great with them," Fara said teasingly, her implication clear: one rascal able to understand another.

Afterwards Fara bought lunch. One day they ate on a swing set at a kid's playground. Fara ate "birdseed," as Mushrow refers to it – nuts and berries – and Mushrow ate a sandwich. As they sat there, Fara said, "Bet I can swing higher than you."

"Go on then," said Mushrow.

Fara swung higher and higher, and Mushrow leaned forward and backward and pumped her legs and tried to catch her.

"Told you," said Fara.

"Fuck off," said Mushrow. "You're an athlete. An Olympian."

Most of the time, they just messed around; they weren't having "deep talks." But every once in a while as she sat next to her in the car or ate her sandwich on a swing, Mushrow confided in Fara about her past. "She pretty much knew everything," says Mushrow.

Fara's not the type to say, *that's so sad.* "She treated it like that's just stuff to move beyond. Fara is not emotional – and when I'm with her, I sometimes act like I'm not either," Mushrow says with a smile.

When they left the fields at the end of the day, Mushrow would engage in daily battle with the bag of footballs: trying to jam the bag into the trunk – pushing one ball down, another ball popping up, the bag not quite fitting. "Fara, you really ought to get a proper vehicle," Mushrow would joke as she tried her damndest to get the Mercedes trunk to close.

Then they headed back to the hostel, zipping along the motorway – and like always, Mushrow was nonchalant. She never told Fara what she meant to her. "If I were to say," she puts on a faux-dramatic voice, "'You've been very influential on my life,' she would just laugh at me," says Mushrow.

"But to know I was coaching and being coached by someone that's made it that far – to know that someone like *that* had belief in me—" Mushrow's voice catches. She can talk about anything else in her life without a hint of emotion. But now she apologizes, goes silent, and takes a second to regroup. "It makes you stop and think, if they believe in me, I must have something."

• • •

MUSHROW SPENT THE next four years playing and coaching with the Street Football Association. The year after Mexico, she traveled to Poland for the 2013 Homeless World Cup as an assistant coach; in 2015 she went to Amsterdam as the general manager.

As she gets her life back in order, gradually football is phased out. Because now she's too busy, now she's got plans – plans that grew out of her experience with the teams. Every trip she goes on, the hungrier she is for another. She wants to see Vietnam, Cambodia, Thailand, and to go there she needs money. So she's working every second she can. She gets a job at a warehouse sealing up boxes; she works at her uncle's bar; she takes orders at a fish and chip shop/Chinese restaurant. She's no longer in hostels; she's living with her uncle, who has taken her in now that she's clean. Her mother too is doing better. Mushrow has a new brother and sister, and when she's not working, she's helping chase them around.

As she's frying fish and sealing up boxes and playing with her brother and sister, she's also dreaming of traveling, of her future. She knows she's not meant for coaching. ("Truth be told," she says, "I don't really know the ins and outs of football, which is kind of a requirement.") But she hasn't lost the idea of herself as a leader – she's holding on to that. When she hears about the possibility of teaching in Thailand, she thinks that's something that could be for her. She knows English a lot better than she knows football, even if she does have a thick Scouse accent. To qualify, she's got to pass the Test of English as a Foreign Language (TOEFL). So now, in between her jobs and taking care of the kids, she's studying, going through questions like, "How would you describe the difference between the words 'alone' and 'lonely?'" More often than not, she thinks she knows the answer.

• • •

IN JUNE 2015, when Fara Williams and the English national team are competing in the World Cup, Mushrow sits in a bar in Thailand, one of around 2 million fans tuning in to watch each England match.[8] There are maybe a dozen other people gathered in the dingy room, mainly travelers like herself, and whenever Fara touches the ball, Mushrow shouts at the television. She tells anyone who will listen, "That's my coach! That's my coach!" England finishes third – their best finish ever – and the media spotlight lands for once on the women. Mushrow texts her now-three-quarters-famous friend: "Looking good on the telly!"

For the next few weeks, Mushrow wanders through Thailand. Her travel buddy gets tired – her legs hurt and she wants to explore via mini-bus. But Mushrow's legs feel good. She wants to walk – wants to go everywhere – and she does, setting out on her own, making friends with whichever other travelers she runs into.

Maybe her favorite moment is taking a little rickety sailboat into the famous Phang Nga Bay. There's a rope ladder up to the top of the fifteen-foot-high mast, and you're not supposed to go up there – it's not meant for tourists – but it feels meant for her. As they sail towards otherworldly mangrove caves and limestone cliffs, the old, battered wooden boat skimming through green water, Mushrow is high in the air, holding on tight – determined not to fall.

A French Football Fairy Tale

GO DEEP WITHIN the Forest of Rambouillet in the Île-de-France. Down meandering roads lined with majestic oaks, past quaint villages, past secretive valleys and star-shaped walking paths where royalty once hunted for wild boar and red deer. Enter a lane – towering rhododendron bushes on both sides – and drive until you reach a clearing, more than sixteen acres of green. This is Clairefontaine, the most majestic football academy in the world. The best footballers, age thirteen and up, pulled from all over France, come here to live and breathe *le foot*.

Nestled within the center of the grounds, beside a cascading garden, there lies the famous *chateau*. On a brass plaque in elegant script, it reads – *Residence de l'équipe de France*. Home of the French national team. The teenaged footballers who sleep in the dormitories a stone's throw away, dot the surrounding fields, and walk the sidewalks will tell you – they all dream of one day "making it to the castle."

• • •

ONCE UPON A TIME, in the mid-nineties to be precise, this *chateau* was home to Zinedine Zidane, Thierry Henry, Marcel Desailly, and Lilian Thuram as they prepared for the ultimate conquest: to bring home the World Cup, to win it on home soil. Together, in the quiet of the forest, under the guidance of Aimé Jaquet, they trained on these fields, slept within these walls, lived together as one family. They were a rainbow of faces and backgrounds – with roots in Algeria, Senegal, Martinique, Guadeloupe – and some in France held that against them; Jean-Marie Le Pen, leader of the far-right National Front party, called them "artificial," and "not a real French team." But then the team that Le Pen had decried kept winning – winning in style, kicking things off with a 3–0 win in front of a multi-cultural crowd in Marseilles. With every win, you could feel the growing current; this felt like more than football. When Les Bleus beat Brazil 3–0 in the final, the whole country went mad – millions celebrating in the street, filling the Champs-Élysées, chanting not "red, white, and blue" – the colors of the flag – but "*noir, blanc, and beur*" – the colors of the people: diversity of both the team and the country celebrated rather than scorned. "*Beur*" is a term that refers to French people of North African descent, like France's star, Zidane, whose face was projected on the Arc de Triomphe. Thierry Henry told the BBC, "Because of the different heritages [on] the team, whoever you were and whatever your background, you could see yourself in that team. It was an amazing feeling."[9]

In one of Jacquet's final speeches to his team, he spoke of the "champion mentality."[10] "We are all World Cup winners, every one of us," he told his men. "You must now pass on this experience," like it was a magical aura that could be bestowed and passed down and continued. Which is exactly what Jacquet aimed to do: having won at the top, he became interested in the bottom. He stepped down as national coach and took control of Clairefontaine. As technical director, he wanted to plant the seeds for the future of French football. And this vision included *football féminine*. In 1998, ten years after Clairfontaine's opening, and riding a wave of goodwill in the year they hosted and won the World Cup, *les filles* were brought into the fold.

• • •

CAMILLE ABILY FIRST READ in *Onze Mondial* that Clairefontaine was going to start taking girls too. "Dad," she remembers saying, "wouldn't it be incredible if *I* could play *there*?" When she was fifteen years old, a letter came in the mail: an official invitation to Clairefontaine. For her mother, this was hard – she didn't want to give up her youngest daughter. But Camille bounced with euphoria and it was impossible to tell her no. Abily packed her bags and took off for a world I imagine as straight out of the pages of *Madeline*, the classic children's story that begins, "In an old house in Paris that was covered with vines, lived twelve little girls in two straight lines." The majority of the future French stars – Abily, Hoda Lattaf, Sonia Bompastor, Louisa Nécib, Laure Boulleau, Élodie Thomis, Laura Georges – came here as teenagers, to live and play and grow up at Clairefontaine. From their dormitory windows, they could see the castle. There was no women's team inside, but Abily remembers thinking, *Maybe one day there will be*.

• • •

IN 1998, ESPN Classics ran a six-part reality show on Clairefontaine that took you right inside *l'académie*, alongside the thirteen-year-old boys – in their dorm rooms, getting weighed in their boxer briefs, taping up magazine cutouts of their favorite players. A teenage Hatem Ben Arfa plays rock-paper-scissors for bunk rights. They walk down meandering sidewalks, take turns trying to shoot a ball through a crumbling, ancient archway in the forest. At night, they sit on the crest of a hill and watch the national team. When training is over, under the glow of the stadium lights, they crowd around, a sea of hands holding out their notebooks for autographs. None of the teenagers thronging the players are girls.

• • •

"*J'AI FLASHÉ SUR la Zidane,*" Louisa Nécib has said. A slang expression, "*j'ai flashé*" roughly translates to falling in love at first sight, being hooked in a flash – which is what happened to her when, as an eleven-year-old, she watched Zidane lead France to the World Cup trophy. Like her, he is Algerian. Like her he is from Marseilles. Like her, he grew up playing on the streets outside his concrete apartment building. This all played into why she loved him – but most of all, she was simply drawn to the way he moved. He was beautiful to watch.[11]

But when she arrived at Clairefontaine in 2004 as a seventeen-year-old, she wasn't about to ask him for his autograph. "I am shy, and I didn't want to bother him," she says.

Then, about a year after she arrived, to her everlasting shock, *Zidane* summoned *her* to the castle. He had heard of the girl from Marseilles – and the talk that her playing style was reminiscent of his own. Ahead of the U-19 UEFA Championship in 2005, coach Bruno Bini told UEFA: "We have one new player who can do everything – it's like watching Zinedine Zidane."[12]

They talked about "everything," says Nécib. It is fun to imagine the two softly-spoken center midfielders standing in the castle comparing notes on their beloved Marseilles, the old port city where fishermen drink Pastis and immigrants from all over the world move together in one sea of music, football, and culture. "My passion for the game comes from the city of Marseilles itself," Zidane told the *Guardian*.[13] "In football and family, I learned everything in Marseilles," said Nécib. "For me, Marseilles, it is everything."

Maybe they talked about her neighborhood, Busserine, and his, La Castellane, and about the difference between playing in the street and playing in the academy. Even though Nécib was playing well – and would be invited to the full national team within a year of being at Clairefontaine – it was still a struggle: she was homesick, and after a decade playing in the street with the guys in her apartment complex, *académie* football was a shock. While she describes *foot de rue*, street football, as "the most beautiful school," she has also said that "you don't learn everything. We so much loved having the ball that we tended to only play when it was near us."[14] When she arrived at Clairefontaine, she knew how to move with the ball; what she had to learn was how to move without it. It's quite possible that she confided all this to Zidane, that he encouraged her, and that they reminisced together about the street.

In the end, he gave her his jersey and wished her luck, and she walked out of the castle and back to her dorm. Maybe when he handed her his jersey, he also passed down something else – the champion quality Jacquet was talking about, that belief. When you are a shy teenager a long way from home, a show of faith from your hero is no small thing.

• • •

FOR LAURA GEORGES, the transition from her old home to her new home was less jarring: she had spent her entire life in a castle. Her Guadeloupian father and three uncles are security guards at the Palace of Versailles, which meant her family was one of the few to live within castle grounds. Their apartment was inside the gardens Louis XIV built for his wife, and Georges grew up using century-old trees as goal posts. "There was no shortage of lawn," she laughs.

Since she had arrived at Clairefontaine, her friends had been on her to get autographs: They would tell her, *Hey, you should go! The national team is in the castle!* And she would shake her head, "Nooo. I don't like this! I don't like this – don't ask me!" she would say. Like Nécib, she didn't like the idea of approaching them. But also like Nécib, she had a hero: Lilian Thuram was to her what

Zidane was to Nécib. Like her, he hails from Guadeloupe. Like her, he played in the backline. Ever since she had watched him in 1998, she had told herself, *One day I will tell him what he means to the people of Guadeloupe.*

One night, finally, she said to herself, *Ok, I'm going to do it. I'm going to go there, and I'm going to wait.* She brought a teammate to the pitch after the national team's practice and, once everyone else was gone, finally Thuram stepped out – he glanced at the girls and said, "How can I help you?"

"*Alors*, Mr. Thuram, please, can I have an autograph?

"No, it is not 'Mr. Thuram,'" he said. "Call me Lilian."

Her teammate piped in: "Do you know she is a big fan of yours?"

Thuram said, "Really?!" and Georges stared bashfully at the sidewalk. He hugged her and started cheerfully to inquire about the player in front of him. As they stood there chatting, Georges thought to herself, *I am so happy.*

One month later, he sent her his entire kit – jersey, shorts, socks.

Every time the national team was back in residency, he made a point of seeing her. They met in a café over coffee; he asked her about her football, she asked for advice; they talked about Guadeloupe. "I was just a kid from nowhere – there was no reason for him to be nice to me," she says. Talking with him, she thought, *This is the type of person I want to be. To be approachable, to be nice.*

Georges will pass it forward: when she attends Boston College on a soccer scholarship, she will be the kind of player who knows every cafeteria worker by name, who eats with the bus driver, who sends autographed jerseys to his mentally-challenged son. She will become a FIFA ambassador for the women's game and will travel around the world in an effort to give other girls the opportunities that she had. In her friendship with Thuram, the beauty of Clairefontaine is on display – a leader of one generation inspiring a leader of the next.

• • •

BUT BY 2010 that mentoring process, the passing down of dignity and greatness, felt like it had failed. French football was in crisis. It took a flagrant handball for the men's team to qualify for the summer's World Cup and, once there, they went down in flames: player boycotts, fighting, mutinies.

The Sports Minister Roselyne Bachelot stated, "I told the players they had tarnished the image of France. It is a moral disaster for French football. I told them they could no longer be heroes for our children. They have destroyed the dreams of their countrymen, their friends and supporters."[15]

Newspaper *Le Figaro* added: "It was almost hallucinatory. This is a psychodrama that will go down in the history of the World Cup. The French team has been reduced to ashes." And then things got still worse: in May 2011, tapes were leaked featuring French Football Federation officials, including '98 team captain and now national team coach Laurent Blanc, talking about imposing secret quotas limiting the number of non-white youngsters.[16] Football, once the symbol of racial harmony, was now the symbol of discord and exclusion.

A month later, when the French women took to the stage for the 2011 World Cup, they were nearly entirely unknown – and felt completely apart from the disgrace of the men. In 2007, they had not even qualified for the World Cup. Nothing was expected of them. But with each game, more and more people watched – and discovered football that made them nostalgic. In the quarter-final against England, 1 million viewers tuned in, television ratings climbing to a record 3.2 million viewers during their shootout.[17] As the football scholar Laurent Dubois wrote, "Their dominance in the game was a surprise to many, and to me, and also a little ghostly: suddenly, I was watching the sort of flowing, graceful, entertaining French football which for the past years had existed mainly in my imagination."[18]

As diverse as the '98 team, there was the feel that these women were the true, worthy descendants: in the midfield, the media lit upon Nécib; newspaper headlines heralded the arrival of "The New Zidane," a petite brunette with highlights, blue eyeliner, and manicured fingernails. When she roamed the center of the midfield, she had a ... *je ne sais quoi* that she had developed on the street. Like Zidane, she exhibited a gift for both the crafty and the breathtakingly simple. In the backline, there were also new heirs: in 1998, the team featured "The Black Guard" – William Gallas, Marcel Desailly, and Lilian Thuram. Now, in Guadeloupe, they started referring to Laura Georges and Martinique-rooted Wendie Renard as "The New Black Guard."

The Thuram–Georges friendship stayed strong: he told her that if the team made it to the semi-final, he could attend the game. France beat England in the quarters, and so Thuram was in the stands to support Les Bleues against the US. France lost 3–1 but that scoreline was misleading: France maintained the majority of possession and took twice as many shots on goal as the Americans. Fans across the world moved closer to the screen – to take in the silky telepathic football that seemed to come out of nowhere, but which actually came out of somewhere very specific: Clairefontaine.

Nowadays, as the teenaged Abily once hoped, *l'equipe feminine* reside in the chateau, training together ahead of international tournaments. The 2012 Olympics and the 2015 World Cup were a continuation of beauty. The technique, the orchestration of passes, the intuitive understanding. These players *knew* each other. Amandine Henry, one of the younger players to come through

Clairefontaine, who won the Silver Ball at the 2015 World Cup, described to me their collective experience: you arrive at the dormitory with your pillow, you spend years of your adolescence together, you argue and make up and have hallway dance parties and blow out birthday candles and brush your teeth shoulder to shoulder. You share the cookies in the care package your mother sends you. You plot and conspire (like the time you try to sneak in hamburgers because you are tired of pasta pasta pasta) – you get caught but decide it was worth it. You watch game after game, you walk slowly up the sidewalks together, bouncing soccer balls on your heads, fall leaves crunching beneath your feet. One day, after years of touch after touch on *le ballon*, you move together into the castle – once the apprentice, now an official member of the national team. All that experience gets into your football. "We are family," says Henry. And you can sense those familial feelings when you watch the women – love, understanding, loyalty – the exact feelings that have been absent from the mutinous men's side.

But Les Bleues cannot quite *win*. The "championship mentality" that Jacquet had hoped the '98 team could instill in future generations is exactly what the women are said to be missing. They still feel too new-at-the-table to close out games; they can outplay the goliaths, but can't take them down. The fourth place finish in 2011, and then again in the 2012 Olympics, is the best they've managed. In the 2015 World Cup and 2016 Olympics, they lost in the quarters. Quarter-final losses aren't enough to rivet a nation. And now, with each calendar year, the players that were once fresh-faced teenagers are beginning to age out: Sonia Bompastor is gone; Louisa Nécib retired in 2016. How long will the rest of that generation stay in the game? Will they fade out before they ever win anything? Will they be remembered if they cannot win? The next generation shows promise: in 2012, France won the U-17 World Cup and in 2015, they won the U-19

UEFA European Championship. Could the two generations merge together and find a fairy tale ending befitting a team raised in a forest beside a castle?

• • •

THE PLOT THICKENS. In 2019, for the first time since the 1998 team beat Brazil and pandemonium broke out, a World Cup will again be held on French soil. In the wake of the terrorist attacks that rocked the country in 2016, racial tension is at a peak and the national psyche is hurting; Marine Le Penn, Jean-Marie's daughter, leads a new era of anti-immigrant sentiment. There is no question that the country could use a unifying event.

It's possible that after decades of the French Football Federation investing in the women's game at the youth and professional levels, the French game could crescendo right at a sweet spot in history: the old stars just young enough; the young stars just old enough; the country just versed enough in the women's game to pay attention.

Recalling the '98 final, Lilian Thuram tells the *BBC*, "I remember just as we were about to walk on to the pitch seeing the Brazilian players, and thinking it was impossible that they could win because they were eleven and we were millions."[19] Will the French women have the chance to know what that feels like? Will their country fill the stadiums, the bars, and the cafes in the same way they did for the men's team? And what about the "you-could -see-yourself-in-that-team" emotion that Henry described – the feeling Georges felt when she looked at Thuram, and Nécib felt when she looked at Zidane? Will the country feel that same powerful sense of identification and unity when they watch the women? Can Les Bleues win? Here's a reverie: another moonlit night on the Champs-Élysées in July, millions out on the cobblestones, horns honking, flags waving, people again united for Les Bleues.

The Football Refugee

SIX MONTHS AFTER her father is executed by the Taliban, twelve-year-old Nadia Nadim, her mother, and four sisters are standing in the dark at a truck stop in Italy, surrounded by a dozen or so commercial trucks. When they get the signal, they take off running. Nadia's mother is carrying the youngest sister and Nadia is in charge of the six-year-old and the four-year-old; she holds their hands as they snake through the parking lot, adrenaline pumping, afraid one of the other truck drivers will see them.

They climb into the back of a vinyl-sided cargo truck – into a small pocket of space behind towers of boxes. Nadia's heart pounds. Her mom says, "No one talks – don't say anything." For the next 30-odd hours they are silent. And scared – but that's nothing new. Fear has been a constant: as they fled Afghanistan, creeping over the Pakistani border. As they stood in the Jinnah International airport, holding fake Pakistani passports, boarding the plane with charging hearts, terrified someone would at any second tap their shoulders and stop them. And now here, as they rattle around in the back of a truck. Allegedly, they will be delivered to London, where they have family, but even aged twelve, Nadia's heard the stories – of smugglers who are criminals, men who take your money and abandon you, or worse. The sisters huddle against their mother for warmth. The truck's uninsulated vinyl sides flap constantly as the truck bounces down the highway – *tat tat tat* – a noise Nadia will remember for the rest of her life.

At some point, they feel the truck slow down, hear its brakes – and now they are all alert, anxious. The driver tells them to get out. Between them, they have only a backpack and one large duffel bag of belongings – clothes, pictures, documentation to prove they are who they say they are. It is 4 or 5am. The sky is purple. They walk along a meandering road for 30 or 40 minutes. There are no cars, no people. The world is empty and silent and surreal. It doesn't feel much like London – it feels like the middle of nowhere. As the sky gets lighter, she can see stretches of green hills, dirt trails, yellow flowers and fields. It's all beautiful but Nadia's not thinking about beauty – she's thinking this place looks *safe*. They've made it – where exactly she doesn't know but that doesn't matter: they are all still together.

They come to an old, powder-blue steel bridge. As the sun begins to rise, reflecting off the steel sides of the bridge, they see an old man walking a poodle. In broken English, her mother asks where they are. He tells them, "Randers. Randers, Denmark – You are in Denmark."

• • •

COME 2017, Denmark will not be the place you want to go if you are a refugee – as the far-right, openly anti-immigrant Danish People's Party has worked hard to make clear: slashing social benefits to refugees by 45 per cent, seizing refugee assets, advertising these cuts in Lebanese newspapers. But that wasn't Nadia's experience of arriving in Denmark sixteen years ago. Nadia remembers nothing but kindness. In this story, Denmark is still proud to be a social welfare utopia, happy to take in the family dropped off on its doorstep.

The man with the poodle points them to a police station. The lone officer on duty listens to their story and says only, "You must be hungry." He drives them to the supermarket and buys them bread, milk, and bananas – which feels to Nadia like the best food she's ever tasted. *This guy is an angel*, thinks Nadia. Wishing them luck, he puts them on a train to Copenhagen, where they are sent to Sandholm Detention Center. The old yellow military barracks feel like a prison and some people there are at their worst, people with wild, desperate eyes that scare Nadia. But they don't have to stay there long: after two weeks, they are sent to a smaller refugee center in Visse, and here Nadia finds her great love – *fudbol*, as they say it in Danish.

• • •

RIGHT NEXT TO the refugee center, there is a patch of woods. If you wander through it, you stumble out onto a football club, sprawling field after sprawling field. What Nadia can't get over is the green, the endless green – a sharp contrast to the war-torn, arid city she has left behind. In Kabul, the number one sport is kite-flying, largely because the only space is in the sky. "I'm telling you, those fields were beautiful – one after another, perfect lush grass," says Nadim.

She is not the only refugee kid drawn to the open expanse of fields. She runs with a pack of six other kids: five boys – one Bosnian, one Armenian, two brothers and a cousin from Iraq – and her little sister Diana. In the mornings they are in class, learning Danish and English, but in the afternoons they come here, perched up at the edge of the woods, staring down at the fields through a chain-link fence. They watch men's team practices, they watch youth club team practices – kids their age juggling shiny balls, dribbling through neon cones, shooting at huge, perfect goals. The refugees can't speak each other's languages (other than the five or six curse words they've taught each other), but watching football, they don't need to – it is visual, it is physical, it is a game they reproduce once they get back to their own ramshackle field in the middle of the refugee center.

There is no shortage of balls: on one of their walks through the woods, Nadia spots a ball lodged up in a tree. She understands immediately: *If there is one ball, there must be so many more – let's go*. The pack of refugee kids scours the woods, shaking the trees, a fantastic, gleeful scavenger hunt. They discover balls upon balls. The new ones, the expensive looking ones, they figure they should not keep – they punt them back to the club. But the deflated ones that seem like they've spent more than a season lost in the woods they take for themselves. They don't have a ball pump, but they head to the gas station and inflate the balls there. One yellow Select ball is Nadia's favorite. She keeps that one, along with three or four others, tucked beneath her bunk bed while she sleeps. As soon as she wakes up, it's out to the field.

None of the kids is good; none of them has ever played before. "We were awful," says Nadim, with a huge grin. Back in Afghanistan, her father – a prominent general in the Afghan army – had given the sisters a classic black-and-white soccer ball. In their walled garden, an enclave of apple trees and rose bushes, the sisters had used it mainly to play dodge ball. It's not until refugee camp that football takes hold. And because they are bad, because they are starting from scratch, they have so much room to improve. Every second outside of class is spent in the pursuit of football: they pull up David Beckham clips on the old, clunky desktop computers and watch German Bundesliga games on the community television, hungry for any game or clip they can come across. And then it's out to try the moves themselves – hours and hours spent with the ball.

Juggling is what they get hooked on first, everyone attempting to top their personal bests. Initially, they can get four or five in a row; then it's up to fifteen and sixteen, twenty and 25. They wage competitions to see who can keep the ball up the longest. One day the oldest, the Armenian, sets the record with 57. Then it's Nadia's turn. "My heart's pounding as I reach the fifties," recalls Nadim. "51, 52, 53 ... I'm close! I can beat him! And then my touch goes wild and I start to scramble ... I'm darting all over the place to keep it up! I get 57 and have to sprawl out ... I jam my thumb on the ground but I get that final touch – 58! My thumb is throbbing but I'm running around yelling, 'I won! I won!'"

It is the greatest distraction, the greatest fun, every touch keeping their minds away from the lives they left behind.

• • •

MOSTLY, THEY PLAY on the refugee center's mini-field – uneven grass, homemade hand-ball style goals without nets. But they also know the schedule of the club fields – and when the practices are over and the fields are empty, they descend upon the grass and go wild. One game they appropriate from the club practices is "Heaven or Hell": in each round of the game, each player attempts to score. Those who score are sent on to the next stage – for another life in Heaven. The last remaining player in the round who has not scored is sent down to Hell – eliminated from the game. "Bye!" the other kids would yell, in Danish, in English, in Armenian, in Dari. It is in this game – everyone mobbing the box, screaming and laughing, picking off balls, shooting at those wide amazing goals – where Nadim discovers how it feels to score.

One of the practices the refugees watch is a team of girls. After four or five months of sitting on the edge of the woods studying every move, Nadia makes up her mind: she's going down there. She's going to ask the coach if she and her sisters can play with them.

As their practice ends and the players walk off the field, Nadia pops out of the woods. The coach is gathering up the last of the balls as she appears at his side.

Her Danish is no good but he can pretty easily see what she is after: "You would like to practice with us? Sure," he says.

Now, Nadia thinks, *I need cleats*.

• • •

NADIA'S MOTHER, HAMIDA, no longer spends nights afraid a rocket will take out her home, cowering from the sounds of mortar and bombs happening all around her. But now she's consumed by a different fear – being sent back. She's struggling – losing weight, crying in the middle of the night. ("I can handle most things, but that is one sound I cannot handle," says Nadia.) Nadia doesn't like asking her for anything, doesn't want to bother her, and she knows there's no money. But she *really* wants cleats.

Nadia brings it up – the practices, the team, the cleats. Many Muslim parents discourage daughters from playing sports: while the Quran promotes physical activity – there's even a passage where Muhammad races against his wife – many believe participation in public jeopardizes a woman's modesty. But Hamida is a freethinker who believes in women's rights. And football may be the embodiment of why she is here: so that her daughters can pursue whatever it is they want to pursue. With the fundamentalist Taliban regime in power in Afghanistan, basic freedoms were taken away: centuries old traditions, like kite flying and bird-keeping, were outlawed. Sports were banished. For females, of course, it was the worst: girls over eight could not attend school; women were not allowed to work; unaccompanied females were not allowed out of the house. "It wouldn't have been a life," says Nadim.

When Nadia starts begging for cleats, Hamida looks at her daughter and says "yes," no hesitation. She doesn't understand football, and doesn't care to, but she's nothing but grateful to the game that has kept her daughters from worrying about all the things she is worrying about. Her daughters have gone back to being kids.

Hamida takes Nadia to the nearby secondhand store, where's Nadia's gotten most of the clothes she has so far – including an old retro green soccer jersey that says number ten. ("All the time I wore that shirt," says Nadim.) There is only one pair of cleats anywhere near her size – Adidas boots that cost 5 kroner and look like they have been sitting on the shelf since 1940. The dust-coated leather is unbelievably stiff. At the center, she tries a bunch of different tricks to soften them: she sleeps in them, she puts them on and stands in a tub of water. Nothing really works but she doesn't care – "I was in love with them," says Nadim.

Nadia, Giti, and Diana don't need the coach to tell them what time practice starts; on day one, they are ready and waiting on the field. For one month, they play with the team. As fun as it was to watch from afar and try to recreate the moves later, it is a thousand times more fun, and more helpful, to try the moves right then and there, with the coach explaining the techniques. "We got so much better, so fast – because, I'm telling you, all the time we were playing," says Nadim. "Of the 24 hours, I slept seven hours, went to school for four, and all the rest of the time it was nothing but football." After dark, she stands under one of the center's street lights and juggles the ball there. While she's juggling, she doesn't think about her father – doesn't think about how she and her sisters would climb on him, how he'd hoist her over his shoulder – doesn't think about that day when he just didn't come home. Or the following months, when her mother searched frantically for him – long nights of phone calls to anyone who might have heard any news. She doesn't think about the day they found out the truth: that he'd been executed in the desert, the Taliban afraid of his influence. She thinks about nothing but the ball.

In her first game with the team, she is so nervous, so excited. She is wearing *real* soccer clothes – a jersey, soccer shorts, socks, shinguards, the whole deal. "It was *so* cool," says Nadim. The coach puts her in the back. She runs crazily, just running everywhere, unbelievably keyed up. And she can't help herself – she keeps darting straight for goal. Within fifteen minutes, the defender has scored three goals. It is the first and last time in her life she ever plays defense.

• • •

NADIA NADIM IS, unquestionably, a goalscorer. She's got that elusive psychological brew of cockiness and nerve, intensity and nonchalance. You can see it even in the way she moves – the 26-year-old Nadim is jaunty and spry, with a lot of hop to her run. Sitting in the stands at Providence Park in Portland, Oregon, I peer down on her during a pregame practice for the Thorns. Each step she takes appears both gleeful and combative, like at any second she may come at you ... or like she's just teasing, like this whole soccer thing is a lark. Constantly, she tinkers with the ball – during drills, in between drills. There are hints of rebelliousness – the occasional f-bomb that echoes across the field, the socks-pulled-up-high-over-her-knees fashion statement, the ball touches while the coach is talking. While everyone else is placidly listening, she is juggling, bouncing the ball on her foot, tiny, secretive little touches as she stands in the back of the huddle. When the forwards head to one end of the field to fire off shots, she is all the time hopping and firing and reacting (angry frowns for misses, *oh yeahs* and fist pumps for makes); it's not hard to see the kid from the refugee center, the one who whooped and shouted and ran around with her arms like a plane during "Heaven and Hell."

After practice, we sit down on a bench on the side of the field. Post-shower, her long dark curls are shiny and wild. She's wearing a beat-up jean jacket over the top of a team-issued black Adidas sweatshirt and splatter-paint leggings – about as individual-looking as team apparel can get. She's holding a plastic baggie with carrots and peanut-butter-and-jelly-sandwich crusts. Like her General father, she too has a presence. An aura that even soccer coaches – not exactly the type to talk about "auras" – take the time to try to describe, fumbling around for words to adequately describe her crackling liveliness. "She's downright radiant," says her former coach, Jim Gabarra of New Jersey's Sky Blue FC. She has a tendency to beam, and to curse, no matter what story she is telling. Both the smile and the profanity seem defiant – like she's challenging anyone trying to put her in a box or typecast her. She is many things at once – a Dane, an Afghan, a Muslim, a speaker of five languages, a Bollywood lover, a wannabe surfer, a soon-to-be surgeon. But, she acknowledges, probably, more than anything, she is also still the refugee who spied on practices from behind the bushes – she is still the kid with something to prove.

• • •

AFTER SIX MONTHS at the refugee center, her family gets the news: they've been granted asylum, and they are headed to the aptly named Rebild. It's a fairy-tale setting: forested valleys and lakes, moors blanketed with cotton grass, heather-clad hills, heaths and natural springs. The Nadims are put up in a big pretty old house with wooden floors and bedrooms for each of them. Their first night, there is a snowstorm and they can't make the heat come on – they huddle in the smallest bedroom, freezing and shivering and puffing out visible clouds of air. But even in the cold, there is the sense of immense gratitude to the country that has given them a chance for a new life. When they wake up, the world is coated in white – a blank slate.

Nadia's mother takes English classes in the morning, works in the afternoons. A principal in Afghanistan before the Taliban took control, she now takes whatever job comes her way – working as a maid, in the school cafeteria, in an afterschool program. The five daughters go to the local school – the only family of refugees. All five understand that, were they still in Afghanistan, there would be no school. And their mom has made it clear: education is everything. She's fine with this soccer business – Giti, Nadia, and Diana are now playing on the local seven-a-side team in Skørping – so long as it doesn't get in the way of school.

The teacher at the refugee center had prepped Nadia's new sixth-grade teacher: this girl is *smart*. The new teacher introduces her with this tagline. On her first day in class, the teacher wages an academic bowl, a trivia contest: she puts Nadia and the other "smart" boy on one team, and everyone else on the other. Nadia blanches – it doesn't matter how smart she is, she still has only a rudimentary sense of Danish. She can't answer the questions right because she can't understand the questions. She doesn't like not being able to live up to her billing and this of course only motivates her more. At home, she works at it: she starts with children's books with pictures, and the workbooks her teacher gives her, where you insert the right word into the blank. She does extra grammar, extra worksheets, extra everything. It's not long before she's running the classroom, speaking Danish with the speed, and slang, of a lifelong citizen.

Socially, too, she's a natural. Sure, there are times she gets into it: once, when she rides her bike to the grocery store, a pack of boys makes a racial slur and throws an apple core at her. But she chucks the apple core right back at them. There's one boy at school who hates her, who holds her Afghan heritage against her; they fight so much the teacher makes them sit together and talk it out in front of the whole class. But these moments are the exception;

in general, she doesn't feel like an outsider. Her family doesn't have the same "stuff" as everyone else – the cool brands, the rollerblades, the computer games – but that too could be solved: Nadia and Diana get themselves a paper route, wake up when it's pitch black outside and take off, chucking papers at doorsteps. First they save up for a computer, then skates. They start with one route and add another, and then another. In Afghanistan, under Taliban rule, they would not be allowed to leave the house; here, they roam the hills out on their own, cover mile upon mile and stake those hills for themselves. "We built our own empire," laughs Nadim. At the end of every week, Nadia and Diana go to the ice cream place, buy five scoops of ice cream, and sit back victoriously, grinning at each other, like, "*Yes*, we earned this."

It doesn't take long before their spoons pick up pace – because even eating ice cream becomes a race to see who can do it faster. ("We couldn't even taste it – our tongues would go numb we ate it so fast," laughs Nadim.) Brushing their teeth, they don't have to say anything – it is understood that they are seeing who will stand there in front of the mirror and brush their teeth for longer. "Always, Diana and I were at each other," laughs Nadim.

In *fudbol*, this constant vying makes both of them better: every day Diana and Nadia head to the field, Nadia taking shots at her sister, the keeper. They study the football on the TV and imitate: "Nah, Diana, you gotta do it like Oliver Kahn – he uses his left arm there," Nadia would say. She puts her sister through workouts: jump here, jump there. She nails the ball over the fence and tells Diana to chase it. After a few months playing for the local, casual seven-a-side team, the coach from the club next to the refugee center calls the Nadim sisters; he gets them to try out with his daughter for B-52, one of the best clubs in the country. At tryouts, the coaches are wowed by the Nadim sisters – yeah, they want them, no question, Giti for the older team, Diana and Nadia for the younger. But when the sisters ask Hamida for permission, this time she says no: it's too far away and she doesn't have money for the trains and the buses; there's just no way it can happen. Resigned, the sisters tell the coach they can't do it. But the coach is keen on solving this problem: the club will sponsor them, he tells them hastily. *We'll pay for the train tickets*. "And then we were like, 'Sick! Alright! Ok! We are coming!'" says Nadim.

For every practice, Nadia, and Diana ride their bikes six kilometers to the train station, take a twenty-minute train ride to Aalborg, then take a bus. This, she says, never feels like a burden: "I wanted to! I wanted to get better! I wanted to win stuff!" says Nadia. And they do – with the addition of the Nadim sisters, they crush everyone. Their coach starts playing the team in boys' tournaments, which would have been unthinkable in Afghanistan, where there is strict adherence to Sharia law. But the sisters are in Denmark, and they believe religion is personal. And Nadia has always abided by her own personal code. The sisters not only play against boys – they beat them, continuing to win by huge margins.

• • •

ON THE FIELD, Nadia wears trademark multi-colored headbands that she sews herself. When I ask her about her first headband, she grins, slightly sheepishly: it started with a pair of underwear. "The elastic waistband was so cool! I loved this band," says Nadim. So when the underwear got too small, she cut it out, made it shorter, hopped on her mother's sewing machine and sewed the ends together. In Afghanistan, women wear hijabs to cover their hair or the face-and-body-encompassing burkas; in Denmark, Nadia wears rainbow-colored headbands constructed out of her underwear.

The headband also illustrates her level of confidence: totally cool with making a headband out of underwear. She has few moments of self-doubt. And, she explains, any time she does feel a prickle of insecurity, she talks with her mom: if she says, *Mom, I think I'm going to bomb that test*, her mother always tells her, *No Nadia, you are going to kill it*. "And whenever she said that, I was like, ah, oh, okay, I *will* kill it!" That self-assuredness goes a long way when she is in front of the goal.

Her other prime goalscoring mental ingredient? Anger. "I have a temper," she says matter-of-factly. "I just get so pissed. It is this feeling of everyone being against you and that I have to show them." Her goalscoring is often prompted by rage – when she goes "red zone." There's the time when so-and-so isn't passing her the ball, so she goes and gets it herself, scoring four goals to prove to that other girl that she should've passed her the ball. There's the game where the referee keeps calling her offside and taking back her goals. When she argues, her protests colored with the profanity and slang she's learned in school, he gives her a yellow. Enraged, she gets the ball on her own goal-line, dribbles up the entire field and puts the ball in the back of the net. She walks up to the referee, her face close to his, and puts her arms out wide, "Was I offside this time?"

"Yeah, he gave me a red card, said he felt 'threatened' by me," says Nadia as she munches on carrots. "I got lots and lots of red cards."

She's learned how to control her temper, to rein it in and direct it. She is never better than when she is angry, and she's totally okay with anger accompanying her on the field. "It means I care," she says.

• • •

DIANA WAS THE other hot-headed sister – though her rage got channeled in a different direction. When they moved her into her own age group and she was no longer playing with Nadia, soccer wasn't as fun. And as a keeper, she hated that she could play out-of-her-mind well and then pay for someone else's mistake.

So she quit. ("She was so good! She definitely would've been on the national team had she kept playing!" bemoans Nadia.) Their aunt Saida often teased Diana – she called her "Boxer" because of her flat nose and her temper, and told her she really should get herself out in the ring. Saida wasn't just being facetious – she meant it. The Nadim women are envelope-pushers. Their other aunt, Aryana Sayeed, is a singer of Afghan pop who eventually shot to fame and even became a judge on *The Voice of Afghanistan*, all in a country in which female performers were often considered to be prostitutes. Since moving to London, Sayeed not only sings, she uses her lyrics to call out the violence and oppression experienced by Afghan women.

So, eventually, Diana takes the cue from her aunts: she tapes up her hands, puts on gloves, steps into the ring, and begins pummeling a bag. Nadia's in the front row for her sister's first fight. As soon as the referee blows the whistle, Diana is on the other girl – she knocks her out with her fist punch. Nadia, beaming, narrates the story, jabbing her fists around. "I was like, *"Daaamn! Okaaaay!"* says Nadia. "I was so loud, I was out of control, I was like, my sister is *sick*! People had to calm me down. They were like, 'Be quiet, Nadia!'"

Both sisters rapidly ascend to the top of their respective athletic pursuits. Diana becomes the number one ranked featherweight boxer in Denmark. Nadia makes one age group of youth national team after another. When she's eighteen, she gets an offer to play professionally for IK Skovbakken in Aarhus, and the whole family follows her there. In Aarhus, they live in a poorer community with high-density housing and increased crime rates. It's considered "the ghetto," but Nadia loves it – because always there is somebody playing in the street. She can look out the kitchen window and see when there's a game and head out. Even as a "professional," she is still down to join the kids in the street.

(The professional soccer player also still runs a paper route with Diana. By now they have saved up enough for a scooter – they get up at 3am and by 8am, they have the entire city covered.)

Many in their ghetto are refugees from Muslim countries. With one daughter a soccer player, another daughter a boxer, Hamida often fields comments from the other Afghans: *Why are you allowing your daughters to play with boys? Why aren't your daughters at home learning how to become good wives?* But Hamida doesn't care; she doesn't believe her daughters are doing anything wrong. And, as anybody can see, her daughters are good, and she knows those gifts could take them somewhere.

FIFA mandates that players not born in their country of residence must live in that country for five years after the age of eighteen before they're able to play on a national team. Denmark can't wait that long; they appeal to FIFA and FIFA makes an exception, deciding that a kid fleeing her war-torn country is not the same as a ringer imported to enhance the soccer team. When she is eighteen, she makes her national team debut.

Once Nadia makes the full Danish national team, disapproval doesn't stop the Afghan community from watching. Once they see what she can do, there is a shift: *We are proud of you*, they say. *Maybe one day my daughter will play soccer like you.*

This means something to Nadia, gets her thinking: where she lives, there are tons of kids, kids she's friends with, kids she plays with. She figures that a club, a chance to play for stakes, can help them in the way it helped her. She and Sam, a friend from her street games, gather up a group of seven or so kids who don't have the money for the local club and make a team. She gets a local sports store to sponsor uniforms so that the kids can feel that same thrill of a jersey that she did. What starts with seven kids turns into seven teams of players, everybody wanting to play. Many of them are girls. As Nadia and Sam run practices, they are aware of the parents watching – mothers in hijab who smile and nod encouragement at their daughters. Nadia, standing in the center of the field, coaches: "Push forward! Go to goal! *Sick!*"

• • •

ALL THE SISTERS understand that their athletic endeavors are still side pursuits. Soccer, boxing – they are just games. Her mother, Nadia explains, still doesn't quite "get it." She'll call up Nadia and tell her there is a wedding or a play or some other family function on such and such a date, and Nadia will say, "Nah, Mom, I can't go – I've got a game with the national team." And her mother will sigh, "Can't you just skip one time? Call in sick?"

School is still the priority. Even as Nadia is playing forward for the national team, she is also applying for colleges. She had wanted to pursue a career in law because she'd seen a Tom Cruise movie that made it look exciting, important. But after a summer-long internship of paperwork, she was bored out of her mind: law was definitely not for her. Business she figured had the potential to be similarly boring, so that too was out. She'd ruled out medicine early on – because it was what her mother wanted. Having married too young to become a doctor herself, Hamida often made it clear that she would like a daughter to fulfill her medical ambitions. And Nadia couldn't just do something because her mom wanted her to. Plus, Giti was already in medical school, and she definitely didn't want to do the same thing as her sister.

But then her high school has a "professions week," where you shadow someone in a field you might be interested in. Nadia opts to shadow surgeons at the private hospital that was close by – not, she says, because she actually wanted to be a doctor, but because she wanted to sleep in; she didn't want to have to take buses and make the trek to one of the other professions.

On day one, she watches a surgeon perform a boob job. Where

there had been nothing, now there were boobs. *Whoah*, she thinks. *That is impressive.* Over the next few days, she watches operation after operation – on boobs, on eyes, on stomachs. She walks with the doctors down the hospital hallways as people thank them, showing true appreciation. She's also doing calculations in her head – each surgery earns X amount of dollars, and they're able to do multiple surgeries a day. They're going to make *a lot* of money. And Nadia wants money. Always, she has wanted a lot of money. Partially because she didn't have any growing up, but more so because she knows that with money comes power. If you have money, people listen to you – you have a better chance of making a difference. And Nadia wants that too.

In Denmark, at the end of your high school career, you fill out your top three preferences for profession and school and hope you get one of them. On Nadia's form, she writes medicine for slots one, two, and three.

But she doesn't tell that to her mother. If she's going to give her mom the satisfaction of hearing her daughter is becoming a doctor – exactly what she'd hoped for – she's at least going to mess with her first. Congratulatory paperwork in hand, she tells her, "Mom, I got in to business school!" Her mom is properly supportive – *That's great, Nadia* – but five hours later, when she tells her mom the truth – "Just kidding, Mom. I'm going to medical school" – her mom squeals and hugs her, yells, "I knew it!" "She was way happier about medicine than she was about business school," laughs Nadia.

From the second Nadia lays eyes on the cadavers, smells the formaldehyde, gets a scalpel in her hand, talks with patients, her reaction is instant: *Oh shit, I love this. This is the best thing ever.*

• • •

HER FIRST FOUR years of medical school at Aarhus University, she plays professional *fudbol* for IK Skovbakken and then for Fortuna Hjørring, the top professional team in Denmark. Then New Jersey's Sky Blue FC in the American League gets wind of the goalscorer and comes after her. She can't pass up the chance to see how she stacks up against the best players in the world. So, for a summer, she goes on loan – lugging her medical textbooks, giant tomes with titles like *Medicinsk Kompendium Lommebog*, with her to Piscataway Township, New Jersey.

Off the field, she squeezes a lot into her schedule: studying at the kitchen table, highlighter in hand; praying five times a day, but only if she feels like it, only if it's genuine, because she never wants to pray just because she is supposed to; even learning how to surf on a giant yellow longboard. While New Jersey isn't typically thought of as a surfer's paradise, there is a shoreline nearby and Nadia's a beach-lover who fully intends to make the most of her American summer. On the field, she scores seven goals in six games – enough to get noticed, enough for people to see that she's not just a good story, she's absolutely legit. Her goals per game average is higher than anyone else's in the league.

She takes a year off medical school so she can follow football where it takes her. In 2016 she is snatched up by the holy grail of women's soccer: the Portland Thorns. She has superstars for teammates: Canada's Christine Sinclair, seven-time FIFA World Player of the Year nominee; United States National teamers Tobin Heath, Megan Klingenberg, Allie Long, and Lindsey Horan; and France's Amandine Henry, Silver Ball recipient. The stadium is the fullest, loudest stadium she's ever played in. It is one more chance to prove herself – to show she is as good as anyone out there.

• • •

I AM ONE of 19,000 loud fans in the stands on September 4 for a game against the Boston Breakers. In a few weeks, Nadia will return to medical school, but right now, she has playoffs on the line – a win will pretty much clinch it. During the national anthem, Nadim stands on the halfway line, taking in the sea of fans whipping their Thorns scarves above their heads. Nadim makes minor adjustments to her headband, nudging it backwards. Now sponsored by Adidas, headbands with logos are readily available, but Nadia doesn't want the same old headband as everyone else. She continues to make her own, buying elastic bands from eBay and sewing them together, making a new one every couple games. Today it is rainbow-colored, maybe as a shout out to the huge LGBT fan base in the stands, maybe just as a way to be bold and bright and different, maybe both. She hikes her socks up over her knee caps one last time, hops on her toes, and waits for the whistle to blow.

Forty-one minutes in she scores a penalty kick. She scores again in the 79th, slipping between the defenders and dribbling around the keeper. And then she scores again in stoppage time – her final goal is a leaping, reaching scrappy header that feels emblematic of who she is as a player. The hat-trick makes her the leading scorer on the team. After the game, she heads to the end of the field in front of the Rose City Riveters supporters section. As thousands of fans cheer, a young girl hands her roses – one for each goal – along with a crown of woven roses, worn over her headband: she is a star.

• • •

IN DENMARK, ever since her national team debut, Nadia is well-known. A Danish news channel filmed a segment on her, following the soccer-player-doctor as she walked down hospital corridors in a white lab coat and Adidas Sambas. (Some of the boys from the refugee camp saw the segment and Facebook messaged her – "So awesome, Nadia!") Playing in the United States has brought a whole new level of exposure. Every day, there is another writer, another website, another photographer wanting to cover her story. She is patient, generous with her time. She has an it's-the-least-I-can-do approach. She's grateful to be where she is – grateful to Allah, to her mother, to Denmark, to everyone who has helped her.

She's plenty aware of the world beyond the field: the week I am in Portland, Kabul is under siege, three separate bombs killing civilians. On Facebook, she posts "Kabul is bleeding ... again," with a crying emoticon. In Europe, a million plus refugees seek asylum, and every week there's another story of countries, including her own, implementing anti-immigrant policies. After a Syrian toddler drowns at sea, her sister Giti posts the line by the British-Somali poet, Warsan Shire: "No one puts their child in a boat unless the water is safer than the land." These journeys of risk and terror are something the Nadim sisters know firsthand. They also know what it's like when a country reaches for your outstretched hand. With every game, every hat-trick, every newspaper article and TV segment, Nadia has the chance to make a statement: *Here's what's possible when you give someone a chance.*

Though most NWSL games are not broadcast on TV, there is a live internet feed of every game; people from all over the world – her mother, the boys she once played with, Afghans – are able to tune in. On Facebook, she has 63,000 followers. One Facebook comment from an Afghan man reads: "I know it is impossible, but I dream of seeing you play for Afghanistan." She will never be a member of the Afghan national team. But one of the thousands of Afghan girls watching her will be. *I want to be a forward like you, I love watching you* – every week there are Facebook messages from kids who follow her. In Afghanistan, the Taliban presence still constricts possibilities for females: there are bombings of schools for girls who dare to attend, and most women still wear the all-encompassing burka when they step outside their homes. But in 2015, for the first time, the Afghanistan Football Federation establishes a women's national team. Nadia and the Afghan national team players follow each other's progress and reach out to each other, occasionally sending messages of support. In Afghanistan it is still a risk for a girl to step on a field. But every day, another steps on the field anyway.

• • •

THE DAY AFTER the Thorns beat the Boston Breakers 5–1, they train at 10am: substitutes go full-tilt while starters cool down, work out tired legs, jog as slowly as possible around the field. But Nadia's not entirely zapped – she's still subject to that giddy-mischievous-kid thing that happens to her when she steps on a field. She hops in goal while a couple of substitutes take shots; she is really enjoying pretending to be keeper, really diving to try to block a shot. She sprawls for it, belly on the turf, feet in the air as she yells, "I was so close! Shit! I almost had that!" Coach Mark Parsons is maybe twenty yards away and when he sees his goalscorer on the ground, I think for a second he will tell her to get the hell out of goal before she gets hurt. But he doesn't say a word, just keeps picking up cones – as though it is futile to try to suppress Nadim.

As the hour-long training wraps up and players start disappearing off the field, Nadim stands with the three or four other players, the substitutes, engaging in the juggling game she's loved since she was a kid: *How long can we keep the ball up?* When things go awry – when the ball gets away from them – Nadia's on the sprint, splaying out, her laughter echoing across the wide beautiful field.

Play Away the Gay

IN 2007, 23-YEAR-OLD Amanda Martin, a goalkeeper from Nashville, Tennessee with blue-green eyes, olive skin, and an aggressiveness in goal that outmatched her size, got called into the front office of her semi-professional soccer team, the Charlotte Eagles. The Eagles were a Christian-affiliated team, run by a nonprofit called Missionary Athletes International. Their mission statement is to use "the platform of soccer to bring trans- formation to their teams and communities through living out and sharing the Gospel." Martin, a devout Christian, had been playing for the team for the previous four years.

She sat down across from the general manager – a quiet, calm man, and her friend of four years. She had spent hours sitting beside him in the minivan as they drove to away games, discussing God and their faith. Now, he looked her in the eye and he was sad. He said, "We feel that it's best if you stop playing with the Eagles. We wish you well with your journey with Jesus Christ."

Martin started sobbing. She said, "I'm sorry, I'm so sorry." For years, she will wonder what exactly she was apologizing for. He said, "I know, I know" and passed her a tissue, and he repeated, "We wish you well with your journey with Jesus Christ."

She was still crying when she walked out of the office. She had just been cut from a Christian-missionary soccer team – was that even possible? How do you get cut from a team you're not getting paid to play on, a team that preached about inclusion and outreach? In the past four years, she'd traveled to Thailand, to Singapore, to India – spreading the word of God – and now they were cutting her? Not because of any shortage of ability but because of a perceived shortage of character? Was it because she'd been a touch pissy that she was not the starting goalkeeper? Had she had too much attitude? Or was it because they'd found out she was gay?

• • •

THE TENETS OF religion and sport often go hand in hand: in both, you give yourself over to a larger pursuit; both rely on unwavering faith – faith in yourself and your ability, faith in God. In both, an authority summons you to do more – a coach's pregame speech and a minister's sermon extol similar values of sacrifice, commitment, and discipline. Many athletes grow up relying on both God and the game. In the American sporting world, several influential sports organizations marry sports with Christianity; Athletes in Action, Fellowship of Christian Athletes, and Missionary Athletes International are all conservative, evangelical sports groups with presences across the world. They work mainly with athletes on the cusp of adulthood, players in the throes of discovering who they are and who they want to be. All of these organizations believe that homosexuality is a sin – which can be incredibly confusing for an athlete like Amanda Martin.

• • •

MARTIN EXPLAINS EVANGELICAL sports: you believe God has given you a gift, and you use your gift to spread his word. "When I found the Eagles – God and soccer together – I thought it was the coolest thing," she says. "My two loves together, what could be better?"

She had first encountered radical Christianity when she was a thirteen-year-old reeling from her parent's divorce. Her mother had left her father. After many nights of eating McDonalds on the floor of her father's furniture-less new apartment, she was desperate for happiness. When her friends invited her on a skiing mission trip, and she saw how incredibly happy they were, she thought, *These people have joy – what is that? I need that.* She was told that if she didn't accept Jesus into her heart, she would go to hell. She wanted Jesus, and she wanted the peace radiating off her new friends. She threw herself into this new world and promised herself that no matter what happened in her life, she would never lose her relationship with God.

From ages nineteen to 23, she played for the Eagles during the summers and formed some of the best memories of her life. From 2004 to 2007, there was no professional league in the United States – which meant she was playing at the top level in the country, while also sharing her love for God. And the Eagles weren't some mid-table W-League team; every year they were contenders for the title. There was something wonderfully intoxicating about communion on a field: players all exhausting themselves, working toward a common goal. They sang songs to the Lord in the weight room before games; they sang songs on the sideline; they prayed on the field, and then prayed off of it. Everyone was unfailingly kind. After training, they coached kids camps. Sometimes they escaped the North Carolina heat and hung by the pool with the men's Charlotte Eagles semi-pro team – "wholesome downtime," as Amanda describes it. "I absolutely loved it."

But there was one part of her life that kept surfacing no matter how hard she tried to keep it buried: she is attracted to other women. In 2017, the website for Missionary Athletes International – the umbrella organization for the Eagles – includes a code of ethics which explicitly states that "any form of sexual immorality (including homosexuality) is sinful and grieves God," although none of the athletes I spoke with were aware of there being any such clause back then. "But it was 100 per cent understood," says Martin. "And even if that had been there, it wouldn't have stopped me from playing on the team. Because I didn't want to be gay. I thought, *I've had girlfriends, I don't want to have girlfriends – this team is going to keep me from doing that. I'm going to get better.*" Part of what she was doing on the team was trying to change who she was.

Martin didn't hide her past; her ex-girlfriend was a part of her testimony. She was not the only one on the team with these feelings. In small groups, over coffee, in the basements of host families, she and a handful of her teammates prayed to be delivered from those desires. "We tried to hold each other accountable," she says. They told themselves, *Everyone has a thorn in their side, and this is ours, the battle we will fight our whole lives.*

Martin – who has a loud laugh, a charismatic personality, and a readiness to hold your gaze – inspires confidence. People talk to her and she talks to them. And when she was dismissed in the 2007 offseason, she wondered if they thought she was "spreading it," if she had just too much of the wrong kind of presence. She had no idea what they had found out, or what about her they no longer thought fit, and she was too afraid to ask. But she knew that she'd never heard of anyone else being asked to leave.

The thing is she *loved* the Eagles. These were *her people*. And that's the part that hurt the most – "her people" didn't want her. In this environment that is all love, all God, they didn't believe she belonged.

• • •

PAIGE LEDFORD IS part-Cherokee, part-Swedish: white-blonde hair, tan skin, angled cool blue eyes and high, sculpted cheekbones. She wore her hair down while she played – the mess of white hair gave us all the impression that she was a feral child from the sticks, which wasn't too far from the truth. She came from nowhere. Nowhere being Ooltewah, Tennessee, a small mountain town not at all known for soccer. She was the only Tennessee player to make the '83 Olympic Development southern regional team, which is where I met her – at camp in Montevalo, Alabama. We were fourteen years old. She stalked the field like a hunter in the woods – deft, smart, quick, and strong. Coaches adored her for the same reason we did: she fit no mold. She was an only child, born to two parents who rarely spoke; she rarely spoke either – which made us, her teammates, all the more compelled to know more about her. There was something so pure and unadulterated and spun-out-of-gold about her that you wanted to protect her, even though deep down you guessed that really, she was the one who could save you.

As we got older, we, her teammates, her lifelong friends, relished every new detail: she, silent wonder, was crowned homecoming queen of her high school. She set a state weight-lifting record: she held the clean and jerk record for the state of Tennessee. She was Tennessee State Mountain Biking champion. She got a perfect score on the math section of the college entrance exam, the ACT (or so the legend goes). She chose Clemson University because of its strong engineering department. In the summer before college, she and I both went to play for the semi-professional soccer team the Memphis Mercury. We lived together, along with Joey Yenne, Harvard's leading scorer, a Christian Scientist with whom I grew up playing in Pensacola, Florida. I'd bought an old Ford truck for $400 from the billboard company where my dad worked; we sat three, sometimes four across the truck cab as we drove through downtown Memphis at rush hour. Paige had picked up a bag of smoke bombs from a fireworks stand and when we arrived at the field, she'd wordlessly toss a few smoke bombs out the window.

Joey and I worked boring desk jobs – her for a law firm, me

filing papers for a vacuum company. Paige worked as a grounds-keeper on a golf course. She wanted to be outside. She was the only English-speaker and the only girl. (Once, she cleared poison ivy out of a bed with her bare hands – maybe because we'd convinced her by that point in the summer that she was invincible. Her entire body and face broke out in a swollen, angry rash, but she just lathered on white ointment and never once complained.) While Joey and I took our paychecks and went to Banana Republic to buy clothes, Paige bought a climbing rock that she nailed to the wall so that she could work on her grip. Frequently, we found her just hanging there in the entryway, suspended in air. Often, she scaled our balcony – parkouring before we knew it existed – and when Joey's lawyer colleagues dropped her off, they leaned across the car to get a better look – "What *is* that?" And Joey would say, "Oh, that's just Paige."

The following year at Clemson, Paige got a girlfriend, Abby. They visited me at Duke and they were flush with love. My normally silent Paige was giddy, chatty, boundlessly happy. She told me, "It is the best thing that has ever happened to me."

Maybe six months later, the next time Duke played Clemson, she told me that she was no longer dating Abby. She kind of scratched her head and said, "Shouldn't be doing that." On her dorm floor, there were a group of Christians – every time she passed them, her relationship with Abby weighed on her conscience. She thought, *Wait a minute, am I pleasing God right now?* She had grown up in a religious school, and while everyone else got baptized when they were around fifteen years old, she declined – she had not wanted to do that unless she felt sure. And back then she wasn't. But now she was digging into the Bible, exploring her faith. "Yup, G. Found Jesus," she said, her manner lighthearted but definitive.

The next summer she again went to play with the Memphis

Mercury (I went home to train in Pensacola). That season she roomed with evangelical Christian Amanda Martin. Paige turned to Amanda: they pored over the Bible together and they visited churches across Memphis. Abby – who was no longer Paige's official girlfriend but who she couldn't quite bring herself to stop seeing – came to visit. Afterward Amanda got it out of her that they were not quite just friends, and Amanda shared that she too had a relationship with a girl. "Amanda and I had the same struggle," says Paige. "I was at that point feeling really conflicted about my relationship with Abby. There was a time when I didn't feel conflicted. But by then, I was thinking, maybe I shouldn't be doing this. I wanted to be a Christian and know exactly what I believed – but I also had such strong feelings at that time for Abby, and it was really hard to stop."

Together they prayed. They prayed that God would help turn them away from their flesh desires, prayed that He would help them lead a holier life. They pored over all relevant passages in the Bible and they both ended things with their girlfriends. The Bible, Paige decided, is clear. "And I wanted to live a life that was in line with my beliefs," she says. By 2005, both Paige and Amanda were playing for the Charlotte Eagles – and both had vowed to leave that part of themselves behind.

Over the next few years, Paige and I kept in touch only sporadically, to provide big life updates. Of which there are several: in 2006 she had a stroke. Because of her low percentage of body fat, she had started using the Ortho Evra birth control patch to increase her estrogen levels. She is one of the dozens of women who, possibly as a result of the patch, experienced blood clots that resulted in a stroke. She was, as always, nonchalant. "I'm okay, G," she said when I talked with her from the hospital.

But the stroke changed the course of her life: while she had intended to make a run for the national team, now she turned away from soccer. And she no longer felt invincible. "It shook me up. I felt the gravity of my life," she says. "I also felt God's protection and care and nearness. I found the promises he made in the Bible to be true."

Six months later, she married Chris, a guy I'd never heard of. Amanda was a bridesmaid in the wedding. In 2007, Paige and her husband moved to Thailand and became missionaries.

• • •

BY THE FOLLOWING SEASON, in 2008, Paige was in Thailand and Amanda had been dismissed from the team. A new team – a mix of long-timers and fresh faces – showed up in Charlotte. Before the first practice, the captain said, "Make sure to bring your Bibles." Heather Dittmer, a soft-spoken brunette with kind eyes, and Ashleigh Gunning, a curly-blonde spitfire from southeastern Louisiana, both just looked at each other. They were best friends and first-time Charlotte Eagles. Neither of them had a Bible.

They headed to the Barnes and Noble and grabbed the "sale" edition. One got brown leather, the other got black because they didn't want it to look like they had matching Bibles, didn't want it to be obvious that they had just bought them. In the car in the parking lot, they ripped off the cellophane, bent the spines, and tried to rumple up the pages so that nobody could tell their Bibles were brand spanking new. They had known that the team was Christian, but hadn't given it much thought – *Yeah, whatever. So we'll pray sometimes. No problem.* Ashleigh did not grow up in a religious home, and when, on the phone, the general manager questioned her about her faith, she had straight up lied: "I told him I prayed about it and that I knew I was supposed to play there. I hadn't prayed about it. But they were the good team and I wanted to play on the good team."

Before Heather signed, the general manager sent her an email:

"Tell me about your relationship with Jesus Christ." Admittedly, Heather had highlighted certain facts to make herself sound more religious than she actually was: she "grew up in the church," she wrote. She just wanted to play soccer and figured she was Christian enough.

But when they arrived, both realized they had tremendously underestimated the God component. This wasn't just an occasional pregame prayer. This was Bible studies every day and singing songs that glorified Jesus along the sideline. They practiced at 7am, their socks wet with morning dew, and afterward, they coached summer camps that integrated Bible lessons into training. This was the part that felt odd to Heather. She understood that vacation Bible studies are common in the south, that this was normal, but preaching to kids didn't feel normal to her. It didn't jive with her personality: "I don't believe in projecting my beliefs out onto others, and that is a huge part of what the Eagles want you to do – give testimony, share your beliefs."

Another thing she did not share: her sexuality. In college she had dated women and men but she was not out. And there was no way she was going to be out here: "It wasn't explicitly stated that you couldn't be gay but it was absolutely understood."

• • •

ABOUT A THIRD of the way through the summer, Heather went out for coffee with a teammate. The teammate casually mentioned having dated a girl and Heather thought, *OK, I can talk to her. It's safe.* So Heather leaned across the table and told her that she was currently talking to another girl on the team, Lydia Vandenbergh. They finished their coffee and left – and Heather had no inkling of what had just been put in motion.

A week later, the players were called into a team meeting in the gym adjacent to the field. They sat in a circle of folding chairs.

The teammate she was just at coffee with stood up in front of the group – and Heather could tell right away that something was up. She said: "I want to confess that I've been having a lot of homosexual thoughts and feeling emotional connections to other females."

Heather stared at the floor and thought, *Oh my God, what is she doing?*

She continued: "I think there are a lot of us who are struggling with homosexual urges. And I just want to be transparent so that we can work through this together."

That was the beginning of what felt to Heather and Lydia like a witch hunt.

• • •

TEAM MANAGEMENT CALLED three veteran players, players who were all married with kids, all long-time Eagles. The general manager said something along the lines of, *Hey, we're hearing some things that we're concerned about, things that aren't consistent with who we are as an organization. We need to find out what's taking place.* He also said that they felt it was best addressed within the team, by the players themselves. Shannon O'Brien was asked to lead the conversation.

• • •

THIS WAS O'BRIEN'S seventh season playing with the Eagles. Ever since she was a fourteen-year-old dealing with her mother's stage IV breast cancer, soccer had provided her truest sense of community: as a teenager, jogging laps around a field with her friends, she found both solace and distraction from "the House of Cancer." She believes that's exactly what God intended. Now, as a 22-year-old, she rejoiced in being able to use the game that had once helped her to bring others to God. On the Eagles, she had found a team that excelled and played to win, but that did so in such a way that the opponent came away with a respect that could help facilitate a conversation about their larger purpose – glorifying God. And here, through this team, she met her husband. Theirs was the first of many marriages between a male and a female Charlotte Eagles player. (The count is up to nine – they jokingly call this Eagles love connection "E-Harmony.") At the beginning of this 2008 season, O'Brien discovered she was pregnant with their second child – so instead of playing, now she was coming to practice as part of the ministry.

But ten weeks into her pregnancy, she felt like something was wrong. At the doctor's appointment, with her eighteen-month-old daughter in tow, the doctor confirmed: "The heartbeat is gone." She remembers her daughter reaching for and knocking over a bowl of candy. As she stooped alongside the doctor to gather up the scattered mints, she tried to process what she'd just heard: her baby was gone.

She drove straight to practice. At the field, along the sideline, she wept, telling herself, *Get it together*. Coach Horton consoled her. As she sobbed, she said, "I know it wasn't that long—" Coach Horton stopped her. "It was long enough – he was your child," he said, hugging her.

Only three weeks later, Eagles management approached her about leading the intervention on same-sex attraction. "It was a heavy ask," says O'Brien. "I didn't want to have to do that. I didn't want to be an authority figure. I broke down. My heart hurt, knowing the level of hurt my sisters were going to feel ... We did not want to hurt anyone. We didn't know how to go about it. We were told this had to be addressed – it needed to be brought into the light. And we really wrestled with what to do. We were actively in a place where we were living our lives by the Scripture – you are called to honor God first and honor and love your teammates second. Knowing it's going to offend and hurt someone ...

Who are you going to offend – God, or your teammate? I didn't want to offend anyone!"

As she deliberated over what she should do, she kept thinking about heartbeats. Because since that hour in the doctor's office, she's been keenly aware that from the second we are born, already our heartbeats are starting to die. "But through God, our heartbeats have a chance to continue to beat – spiritually-speaking because of our salvation in Christ," she says. And she thought, *I have sisters on this team whose heartbeats are literally going to fade – God doesn't want that, he wants them to pursue his Promised Land.*

So she reached her decision: "We can be passive and not address it and just not say anything and let them have to deal with it on their own – which is actually not very loving. Or, I can bring it up from a loving place knowing that it's going to create conflict. These girls were dear to us, but the authority on our life is Christ and Scripture."

When O'Brien stood up to lead the meeting, no sound came out of her. She started to cry. Eventually she got out that there was a sensitive subject to discuss – that some things had been brought to management's attention. Then she sat down. The two other senior teammates led the meeting. They emphasized the Bible's stance on homosexuality. They made it clear where the Eagles stand and that "engaging in homosexual behavior" is unacceptable.

At the end, another Charlotte Eagles alum stormed in, guns-blazing, her voice emotional, angry, nearly hysterical. "I can't believe any sort of homosexuality would be going on in this team. You should be so ashamed. You have no right – you are staining our name. As Christians this is not what we stand for. *We* are *not* gay. How dare you bring this to the Eagles." Everyone stared at the floor.

Nine years later, O'Brien is straightforward about her remorse:

"If I had to do it over again, I would have done it differently. When we bring things into the light, there is opportunity to heal, as opposed to keeping it in the darkness ... but it has to be done so helpfully, and gently. And in hindsight, private conversations would have been a wiser choice. The way it was done – everyone felt blindsided – and for how they felt, dang. That was a miss. And that's Scripture – *Go to them privately*. That's not what we did."

• • •

THIS WAS LYDIA VANDENBERGH'S third season on the Eagles. It was the first season anyone had mentioned the word "homosexuality" out in the open. The past two seasons, players – including herself – had prayed about same-sex attraction in secret; all judgment was unspoken, assumed, and harbored in the hearts of those dealing with feelings themselves. Vandenbergh was a self-described people-pleaser. If people told her it was wrong, part of her believed it too. Her friend, Amanda Martin, had been mysteriously dismissed from the team in the offseason, with no explanation ever provided to either Martin or her teammates, and since it was the offseason, nobody had asked. Never had homosexuality been talked about directly, in public, whole team present.

Vandenbergh is attracted to both men and women and has had relationships with both. "Sitting there, I was freaking out. I was worried I was going to get kicked off the Eagles," says Vanderbergh. "I hadn't told my family, and I was scared I was going to be outed. I didn't know what was going on.

"I told myself, I just need to get through this summer. I'm going to sit in the back and not say a word. I just wanted to play soccer. I was very non-confrontational. Now though, if it had happened, I wouldn't stay quiet."

Like Amanda, she had so many good memories of the Eagles.

In the seven years that came after her time with the Eagles, she went on to play professional soccer in the United States, Denmark, Australia and Brazil. The higher up you go in sports, the bigger the egos and the tougher the competition. But the Eagles was a respite from all that – it was the most relaxed she'd ever been. "The pressure was off," she says. There was less of a focus on results and more of a focus on who you are as a person, who you want to be – and that was empowering. Playing for the Eagles, spending all that time turning inward, she was thinking about what she wanted out of her life – and not just in terms of what she could contribute on the field. Life is larger than that, which is one thing she learned while doing missionary trips across Thailand and India. But she also learned that who she is – bisexual and someone who believes you can love anybody you want – is not somebody the Eagles are okay with.

"It was a bubble – a bubble I wanted out of," she says. "I don't fault them for their belief system, but it is not mine. They think what they are doing is right. But I don't think it's right to treat people that way. I thought, *I'm done with the Eagles, I am not coming back here.*"

She stopped talking to Heather and just tried to get through the season.

• • •

HEATHER'S HOST FAMILY – a "heteronormative, upper-class Christian family" who lived in a big house in a wealthy neighborhood – made it clear they didn't want her there. They asked her to come in through the garage and go straight up the stairs because they "preferred that she not be around their children." While the other players ate family dinners with their hosts, she was never included or invited. She was told to keep her food in a separate fridge. It felt tense and weird, and she didn't know what they'd been told about her, but she knew she needed to get out of there. She went to live with Ashleigh's host family.

Over the course of the summer, Ashleigh, Heather's long-time best friend, had become a devout Christian and a big believer in the Eagles. But Ashleigh was furious about how they had made her best friend feel, and she tried to shield Heather from the gossip.

"I love the Eagles, I love what they strive for ... what they did for me as a young female athlete, what they try to do for other young female athletes. But they aren't perfect and it infuriates me, the mishandling – the very, very much mishandling – of the situation. I want to protect anyone I care about from ever being made to feel that way," she says. "Heather is my best friend. She has a heart of gold. I love her."

• • •

NOT LONG AFTER the meeting where senior players broached the subject of homosexuality, the team was staying at a Holiday Inn for an away game. Shannon O'Brien knocked on Heather's hotel door and asked her to come into the hallway. Heather could guess what it was about and told herself, *Don't cry. Don't cry.* She sat down on the AC unit at the end of the hallway. O'Brien said, "I know one of the gay people is you. That is a sin, you will go to Hell for that. That's not God's Will for your life." Heather didn't say much, didn't affirm or deny anything. Afterwards, she cried in her hotel room. "Through everything I just stayed silent and tried to pretend it wasn't happening," she says.

When I ask Shannon if she remembers talking with Heather in the hallway, she says yes but that her recollection is vague. When I describe Heather's account and ask if that's how she remembers it, she says, "If that is what her memory is, that's all that matters – that breaks my heart. I feel awful. For Heather to feel condemnation from me in that moment – this is a hard truth for me to hear. She needed to know that God loved her in the midst of anything she was wrestling with, and that I didn't communicate that to her ... that breaks my heart. As a Christian, as a teammate, as a human, I got it wrong. My heart was trying to be clear-minded, my tact and tone was awful – how it was communicated was wrong. That was nine years ago – I wounded her that deeply – I want to apologize. That wasn't OK; no one should be shamed."

She adds, "But that's the gospel – we fail and there is hope in redemption. I definitely think I'm still learning; if that moment happened today, it would be a totally different conversation."

• • •

DURING GAMES, HEATHER rode the bench. She had never ridden the bench in her entire life. She was a four-year starter and scholarship player at Division 1 school Western Carolina – a school she chose because it was in the middle of the Smoky and Blue Ridge Mountains. She remembers standing in the center of the field on her recruiting trip, all the mountains rising up around her. She is fourth on the list for career points in the school's history. Her senior year she captained the team. She was also a starter for her last W-League team, the Cocoa Expo. And while every single other bench player for the Eagles got minutes, she didn't. They never played her. It was odd to go from being a captain of a team to feeling like a pariah. She didn't want to be a downer presence so she made it her focus to be the leader of the reserves. Nearly every practice, they finished with a full-sided scrimmage, the starters versus the subs; she knew this was the closest to a real game that she was going to get – and she was the rallier. "It was very important to me to be positive and encouraging," she says.

She didn't quit the team, didn't even think about quitting.

"Part of it was stubbornness. I thought, *You guys are just going to have to stare at me this whole season. You are just going to have to deal with the gay girl on the bench.* But the other part was love of playing. Because after twenty years of playing, the game was a large part of my identity. No matter what, I got to play every single day, and I needed that at that time. Soccer was the thing that rooted me – I thought it was worth it."

Heather was not invited back next season, nor would she have gone.

• • •

WHEN I ASK Pat Stewart, President of the Eagles and Missionary Athletes International, how the organization handles homosexuality, he responds with the following statement: "MAI's approach to homosexuality is to view it in the context of expressed standards of Biblical sexual morality. We believe that heterosexual marriage relationships and celibate single lives are God's pattern for human beings. All players for MAI teams must agree with the MAI statement of faith and abide by a Standard of Conduct which includes a commitment to that Biblical standard."

Missionary Athletes International updated their statement of faith and Standard of Conduct in 2015 to include a clause specifically addressing homosexuality – "to be upfront about who we are."

On a phone call, I ask whether he could understand how – if you believe that being gay is not a choice but the way you are born – how that sounds like discrimination. He says, "I could understand how someone would feel that way. That's the difficult part of the issue around identification as gay – whether or not it is a choice. If they feel they don't have a choice, that they're in a position where they can't escape it, that's a hard thing. I hear their personal pain in all of that, I'm not dismissing that experience.

At the same time – I look at players' experiences, like Paige – how do you distinguish between those that are able to choose and those that aren't? I think there are those out there who do need to hear that they can experience something different. That there are those who, by coming to Christ, had their identity change.

"This is not an easy issue. We want to have relationships that allow us to have dialogue, to deal with people who don't believe the same thing. But we also have to be true to our mission – God glorified, lives transformed. That's our heart in this: we do feel we have a calling that we are honoring; we don't want to do it in a way that comes off as discriminatory or judgmental. We just want to be faithful to who we believe we are called to be as an organization."

But it's hard not to sound discriminatory when the bottom line is that you're an organization that doesn't want gays.

• • •

BY THE END of the summer, Heather was disenchanted with Christian morality. "I wanted to break religion apart and try to piece it back together myself," she says, "because what I experienced on the Eagles did not line up with universal truths expressed in these texts." She read everything she could get her hands on, every holy book, every history of world religion. She read Thomas Merton, Mary Oliver, Kahlil Gibran, Eckhart Tolle, Wendell Berry – writers focused on spirituality and meaning found in nature, outside of the church.

In 2010, she wanted out of the South and moved to California, where culture is not so saturated with religion. She took a job as an assistant coach at a college and then she left soccer and went to graduate school at San Francisco State, where she got her masters in literature and philosophy. At SFSU, it was another extreme: "Now I was the only person with any semblance of a belief in God," she laughs. There, they were making sense of the world without God, and she was fascinated by this perspective as she continued her own process of discovery. Outside of the classroom, she started a nonprofit called Upward Roots, which focuses on empowering youth in under-resourced neighborhoods in Oakland through youth-driven community service projects.

In the summer, she walked the Camino de Santiago, the famous pilgrimage across Spain. For 540 miles she walked alone and thought. She started in France, climbing the snowy, rugged Pyrenees where it is windy and cold. Her feet became massively swollen. Her legs were noodly and weak; she was sorer than after any preseason. She was walking at the bridge of seasons and as she descended into Navarra, wine country, it became summer, the sun heating her face and lighting up the vineyards and green rolling hills. Then it was on to the Meseta, the Spanish tableland, a flat, arid plateau with vast skies and dry heat, where the path is straight and never-ending.

For most pilgrims, the end of this journey is the Santiago de Compostela Cathedral, the reputed burial site of St. James the Great. But the path continues all the way to the western coast of Spain, and she knew that was what was right for her. "A Catholic cathedral did not feel like the natural end to my journey because my spirituality is not focused on doctrine," she says. "The coast, the natural end – that felt way more poetic and perfect for my understanding of spirituality." She walked 55 more miles, through eucalyptus forests and beyond, until she could smell the sea salt in the air. Finally, she arrived at Finisterre, a word that means "the end of the earth." And maybe that's what it took – maybe she needed to literally walk to the end of the earth to figure out who she was, but as she stepped into the ocean, she felt entirely happy in her own skin.

When she returned to the United States, she coached at the Julie Foudy Sports Leadership Academy. There, in walked Kelsey

Davis – a fellow coach and a former professional soccer player. Even though marriage between two women was not yet legal, in the strangest feeling of her life, she took one look at Kelsey and knew, *This is going to be my wife.*

• • •

SEVERAL YEARS EARLIER Kelsey Davis was in Germany with the United States under-23 national team, sprawled out on her hotel room bed, reading *Winesburg, Ohio* with rain pelting on the window when she came to a realization: she didn't want to be an English major, didn't want to write 26-page papers about novels. Not when there was this other giant mystery rattling around inside her: how her sexuality fit with Christianity. In high school, she had found girls the same year she found Jesus, and at the Fellowship of Christian Athletes Bible study groups at her high school, homosexuality kept coming up – as something to be overcome. ("If I had a dollar for every time I 'prayed away the gay', I would be a billionaire," says Kelsey.) But she was tired of listening to other people's opinions. She was tired of reading the Bible – these words on a page that weren't even originally written in English. *What's lost in translation?* she wondered. *And is God bound to these pages, or is He bigger than that? Who is God in this world?* She wanted to figure it out for herself – to become an investigator researching a case.

When she came back to college from national camp, she told her advisor that she was switching majors to theology. "I was prepared for the worst. I was ready to discover that no matter how many theological gymnastics you perform, there is no way to reconcile homosexuality with being a faithful Christian," she says.

Davis's father was a lawyer and a thinker and her pal, and she'd grown up discussing the big topics with him – philosophy, religion, sport, and the meaning of life. ("It was actually easier

Allie Long, playing
for the Portland
Thorns
© Corri Goates

Rail banner created by
the Rose City Riveters
in honor of Allie Long's
Olympic journey
Courtesy of author

"Baby" (Asaya), Augustine, Njoya, and Dani, on the flight from preseason in Turkey to Russia, to begin their season playing for FC Voronezh
Courtesy of Dani Foxhoven

Liverpool Homeless Football Club
Courtesy of Becca Mushrow

Becca (second from right) and Emily (center) coaching with the Street Football Association
Joana Freitas and the Street Football Association

Nadia Nadim, celebrating a goal for the Danish national team
© Anders Kjærbye – fodboldbilleder.dk

The wedding ceremony of Heather and Kelsey; Heather's teammate
and best friend, Ashleigh Gunning, to the couple's left
© Ryan Green, 30 Miles West Photography

Alinco's niece and mother in front of
the home Alinco built for them
Courtesy of Christina Onye

Alinco (right)
with her Nigerian
teammates for
the Washington
Spirit, Ngozi
Okobi (left) and
Francisca Ordega
(center)
*Courtesy of Josephine
Chukwunonye*

Marta playing for Santos FC in the Copa do Brasil 2009
© Ueslei Marcelino/Agif/Gazeta Press

Melissa Barbieri, holding her daughter following an Adelaide match.
© Adam Butler

Gaëlle, cooking dinner in Eskilstuna, Sweden
Courtesy of Kim DeCesare

Gaëlle, wearing
her traditional
Cameroonian clothing
Courtesy of Kim DeCesare

Erin Regan, former goalkeeper for the Washington Freedom, on duty as a firefighter with the LA County Fire Department
© Kate T. Parker

The tifo created for the Portland Thorns' 2016 season finale
© Craig Mitchelldyer

Hailey, a capo, leading the supporters at a Portland Thorns game on June 7, 2014

to tell him I was gay than it was to tell him I was becoming a Christian," she says. "When I told him I was gay, he said, 'Great.' When I told him I was becoming a Christian, he said, 'We need to have a talk.'") Her father taught her about what true debate is, and that influenced how she conducted her investigation: if she were in a court of law, she would need to be able to understand the other side – the people who tell her you cannot be a Christian and be gay. But as she conducted her investigation – talking with the university's Catholic priests and studying Scripture – she was surprised to discover that all is not bleak, that the Bible is clear on exactly nothing. The priests didn't condemn her; they told her to bring up her questions with God, and she did that. "They showed me nothing but love. As a human to human, they allowed my process to be a faithful process," she says. "I found my first taste of who God might be in the world."

In June 2009, the summer before her senior year, her father killed himself. She was an only child. She could not make sense of life without him. A week later, she went to an under-23 national team camp. "Soccer raised me. It was my family, my formation, my craft. It was the spine of my life. The people involved with the national team – my teammates – were my best friends; my coaches were parental figures. National camp was the most rational thing I could think to do. It was my stabilizer."

But right away, in an exhibition game she broke her jaw. Now playing couldn't help her. Her jaw was wired shut for six weeks. She lost 25 pounds. "I was in intense, deep darkness," she says. "The depth of my grief catapulted me into a series of questions: Who is God? And where was He? Why couldn't Jesus and the Holy Spirit save my father from his mental illness? I prayed for things that didn't come through – my prayers weren't answered." A priest walked her through these questions. "Using the Biblical text, he helped open up a world for me to process my grief in a way that was incredibly honest. And that taught me that God can handle our honesty. And that connected to my sexuality."

She rebounded from her injury, got her first call-up to the full US national team at the end of her senior year, and got drafted to the Chicago Red Stars. Then she tore her ACL and was out for the season. That summer, she wanted to go on a mission trip with the Fellowship of Christian Athletes (FCA) to Kenya – wanted to be on a field, teaching girls about the game that had meant so much to her while sharing her love for God. To go on the trip, she had to sign a piece of paper that said she wouldn't engage in homosexual behavior.

"Being able to teach young women soccer in Kenya was more important to me than my sexuality. In hindsight, it was incredibly dishonest – to FCA's credit they were very clear what their expectations were. I wanted to go on the mission trip so badly that I was willing to check the box and deny my identity so that I could do mission work. Today I would never check that box."

Following the mission trip, she was on FCA's radar. Someone from the organization reached out to her before her next WPS season. They wanted to feature her – a professional athlete who is a Christian – in a newsletter and on their website; they wanted her to write a blog. In her reply, she told them she would love to but she also wanted to let them know that she is gay. Their response: *Thank you for your honesty and for letting us know*. They no longer wanted to feature her or have her write a blog. "And yeah, that hurt," says Kelsey.

Her next season in the WPS she tore her other ACL. And then the WPS folded. It was time to say goodbye. She threw herself into coaching – which led her eventually to Julie Foudy Leadership Camp, which led her to Heather.

They got married twenty miles north of Nashville, in a little clearing along a creek, surrounded by 50 of their closest friends and family – that included Kelsey's mother and uncle, and Heather's mother and older brother. Heather's father and little brother did not come. Her father was matter of fact and unapologetic. "Marriage is between a man and a woman," he said over the phone. Her little brother was more tearful – he worshipped her. He was her training buddy: she'd dribble around him in the front yard; he'd fetch her balls; she taught him to play. They did everything together. But he was active in Campus Crusade for Christ, an evangelical organization that does not support gay marriage. There were tearful conversations and she tried to tell him, "*Come*, *you will regret this*."

It was June and was supposed to be unbearably hot, but it was cool and there was a late afternoon glow, sun streaking through the trees. They centered their wedding around a verse in a Wendell Berry poem, "A Country of Marriage":

> Sometimes our life reminds me
> of a forest in which there is a graceful clearing
> and in that opening a house,
> an orchard and garden,
> comfortable shades, and flowers
> red and yellow in the sun, a pattern
> made in the light for the light to return to.
> The forest is mostly dark, its ways
> to be made anew day after day, the dark
> richer than the light and more blessed,
> provided we stay brave
> enough to keep on going in.[21]

Heather works for Thistle Farms, a global community of women healing from addiction, trafficking, and prostitution. The survivors are provided full wrap-around care for two years, including jobs in the social enterprise. Kelsey is in Vanderbilt divinity school, which has a long history of fighting for civil rights in the midst of a conservative South. Divinity students are a smattering of folks from all walks of life – black, white, gay, straight, community organizers, priests, former athletes. Like Missionary Athletes International, the divinity school too has a statement of beliefs,[22] which includes a commitment to seeking "justice, inclusion, and respect for diverse kinds of human beings" and to tackling racism, sexism, and "civil discrimination based on sexual and gender identity."

If undergraduate school was about investigating the "No, you can't be gay" side of Christianity, graduate school is about investigating the "Yes, you can."

Of the "no" side, Kelsey has this to say: "I can respectfully and theologically understand how they hold the belief system that they hold. I don't agree with it, and I don't believe that it ultimately promotes God's mercy, and love and justice in the world. I don't believe that belief system is echoing the kingdom of God. People are getting left out, they're getting left behind."

And here is her "yes": "Because of my faith, I'm married to a woman. Because of who I believe God to be – a Being that creates diversity in the world. I was able to accept myself as part of that diversity and therefore was able to be with who I love in this world. By being with Heather I am living more faithfully into who I was created to be."

Together, she and Heather attend St. Augustine's Episcopal Chapel, fully embraced by their community. Here, you are not told what Scripture means; you are encouraged to interpret Scripture for yourself.

When Kelsey was seventeen, and first telling her father that she was becoming a Christian, he made her promise that she would never preach at anyone, that she would always keep listening, always keep respecting people's points of view. Her faith isn't centered on converting or convincing, but on the idea that there is a place for everyone, that a door is open.

• • •

WHEN I SKYPE with Paige, she has various beautiful, white-blond children in the background: Roman, Deacon, Hannah, and Molly.

Sitting in front of the green chalkboard from which she home-schools her kids, she fills me in on her life. While Paige was always someone of few words, she has, she says, worked on that. Because after all those years of silent family dinners, of a quiet you felt you could fall into and never come out, she doesn't want that for her own family.

She tells me about her husband Chris – how, initially, she liked him because he could do backflips and handstand push-ups. While other couples court each other via dinner and movies, Chris and Paige worked together on acrobatics. She says that what she loves about him now is that he's "not stuck in one place," that he's always seeking to learn. Neither of them has ever played music in their life, but now he's learning the banjo and the mandolin and she's learning guitar. He's getting his masters in Biblical studies, and Paige says their faith is stronger than ever and that she tries every day to live her life according to Scripture. She still believes that in regards to homosexual behavior, the Bible is clear. "I don't view myself as on higher moral ground, I'm not pointing fingers; Jesus doesn't let you do that." But yes, she does believe that it is a sin.

"I feel sad – my favorite people that I've ever come across are gay. I strongly believe what I believe – it's my identity – but it puts me on the other side of the fence from people I really love," she says. "I'm not trying to build walls."

• • •

AMANDA MARTIN SPENT, in total, ten years trying not to be gay. She listened to everybody she possibly could, from both sides of the aisle – from the homosexuality-is-a-sin crowd to her friends who said things like, "That is all bat-shit crazy."

In 2013, she met a beautiful, tall blonde who had never kicked a soccer ball in her life. She had nothing to do with that world. She's also not religious. And, after an entire life of soccer and God bleeding into one another, it is profoundly comforting to be around someone who isn't centered on either.

Before her wedding, she knew she had to tell Paige. She hadn't given Paige – her once best friend – a life update in six to seven years. Paige didn't know she was dating a woman, didn't know anything. It wasn't an easy phone call for her to make. "We went through this together. I *helped* her leave Abby. Our lives took drastically different turns: she became a missionary, I married a woman," Amanda says. And even though she no longer believes that who she loves is a sin, she knows that Paige does. "And I felt like I was letting her down," she says. She sent her an email and Paige's response was kind, as she knew it would be: "I just want to say I wish you the best. I love you and I'm praying for you two. Tell Jenna hi, I look forward to meeting her in the future."

In a candlelit room with open beam ceilings and brick walls, Amanda's wedding officiate read from the 2015 Supreme Court decision holding that the Constitution guarantees same-sex couples the fundamental right to marry: "It would misunderstand these men and women to say they disrespect the idea of marriage. Their plea is that they do respect it, respect it so deeply that they seek to find its fulfillment for themselves. Their hope is not to be condemned to live in loneliness, excluded from civilization's oldest institutions. They ask for equal dignity in the eyes of the law."

As for God, Amanda has not broken the promise she made to herself when she was thirteen years old. She still believes in God, but her faith looks a lot different now than it did then. She's not ready to step back into a church. She lives in a suburb of Nashville, in the conservative South. "I don't want to expose my family, my new wife and the kids we one day want to have, to a community that doesn't validate us."

Nowadays she is proud of who she is and active in fighting for equality. When Tennessee legislators passed a bill that would allow mental health professionals to deny patients treatment on the basis of their sexuality, Amanda reached out to her senator. They met for two hours, and she tried to express how incredibly hurtful and harmful it would be to seek help and be turned away on the basis of your sexual orientation. He tried to say that the bill actually had everyone's best interest in mind: that it would not be healthy for a gay person to seek mental health treatment from someone who doesn't support their right to express their sexual orientation. "So what we're trying to do is shut the door softly," he said. But this much Amanda knows: a softly shut door can hurt the most.

Alinco, the Super Falcon

THIRTEEN-YEAR-OLD Josephine Chukwunonye has several bunches of bananas stacked high on her head as she weaves through the Ajegunle boundary market in Lagos, Nigeria. Each afternoon for the past four or five years, she has been out here, one person in the throng, everyone hustling and moving and shouting and selling. With a population somewhere between the UN's estimate of 11.4 million people and the city's own estimate of 21 million, Lagos is the biggest city in Africa and it feels like it. Normally, the market overwhelms her – the press of people, the incredible noise: the jackhammers, the car horns, the motorcycles, the line of buses and the drivers yelling routes. ("It's so loud you hear nothing," she tells me.) And the smells – car fumes, spilled petrol oil, body odor, beans, dust. ("It smells *bad* – it smells like *everything*.") But on this day, she doesn't hear or smell anything. As she leans down into each car and runs up to the yellow mini-buses, calling out, "Bananas, Bananas!", she moves with special, private conviction, her face flush with what feels like a secret. Because what the drivers and passengers and fellow peddlers don't know is that yesterday her life changed: yesterday, a coach knocked on the plywood door of her family's one-room shack and told her parents that their daughter has what it takes to be a professional soccer player.

Now, she needs cleats. Her mother, owner of a roadside fruit stand, the primary family breadwinner, had said there was no money for cleats, but Josephine had kept at her until she'd clucked her teeth and said, *Fine – you will earn them*. Josephine could keep ten cents out of every dollar. Which means that now, every banana she sells gets her one step closer to cleats, to football, to her future.

• • •

ELEVEN YEARS LATER, Chukwunonye is a 24-year-old playing professional soccer in Vittsjö, Sweden. She sits in a two-bedroom flat with a modern abstract-print rug and talks with me via a WhatsApp voice call. "I was so concentrated on those cleats – you don't even know. Nothing else mattered," she says, and it is easy to imagine her shaking her head and smiling into her hands. This first time we talk, you can hear the smile in every story – even when she tells the serious stories, recounting her poverty growing up: "It was bad. And when I say it was bad, I mean it was *bad*. No one should live like that."

The second time I call, she doesn't answer. The third time I call, the tone of her voice has changed. Because in the time between that first phone call and now, she has gone to the doctor, and she is scared.

She had ignored and ignored the pain in her knee. She had won "Player of the Game" in her very first game with Vittsjö GIK and had won it again several games later. She played every minute of every match. Until she couldn't. So finally she admitted to her pain and got an MRI. The man in the white coat with the scan of her knee in his hand told her she needed surgery. When she asked her coach whether the team would extend her contract, he said they would have to wait and see.

So now she's in the "waiting" phase. She has too much time to think. The past is on her mind all the time. (This was always the case, but now her memories are accompanied by panic.) She thinks about the one-room cinder-block home where she grew up. No electricity, no water. Her family slept seven across the dirt floor – mother, father, aunt, sisters, and cousins up against each other. There wasn't enough space to turn over. It was unbearably hot. In summer, she slept outside where it was cooler, even though there were rats. Each time they brushed up against her, she'd stand up and scream. The other people sleeping outside would fuss at her – "Girl! Why you screaming in the middle of the night?!" She'd lie back down and stare at the stars – so many stars – brushing away rats and roaches, real and imagined, and telling herself all the time, *One day I will get out of here. One day I will live somewhere else.* And that has happened – she has changed her life and changed her family's lives. But now her biggest fear is that she will be sent back to the poverty she has spent her whole life trying to escape.

• • •

WHEN JOSEPHINE was born – the third baby girl – her father disappeared for four days. He had dreamt of a son, had imagined showing his boy to his brothers. Instead, another girl. His family would deem him a failure: he had not continued the line. He would not be welcome in his own village, where they believed that women could not achieve anything. This new baby was just one more mouth to feed before she was one day married off.

If her father had suffered disappointment, he wasn't the only one. Always Josephine was in his ear: "Dad, why are we poor? Why are we like this? Dad, why don't you have any money? Why do other people have two rooms when we only have one?" She hated their house – if she had a bad dream, she'd say, "Dad, it's because of this house." Constantly she'd plead, "Mom, let's move somewhere else, let's move somewhere bigger." They'd look at her affectionately, quizzically, shake their heads and wonder why she was so stubborn, and then they'd get on with surviving. Every morning her mother woke up at 4am, and made her way in the darkness to the big market to buy the bananas she'd sell down at the local one. Her father left for the wharf, where he tried to find work. Josephine woke up at 6am. Her job was to fetch water. The closest spigot was a ten-minute walk away. She made nine or ten trips back and forth to the spigot to buy water, each time filling up a basin and carrying it home on her head.

School started at 9am. In class she listened and tried, but as soon as it was over, all her attention was given to football. She and her sister Christina played with the boys in the slum, out on the rocky clay streets when they were younger, then on the dirt field by the military barracks as they got older. Ajegunle, the slum where the Chukwunonyes lived, was often referred to as "Jungle City" for its wild, aggressive feel; it had all the standard trappings of a slum – an absence of job prospects, a surplus of drugs. But the military field that bordered it had a somewhat mythical reputation: more than a few boys who played on that field had ridden the football ticket out of there. They found professional careers in Nigeria, in Tunisia, as far away as Sweden. Josephine dreamt of doing the same. People around the slum pointed out the obvious – *but you are a girl*. They told her she smelled bad, that her clothes were bad, that she was dirty, that she was looking like a guy, that football wouldn't get her anywhere. But ever since she saw the Nigerian women's national team on the TV during the 2003 World Cup – Mercy Akide, Christy George, Perpetua Nkwocha – she knew that it could.

Her father didn't approve. When she and her sister came home with legs coated with dirt, he chased them with a broom and yelled at them – *football is not for girls* – speeches she barely heard. One time he had actually watched her: it was a game between their part of the slum and another part of the slum, four kids against four other kids, and the atmosphere was jovial, raucous, alive – he'd discovered that his girl was the best, easily the best. He had yelled, "That's my baby! That's my baby!" Yet even that day had not changed his mind. His three daughters were tiny, girly things; he did not want Josephine and Christina to start acting and dressing like men.

So when that coach – Coach Tico – first showed up at his door, he told the man, "I will have you arrested if you do not leave."

But Josephine had cried and begged: "I will *die* if you do not let me play football," she pleaded. He stared at her and hesitated, and then he heard the coach out: this man was saying that his youngest daughter could be great – that football could give her a future. In Nigeria, futures weren't easy to come by. He knew this firsthand. So he gave in: he said only that she had better stay in school, and that she had better not turn into a man.

She started traveling away from the slum on school breaks. Coach Tico packed up a handful of hopefuls and took them to Elekan Beach. For a month or so they'd camp out at a house a couple of miles away, then walk the twenty minutes to the beach. They had no gyms or weights so they used the sand to build their thigh muscles. They ran in the mornings and the afternoons, and then again at night, Josephine wearing the secondhand cleats she'd earned selling bananas.

When she came back from camp, her father would take one look at her rod-like legs and her absence of curves and fuss. "This is what I am talking about – look how skinny you are becoming! Like a boy! Your legs are little sticks!" He started calling her *Paco* – a pidgin, Creole term for driftwood. At dinnertime, she and her sisters would finish their portions and just sit there, looking at him – he'd feel their eyes on him and laugh, wipe his hand over his face, and push his food toward them: "Don't know how any man with children ever gets enough to eat!"

Her skinniness earned her another nickname, the name she

has gone by ever since. She was out on the military field training with Tico and it was windy – big gusts blowing her around.
Everyone else was training like normal, but she was just fighting to
run straight. Seeing her battle the wind, everyone started to laugh.
Someone was reminded of a comical TV character named Alinco,
a famously skinny boy on the popular Nigerian show, *Papa Ajasco*.
"Alinco, Alinco!" they chanted as she struggled in the wind. She
sat down on the field grumpily – *Wind can't blow me around if I'm
on the ground*. When she sullenly told her father about it later, he
laughed and laughed. "Alinco," he said, as though christening her.

• • •

IT WASN'T LONG before another coach knocked on her door, this
one a professional scout. He came from far away, from another state
altogether – Cross River State, at the southernmost tip of the country. He stood at the door, telling her mother, Chiwendu, that he
wanted to take her sixteen-year-old daughter to Calabar so that
she could play for one of the finest professional women's teams
in Nigeria, the Pelican Stars. The bus was leaving the next day.

"No," Chiwendu said. "You cannot take my baby. My daughter
is too small; she is too young. Who would take care of her?" The
coach promised he'd take care of her himself, but still Chiwendu
said, "*No*." Again, Alinco cried and begged until finally, with a sigh,
her mom said to the coach, "Just promise me you won't let her get
hurt." Alinco leaped up, screaming and hugging and kissing her
mother, who batted her away and cried. The next morning, Alinco
and half a dozen girls took an eleven-hour bus ride to a new life
in a new state, playing professional soccer.

• • •

A QUICK HISTORY of Nigerian women's professional football:
In 1989, the hugely popular biennial National Sports Festival,

initially created to restore national unity in the wake of the 1970 Nigerian Civil War, added women's football to the docket. The sport received unprecedented interest and attention. In response, in the nineties, the Nigerian Football Federation created a women's national team, as well as a league – making Nigeria one of the first countries in the world to support a women's league. Prominent Nigerian women, namely Princess Bola Jegede, businesswoman Gina Yeseibo, and First Lady Maryam Babangida, made substantial donations to get the league off the ground. Yeseibo, well aware of the cultural stigmas they were up against, donated 100 trophies bearing the names of influential male figures around the country – a savvy attempt to win the support of Nigerian male leaders and shift cultural thinking. These moves paid off – the Nigerian national team, the Super Falcons, has dominated the continent. They won the first seven African Women's Championships (later renamed the Africa Women Cup of Nations), and in their first twenty years of existence they lost only five games to other African teams. A 2001 BBC article declared the Nigerian women's league the continent pacesetter.[23] Players receive a signing fee ranging from $800 to $2500 and make a monthly wage between $50 and $200. While that's only a few dollars a day, in Nigeria, an estimated 100 million live on less than a dollar a day.[24] With their playing salary, the women are able to support their families.

That's not to say the Nigerian league is some kind of utopia; it has been hammered with the problems ubiquitous in any women's league: financial struggles, stigmas and stereotypes, utter media indifference, and a dearth of sponsorships. A Google search on "Nigerian professional women's soccer" turns up a smattering of news articles, none of them good: companies are hesitant to be involved due to the "perceived lesbian problem"; and the belief that playing sports turns you into a man is still very much alive. Players sometimes go months without seeing their salaries. Teams often forfeit away games, unable to find the funds to travel. Still, the league has survived for nearly 30 years and Alinco's generation of players grew up knowing it existed, knowing that it could be possible to make a life out of football.

• • •

IN 2008, WHEN Alinco arrived at her new home in Calabar – an apartment with a toilet and a kitchen – she couldn't believe it. "I thought, *whoah*," says Alinco. "I said to myself, 'One day, I'm going to build a house like this for my family.'" When she talked to her mom on the phone, she told her this: *Mama, I'm going to save up my money and build us a house with a toilet and a kitchen.* Her mother scoffed. "I told her, 'Alinco, you are just dreaming,'" recalls her mother. "Do you have any idea how much money that would take?" But Alinco wasn't dissuaded, even though she had not received a signing fee from the Pelican Stars. "They said to me, 'You are too young! What do you want money for?'" says Alinco. "I said, 'My mom is selling on the side of the road. What do you mean I do not need money?'" She convinced them to pay her a monthly salary. The first season, it was only 700 naira ($22) a month, half as much as the minimum for the professional league that the BBC had reported seven years earlier. But it was still something – for the first time, Alinco had a way of making money on her own.

After years of playing on sand and dirt, anticipating slopes and sliding on gravel, she was now for the first time playing on grass. Let loose on that smooth, consistent surface, she was astonished by her speed: "I felt like I was flying!" No one could touch her. She was the youngest (sixteen), the smallest, the fastest, and she could keep running the longest. Her older teammates, a couple of whom were on the Nigerian national team, took her under their wing. Super Falcons forward Christy George helped fine tune the youngster on the field, emphasizing possession of the ball, and her roommate – the oldest player on the team – watched out for her off the field. There was not a limitless supply of food; if you headed to the cafeteria after training instead of before, the food was frequently all gone. Alinco learned to keep a cooler in her room and stockpile the food so there would be enough to eat when she returned from the second training.

At night, she talked to her family on the phone. Her father may have been the one who fought her the hardest, but he was also the one she talked to the most. He was no soccer aficionado, and his unease over his footballer-daughter hadn't exactly subsided, but he would call to check in anyway. The conversations were reassuringly the same: first, always, he said, "I hope nobody kicked your leg." Followed by: "How was the game? How did you play, Paco?" Then they'd talk about nothing, for an hour or more. "My father was a yabber – he could talk to anybody who walked by," says Alinco. He liked to tease, to chide – he might call out in pidgin, "Look at that hair – looks like you haven't brushed it in days!" And somehow it was always funny. "He could make anybody laugh," says Alinco.

But on the serious matters he stayed silent. He didn't speak of the Nigerian Civil War in which he had fought, didn't joke about the bullet hole in his left leg. When her sister Christina read books about the war and asked him about it, he said only, *Please, do not look at me differently, my daughter.* When tribal friction broke out around the slum and young boys started killing each other, he would say, quietly, "If they had known the Nigerian Civil War, they would not be doing that." But he never said more than that. He also never spoke about his own parents – or the way his family had turned him out. He never spoke about the things that bothered him – about how it felt as an Igbo man to struggle to support your family.

Most of the time he found work dealing with exports when the international tankers came into the wharf; but they had to call your name, to choose you, and sometimes they did not. There was one day when Alinco came upon her father unexpectedly: she had left her school and gone to train at another school and she'd seen him, on the road outside the wharf, just sitting there with the other out-of-work laborers, waiting, hoping. She did not let him see her – just stared at him, his face absent of the liveliness and humor she was accustomed to finding there. *So this is what he does every day*, she thought to herself with a sinking feeling, instantly regretting all those times she had pestered him – *Daddy, you've got to give us money so that we can go to school*. After that day, seeing his blank face out by the wharf, she never bothered him again about money. *One day*, she told herself, *I will make him so happy*.

• • •

IN 2008, SHE got her first chance to do that: for the first time, FIFA was hosting an under-17 Women's World Cup, and Nigeria was creating a team. At the first tryout, a hundred-some girls were invited. Every day, they told three or four not to come back. The day before they announced the final roster, she stayed up all night – everybody did, no one was able to sleep. On the phone, she talked with her family for hours – already planning, talking about all they would buy, how big a room they would build. She was animated – not nervous, only excited. "I *knew* I was going to make it. I could see it in my coach's eyes," says Alinco. And the next morning, as the coach read out the list, sure enough, he called out: Josephine Chukwunonye. Her name was printed in the newspaper alongside the other teenagers who would represent Nigeria.

So began a slew of firsts: Her first time on a plane, to New Guinea for a qualifier. ("I was shouting, 'Jeez God! God, please don't kill me!'" she says, laughing.) Her first time traveling to Europe. (Her mother made a special visit to their church to proudly announce the news: her daughter had gone to Germany!) Her first time seeing so many white girls, and her first time seeing lush, lush grass. Her laughter rings merrily through the phone as she recounts the memory of playing friendlies in Germany as they prepped for the upcoming U-17 World Cup: "I was bending down and touching the grass! I wanted to know if it was real! I was staring at the white girls – is this what I'm watching on the TV? I wanted to touch their skin. I whispered to my teammate – *Have you touched anyone? Does their skin feel like ours*? And I just kept saying to myself, *I'm in Europe – I'm in white man's land. God, I thank you for making this happen.*" Then, on the phone, she grew more subdued: "I was crying, it was so amazing. In Nigeria, there is so much suffering. Even if you go to school, there are no jobs when you get out. Here there was so much opportunity. How I wish we had that kind of opportunity in Nigeria! It was a miracle to be in this place, to be living like a white man."

In May, Chukwunonye travelled to New Zealand for the main event, the U-17 World Cup. It was going to be televised. She called home and told her mom she had to find a way to watch the game the next day. Her mom was hesitant – while there were a few people in the compound who had TVs, there was no electricity and watching a game meant buying petrol oil to make the generator run. She couldn't spare any money, and she didn't want to put anyone else out. "OK, no problem," Alinco told her mother.

But the day of the game, her mother heard shouting. And then people were running for her, pounding on her door: "Come and watch your daughter! Come and watch your daughter! She is playing for the national team!" She ran through the crowd – so many people watching – and stared at the screen: "My *pikin* is inside the television! My *pikin* is inside the television!" she shouted. Later, when she talked to Alinco on the phone, she told her daughter, "Inside the TV you were so big! When you come home, you will be so small!"

"That is only the camera, Mom," Alinco said, smiling and proud.

When Alinco returned home, she put a stack of cash – $300 USD – on the table. The whole family gathered around it. No one had seen a US dollar before; no one had seen this amount of money before. They stared at the stack, they touched the bills, they laughed. Her mom turned to her dad – she did not go easy on him: "You see now! You did not want this girl baby! But you see now what this girl baby has done for you! All that time you did not want her to play – but now you see!"

Her mother picked up a handful of bills. "Dollar! Dollar! Dollar!" she sang as she danced, rubbing the dollars up and down her arms. "Thank you, God!" she shouted.

• • •

EACH TIME ALINCO got paid, by both her national team and her professional team, she socked nearly all of the cash away – for the house she was determined to one day build. Her second season with the Pelican Stars they paid her twice as much as the first, and after that, she was scooped up by the Port Harcourt River Angels. Their roster boasted nearly all national team players. They paid her 60,000 naira ($190) a month. All the players lived in a large peach stucco building donated by the government – a house Alinco describes as beautiful, with big white windows and a small balcony where the players sometimes hung their clothes to dry. It was an easy walk to the field, where they trained twice a day. "In Nigeria, even if they say it will be one hour, it is always three," laughs Alinco. They played their games in empty, two-tier, cavernous stadiums. For playoffs, their games were scheduled ahead of the men's team's games, and the men's fans often turned up early – on those occasions, there would be a thousand or so supporters in the bleachers. They watched, hooted and looked on with interest, as though it were an intriguing spectacle. But most would not show up in those stands again until there was another men's game.

I ask about little girls: "Were there young kids who came to the games and wanted to be like you – kids who would ask for your autograph?" At this Alinco laughs loudly. "Our autographs? What would they do with that? They don't want our *autographs*. They want *money*, they want *food*. They are *hungry*." Always, Alinco was aware of that. To the kids who lingered around the stadium, and to the kids around her old slum, she gave away old cleats, promised other kids her next pair, handed out old jerseys. (Again, I show my ignorance when I ask, "Your team jerseys?" Again she laughs: "No, no, no – just my personal football jerseys. If I gave away my Nigeria jersey, they would tell me to go and get it back.")

For six years she played with the River Angels – they ate together, scrubbed jerseys together, danced together, dreamt together, and won championships together. At the end of each season, dressed in their finest traditional clothes – blue and white taffeta, satin sheaths – they celebrated Thanksgiving together. They attended each other's weddings and shared holidays when they were unable to make the journeys home. A few players were from well-off backgrounds, but most came from areas like Alinco's. Although their salaries were sometimes sporadic – they'd go four or five months without getting paid – when the money did come, each player gave it directly to her family. Many players were the primary family breadwinner. The team manager and team coach were encouraging, reinforcing what the players already knew:

"Understand that women's football will not last forever for you. Build your family a home. Put the money into a better life, into something that will last – so that when your football days are over, you will be able to say, 'This is what I built for my family.'"

• • •

IN MAY 2010, when she was eighteen years old, Alinco got her first call-up to play with the senior national team in a friendly against North Korea. During a stopover in China, she took a portion of her first national team payment and went shopping for her father. She bought him all new clothes – a pair of nice pants, nice shoes, and a brand new silver watch that she planned to get embossed. All those years he saved his food for her, now was her chance to buy for her father the things he hadn't been able to buy for himself.

In the days before the game, her phone was quieter than usual. Normally, people were texting her, sending her messages and good luck but this time her phone stayed silent. She didn't think about it too much. She was too full of nerves, too consumed with standard first-time-on-the-big-stage insecurities – *I am too small, too young; these women are too good*. Before the game started, she watched the Koreans – she can remember the sound of their cleats hitting the concrete tunnel in unison. "They warmed up like soldiers," she says, everything precise and emphatic. During the game, from her spot defending the other end of the field, Alinco admired the North Korean backline – they were one in-sync unit. The Koreans beat them 3–0, a humbling opening to Alinco's career.

After the game, her phone was still silent. Her father had not called to say, *I hope nobody kicked your leg*. When she called him, he didn't answer. No one answered.

Once she was back in Nigeria, riding a public bus back to her home, finally someone picked up. Her friend Nwabueze delivered the news: "Your father is dead." He had fallen over outside their home.

On the bus, Alinco was alone with her grief, alone with her disbelief. *But my daddy is funny. My daddy is full of life. How can someone so alive be dead?* She wished suddenly that she had never played football. Because football took her away from home, away from him, and if it hadn't, maybe she could've been there beside him. "How I wished I was there," she says. "Maybe he would've talked with me." Because she knows that what killed him was all his worrying, all those thoughts he kept to himself. "He was thinking too much – so many men in Nigeria, they have no jobs, they are thinking too much. That is what killed my father.

"If he would've just held on, he would've seen, things were about to get better," she says. "He never got to see it get better."

• • •

ALINCO REMEMBERS ONE eerie night she spent back at home in Ajegunle. She and her sisters had never experienced death before. They could not shake the feeling that he was still there with them. They kept looking to the chair where he used to sit while they went to sleep at night. After a fourth sister was born, he was the one who had swatted the mosquitoes off her as she slept – he had swatted the mosquitoes off all of them. Now, Alinco kept imagining him still sitting there, still swatting at the mosquitoes, still watching over them.

They buried his body in the village where he grew up. The sisters had only been there once before – when their father had taken them to meet his mother, father, and brothers. Alinco had only been seven at that time but she would never forget what her father's family said to them: "They called us all prostitutes. They told us we were nothing. That women were nothing. They told us we were unwelcome there." They had never planned on returning to that place, but it is traditional for an Igbo to be buried in his own village. So, they returned. Death had not changed her father's family's stance: again, Alinco, her mother, and her sisters were told they weren't welcome. Again, they were told they were nothing. "It is your fault our brother is dead," they told her mother. They said that it was her inability to produce boys that killed him. They did not help pay for the casket or the burial. The Igbo elders in Lagos and her father's friends around the compound pitched in for the casket, and eighteen-year-old Alinco paid for the funeral. Her father was buried in the clothes she had bought for him in China, silver watch around his wrist.

Shunned by her relatives as she put her father in the ground, it was her teammates who made it better: they traveled the five hours from Port Harcourt. They squeezed her hand and held her sobbing mother. With their songs and their dancing, they transformed the funeral into something loving and lively. She did not have a village or a circle of family, but she did have her team.

When she left the village, her intentions had crystallized: "Mom, now you see, we don't have a village to call our own," she said. "We cannot live in Ajegunle forever. We have to start making plans for ourselves." At eighteen years old, she understood: it was up to her. There were no uncles to turn to, no support system to help their family of women. She knew then what she still believes now: "I have no one to run to but God."

An old friend told her about an area outside of Lagos where land was cheap and she made up her mind: *I will buy that land*. Her mother again scoffed, but her protests were more half-hearted – by now she had begun to believe that her daughter would find a way to do whatever it was she said she was going to do. So she too started saving every penny she could. Two months after her father's death, Alinco bought the land in her mother's name.

It would take her five years to build the house: it went up little by little, room by room.

• • •

IN ALINCO'S ROSTER pictures through the years, she smiles, but only slightly, her lips closed. She has a high forehead, arched eyebrows, graceful cheekbones and one eye that is very slightly larger than the other, a result of childhood measles. (She's self-conscious of the eye – though she knows her sister is right – it doesn't matter so long as she can see.) Her face looks unquestionably serious, as well as intelligent and slightly apprehensive – suggestive of a shy, cautious personality. But a video clip from the 2012 U-20 World Cup gives an altogether different impression:[25] ahead of the Nigeria–South Korea game, both teams stand in single file line in a tunnel. The South Korean players rock from side to side, quiet, smiling hesitantly as they watch the Nigerians, who are all song and dance. They chant a call and response – "Okay, okay, okaya – *Okay!* Okay, okay, okay, okaya – *Okay!*" Alinco emerges from the back of the line performing a forward-moving dance solo. She dances the *etighi*, a modern dance originating in Calabar – bent slightly at the waist, arms swinging in time with her hips, left, right, one foot down, then the other. Her face is radiant, playful, taunting – her jaw pushed forward, lips pressed together, tiny dreadlocks in motion. She exudes a sort of ecstatic confidence – like she is all-powerful on the field.

As the center back, she strips the ball off of incoming forwards in a way that is absolute and intimidating. She also distributes coolly and definitively, like she's in charge of providing the calm for the entire team. Although she can sprint with the best of them – nobody beats her – she doesn't rely solely on her athleticism. Each touch on the ball demonstrates a self-assured savviness: she has a tendency to roll the ball with the bottom of her cleat – a flourish not that common in a defender. It's the sign of someone who relishes every touch. More than anything, she gives off the impression that she is about to spring – that at any second she will come at you. Which is exactly what she does.

The hunger is palpable – and it's not just about "love of the game." It's hunger for a better life. Every game is a chance to help her family, a chance to open her world. Her life and her family's lives ride on every touch.

• • •

THE WORLD CUP is of course the biggest stage there is – she and every other player on the Nigerian team is fully aware that this is their chance to be seen. The Super Falcons have something of a World Cup curse. Only once, in 1991, have they advanced to the quarter-finals. In the 2007 and 2011 World Cups, they landed in the "Group of Death," losing close matches to some of the top countries in the world. They failed to make it out of group.

In 2015, they once again landed in the Group of Death, but Alinco and her teammates were all hope. Just one year earlier, a good portion of the roster had wowed the soccer world at the U-20 World Cup; while they ultimately lost to Germany in the final, they had dominated the game, and most watching the tournament would have described the Nigerians as the most talented youth side in the world. Now, one year later, the senior side was composed of many of the same players, twenty-year-olds eager to stun the favorites in their group – Sweden, Australia, and the United States.

While the Women's World Cup gets nowhere near the same level of interest as the men's in Nigeria – businesses don't close, people don't stop what they are doing – it is still their best chance to make their country care. And, although there are no TV ratings to confirm it, the general feeling is that viewership has gone up.

"And in Ajegunle," says her sister Christina, "*everybody* was watching." The entire slum gathered around TVs at bars, in restaurants, in friends' homes – everybody there to watch Alinco.

In their first game, they tied Sweden, the perennial powerhouse – not a terrible start. Next they faced Australia – and lost 2–0. Their final group game was against the United States, the top country in the world. As she walked out of the tunnel, listened to the US anthem and then sang her own, she had a feeling: *Nigeria is going to win.* Any player is familiar with that psychic pregame sensation, where you already know what the outcome of the game will be. It is rarely wrong. "I had *fire* in my chest," says Alinco. But they didn't win. She was astonished to have lost – to have had all that desire and belief and still to lose. It was one more World Cup without advancing to the next round.

But Alinco's "fire" didn't go unnoticed. After the World Cup, she received two offers: a three-year contract to play in Sweden; and a contract to finish out the American professional season with the Washington Spirit. The Swedish offer was the smarter, more stable option, but she could not pass up the chance to go to the United States. She and forward Ngozi Okobi would join fellow Nigerian national teammate, Francisca Ordega, who had played for the Washington Spirit the previous season.

Every Nigerian, Alinco tells me, footballer or not, dreams of an American visa. One of the players on the Nigerian World Cup team, Courtney Dike, is a Nigerian-American who grew up in Oklahoma. "I tell Courtney that she should get down on her hands and knees every day and thank her parents for bringing her to the United States," says Alinco. With the opportunity to play in Washington Alinco couldn't help but dream – maybe she too could bring her family over. When she told her mother that she was headed to America, her mother cooked a feast and invited the whole family into their home. "We celebrated in a *big* way," says Christina. "My mom cooked vegetable soup with everything in it – crawfish, snails, everything. We were all like, '*Wow*.'"

Christina has a four-year-old daughter, Zion, whom Alinco describes as "the love of my life." She is the one Alinco thinks about the most. Zion wants to be a ballerina after first seeing ballet on the show *America's Got Talent*. She turned to Christina and said, "Mommy, what are they doing? What kind of dance is *that*?" She loved the pink tutu. When her mother surprised her with one, she screamed, "I love it, I love it, I love it!" Since then, all the time she wears the tutu and dances around the house, which makes Christina smile sadly. While Nigerian culture emphasizes dance, ballet is a Western dance not broadly practiced in their country. "There is no 'ballet' in Nigeria," Christina tells me. But if she can find a way to get her daughter to the United States, maybe she will have a chance. Her hopes ride on Alinco.

• • •

BEFORE ALINCO LEFT for the United States, she took her mother furniture shopping. The house she had started building five years earlier was finally finished. Her mother did not think they needed to go furniture shopping – "What about our old chair from Ajegunle? We do not need a new chair," her mother said. But Alinco insisted. She told her mother to pick out anything she wanted.

Up until this point, her mother had held it together. She didn't cry when they bought the land, didn't cry when they walked around the finally completed home. But right there in the middle of the furniture shop, she lost it. "I have never sat on a sofa before," she said, voice trembling as she sat down. "Never did I think I would sit upon a piece of furniture like this in my lifetime." Alinco and the store employees came over to steady her. Alinco began to bargain with the employees – she got them down to

200,000 naira ($600) for two chairs and the sofa. Her mother overheard this figure and was beside herself.

"My mother thought it was too expensive. But by this point in my life, I am privileged – I have seen so many things. I have gotten to travel all over the world. I have gotten to shake the President's hand. I've seen the insides of so many nice homes – I studied the interior decorations, all the time I paid attention, I planned the house I would one day build for my mother."

As Alinco placed the order for the couch, her mother shouted, "If I'm dreaming, I do not want to wake up!"

• • •

A MONTH LATER, after her American visa was finally processed, it was Alinco's turn to pinch herself. The dream of the United States did not fall short. She describes her impressions in one excited rush, like she doesn't know where to start: "I saw so many things that are different! In America, they made football so fun! You get to play with joy! Football is not suffering! You can be playing football and be happy! And the fans – they are *real* fans. They know who you are, even if you are on the bench! I was feeling like a nobody – yet they still support you! They support you even when you lose!"

In Nigeria, when you are training twice a day, running sprints all the time, playing games in front of empty stadiums, with no guarantee that you will see your paycheck this month or even the next, football can feel like a job. In the United States, to her amazement, she discovered they trained only once a day – one compact 90-minute session. (To be safe, Alinco ran on her own after practice – 100-yard sprints – because she didn't want to lose the hallmark of her game, her ability to run forever. "I had to do something – I had to make sure I was still ready when the national team called," she says.) The tactics, the drills, the instructions, the focuses – it was all different. After six years playing for the same team, repeating the same drills, it felt fantastic to be constantly learning something new.

"And after practice, the day is your own! They work jobs, they go to school!" Which is something Alinco dreams about. In Nigeria, she explains, football and school are not compatible. Most players are forced to choose, and Alinco is lucky to have even finished primary school. But after spending her entire life running and playing and sending money home, seeing the Americans – most of whom have families who support them – she sometimes let herself imagine what it would be like to do anything you like. It was hard not to gape at the Americans.

"I am not of their class – I cannot afford to buy what they're buying. I can't afford the shoes they are wearing. The US national team players, they are rich – when I heard what FIFA pays them, I could not believe it. That was the first I'd heard of FIFA money. In Nigeria, they just keep the money. How I wish I had that kind of money! Sometimes their mothers came into town. They are 55, 60 years old, but they look *so* young! So much younger than my own mother. She is also 55 – but she looks so much older. And their mothers would 'take them shopping.' Never in my life has my mom taken me shopping."

The three Nigerians playing for Washington Spirit didn't go shopping – they reminded each other not to try to keep up. They continued to send their paychecks home to their families.

By the time their visas had finally come through, it was the end of the season, right before the playoffs – a difficult time for a defender to break into a lineup. But Coach Parsons got Alinco ten minutes at the end of one game, twenty minutes at the end of another; and she was all hope for the next season.

But in September, she heard the news: Parsons would no longer coach the Washington Spirit. A new coach, Jim Gabarra, would come in for the 2016 season. Initially, Ngozi and Alinco hoped they would have a chance to try out – but they were waived immediately, before the new coach even gave them a look. "That's fine," Alinco says, her voice flat as she describes it. Then she adds, "I had to call and tell my mother. She cried." After only three months, the dream of the US is over.

• • •

WHICH LEADS US TO her current life in Vittsjö, Sweden. After Ngozi and Alinco are released by the Washington Spirit, they both sign a one-year contract with Vittsjö, with the option to extend. Originally, the thinking behind the one-year contract was that they could leave for a higher-ranked team. Now, Alinco waits for surgery, and hopes to God that the team will extend her contract.

Nobody on the Nigerian national team, Alinco says, has ever had surgery. In the Nigerian women's league, nobody even got MRIs. "MRIs cost money," she says. "If you hurt your knee, they send you to the local native. He just rubs roots and herbs into your skin." And you keep playing – she knew so many who played through pain worse than hers. "In Nigeria, we believe surgery is bad," she says. Surgery could mean your career is over. And her career cannot be over. Her Swedish teammates who have had much more intensive surgeries than the one she is slated for, assure her that her injury – a meniscus tear – isn't a big deal, that she'll be better in no time. She hopes desperately that they are right.

The Swedish season ends and her Swedish teammates go home. Her roommate, Ngozi, also leaves – for the Africa Women Cup of Nations – a tournament Alinco would have been play-ing in too were it not for her injury. On November 2, she has the operation. Three guys she grew up playing with in Ajegunle who have also followed the game to Sweden come visit her at her apartment. They bring her Nigerian food, plantains, yams, and fish. They stay and talk and try to cheer her up and then they head back to Malmö. From the couch, she follows her team in the Africa Women Cup of Nations. She feels incredibly down. She wants to start rehab, wants to start immediately getting better; she does not like sitting around and waiting.

On Sundays, she takes the train to Malmö to attend church. Initially, she and Ngozi went to the local Catholic church. "It was so quiet! Only the old people go to church in Sweden! I'm telling you, you will never see a young white girl at church in Sweden." But after one service in Swedish, listening to praise they couldn't understand, they sought out the African church, where sermons and songs are in English. Standing beside other Africans, she can sing words she knows.

For much of the day, she scrolls through the internet. She reads a story on Facebook about the rapper Akon – how he sold his Lamborghini and his diamonds, how he is working to bring reusable energy to Africa. *Wow*, she thinks. *I did not know that he has a heart of gold.* Continuing to browse Facebook, she sees a picture of an African boy bending down and drinking water out of a mud puddle. She looks at that picture and aches. "Looking at the photo, I am remembering where I came from," says Alinco. The jarring disparity between her old life and her new one is always on her mind. She has a talk with herself – admonishing herself for moping around, reminding herself of how good she has it and how much suffering is out there: "When you are living in the white man's land you have to appreciate *everything*," says Alinco. She swaps out her WhatsApp profile picture – it had been a picture of her with her hair done into chic knots, wearing gold hoop earrings, a belted pea coat, and a camel colored scarf – a refined Swedish-looking outfit. Instead she puts up the picture of the little boy sucking up the rain puddle. She won't forget where she came from, and all the people who are still suffering, she tells herself.

On December 4, she receives news from her agent via text: because she was not able to finish the season, the team manager will not sign her for another season. Back in her apartment, she cries. She repeats to herself, *I have Jesus, I have Jesus so I am strong.* The coach comes to see her – apologizes and tells her that if it were up to him, he would keep her.

As she rehabs her knee, a new agent searches for a team that will sign her. In February, she signs with a small club, Asarums IF. While Vittsjö play in the top tier of the Swedish league, her new team is in the fourth tier. She will trust in God – and she will keep praying, that her knee stays strong, that she will prove herself, that she will be able to continue to provide though football.

Magic, Hope, and Brazil's Number 10

BRAZIL IS KNOWN WORLDWIDE as the land of magicians.[26] There's even a word for the specific fusion of sorcery and skill embodied by so many of the nation's players: *ginga*, the Portuguese term for a certain kind of sublime deftness on the pitch, something incorporating both the sway of hips and unfettered imagination. This quality is not confined to the professionals; there are glimmers of *ginga* everywhere – in the seven-year-old who dribbles up and down the slope of a favela skateboard ramp; in the barefoot 70-year-olds who smell like aftershave and Icy Hot and play away the morning dew; in the waiters who walk to the court at midnight to play after their shifts; in the bronzed bodies who juggle up and down Ipanema beach, Christ the Redeemer hovering up above.

In the 2014 men's World Cup, when the world made its pilgrimage to Brazil, the tournament itself felt like it was under a spell: endless goals in group play, drastic reversals of fortunes, impossible injury-time saviors. Even the spectacular failure of the Brazilian men's side felt otherworldly, with the squad too thoroughly ravaged in the semi-final for it not to have been fated. After more than a decade without a World Cup victory, Brazil forsook *ginga* in favor of a more aggressive determination to win at all costs, leading the World Cup in fouls committed. The 7–1 loss handed to them by the Germans felt like a reprimand from an angered pantheon, a sign the team should get back to the magic and beauty it is known for.

The exception of course was Neymar – he was the totem representing all the *ginga* of the past, his pedestrian teammates throwing his extraordinary ability into sharper focus. When the striker injured his vertebrae in the quarter-finals, the country mourned the loss of its magician.

But Neymar wasn't the country's only hope. For more than a decade, another player had conjured magic in the name of Brazil – but for many of those years, that magic went unseen.

• • •

FEBRUARY 19, 1986. In Dois Riachos, a small, forgotten town in the northeastern highlands, where there is nothing but scorched earth, wind storms, and wandering goats, Marta Vieira da Silva is born. There, in the dust, she discovers her powers over the ball. At fourteen, she hears of a women's side for Vasco de Gama and takes a three-day bus ride to Rio de Janeiro, beginning her life as a nomad.

Three years later at the 2003 World Cup, she appears like an apparition before the world. She is seventeen years old, and she is incredible. Her face is striking – dark eyes that are equal parts intensity and mischief, high cheekbones, and a wide, white-toothed smile. She is twiggy, so light she could lift off at any moment. At 5'4", she's three inches shorter than Messi. She has a short torso, high hips, and long limbs. Off the ball, she has a tendency to hunch, which makes it all the more dramatic when she springs to life. She prowls the wings – walking, walking, walking, and then – one quicksilver, airborne launch forward. When she's mid-flight, it can be difficult for the spectator's eye to track what's happening; the ball seems to flutter in and out as she improvises, invents and streaks past defenders.

These capacities alone are enough to captivate, to make anybody watching drift into a kind of fugue state, but she has another power, maybe her greatest power: she communes with the goal. While the Brazilian men's side has featured a continuous carousel of players gifted in the art of the dribble, only one ended the sprees of footwork with goals, buckets of goals: Pelé, Brazil's greatest goalscorer of all time. Nearly 50 years later, another goal-sorcerer had appeared. In her first six games with the national team, Marta scores sixteen goals. That's 2.7 goals per game. In her first World Cup game against South Korea, she scores in the fourteenth minute and is named Player of the Match. In her second World Cup game, playing Norway – the number two ranked team in the world, reigning Olympic champions – she acts as "playmaker and provider supreme" as FIFA puts it, creating seemingly everything in a surprise 4–1 rout. Only one of those four goals is all hers, but it's a statement: she slips through three defenders and launches the ball into the net with a reeling, free-falling finish, like an exclamation point after an explosive dance.

Her performance feels like a meteor shower – every touch an explosion of magic – and anyone watching would attest to having witnessed something rare. A professional coach in Sweden tracks down a Portuguese speaker and calls her eight times a week until they can convince her that they are serious – that they want her to come to the country that sits just below the Arctic Circle. But in Brazil, they aren't watching. Because Brazil doesn't care about women's soccer. *Futebol feminino* had been popular in the early 1900s, with up to 40 women's teams in Rio de Janeiro alone, but it was banned in 1941, an embargo that wasn't lifted until 1979. The law stated that "women will not be allowed to practice sports which are considered incompatible to their feminine nature." The concept that women playing soccer is "unnatural" hasn't entirely faded. When I spend the 2005 summer playing for Santos, no one comes to our games or even knows a women's side exists. And when I talk to the taxi drivers, the waiters, the açaí vendors, the kids on the beach, nobody has heard of Marta. In Brazil, it would be two more years before anyone took notice.

In June 2007, Brazil hosts the Pan American Games, which means Marta has her first chance to play for the *seleção* on home soil in a game that matters. Against Ecuador, Marta scores four goals. Against Canada, Marta scores five goals. In the beginning, the stadiums aren't full, but with every game the murmur grows. In Brazil, word-of-mouth is everything: in *Futebol: The Brazilian Way of Life*, writer Alex Bellos gives a disclaimer that in this country "The written word is not – yet – as trusted as the spoken one." Stories spread of a girl who has scored as many goals as Pelé, and who has done so in equally spectacular fashion. By the final, 70,000 pack Maracanã stadium. For the first time, the women's side look out at a Maracanã – the spiritual home of Brazilian *futebol*, place of heartbreak, jubilation, and myth – that is filled for *them*. They crush the mighty United States 5–0. Marta scores twice and assists two others.

You could say it took four years, or you could say it took three games – either way, Brazil is suddenly aware of another magician in their midst. *Ginga*, it turns out, overpowers prejudice: Brazilians can't resist what Marta can do on the field. Pelé, who witnessed Marta's performance, calls to congratulate her. "It is true what they say," he tells the press, "she is Pelé with Skirts." He adds: "And I think she has an advantage because her legs are prettier than mine."

Not everyone loves the legs quip, nor the moniker – deeming the "skirts" add-on distasteful, and believing that Marta should be appreciated in her own right. Marta herself has said she was overwhelmed by Pelé's support. The most famous player in history called her up to congratulate her and sang the praises of a team that had largely been ignored. Unlike FIFA's Sepp Blatter, who proposed that women play in skirts "to make the game more interesting," Pelé was not actually suggesting women should play in skirts; in a country that has always appreciated beautiful women, he was, in his way, noting their contribution to the beautiful game.

Months later, in the 2007 Women's World Cup, she again electrifies. In the semi-final, once again facing the United States, Marta backheel-juggles the ball around one side of the defender, pirouettes around the other, then slots the ball into the back of the net. It was, in the words of *The New York Times*, "a circus act" – easily one of the most breathtaking goals ever scored in men's or women's history.

The morning after, I am again in Brazil, this time making a documentary on pickup games around the world. As I stand on the main road in and out of Rocinha, the largest favela in Rio de Janeiro, Marta is everywhere: MARTA MARTA MARTA exclaim the headlines on the morning papers hung over clotheslines. In the small neighborhood bars, dozens of men gather around televisions. As they wait for their coffee to brew, they watch and re-watch the highlights, reacting, appreciating. She has arrived.

Between 2006 and 2010, Marta wins FIFA World Player of the Year an unprecedented five times in a row. On the professional level, she has kept pace with Pelé: he scored 650 goals in 694 appearances; as of March 2017, Marta has 358 goals in 321 games. For the national team, Pelé scored 77 goals in 91 national appearances; Marta has scored 105 goals in 101 national games. But Pelé won three World Cups; Marta has won zero.

• • •

IN DECEMBER 2011, Marta and Neymar played together in a charity match. After the game, the pair high-fived, lacing their hands together, looking equally impressed by the other. When the reporter said, "Here we are with two crack players" (*"craque"* being the ultimate compliment in Portuguese), Marta responded shyly, "He's *more* crack."

"Nah, nah," Neymar said. "She's the best in the world. I am so happy to have her here, to at least have the chance to play with her."

Marta and Neymar are both jaunty tricksters who invent and surprise, both wearers of the iconic number ten jerseys, both Pelé's successors. Their paths have intersected, dovetailed, and diverged in astonishing ways. While it's well-known that Pelé and Neymar played for Santos FC, it's less well-known that Marta did as well, in 2009 and then again in 2011. Largely because Marta was playing, 13,000 people came to watch the women's Copa Libertadores final. Santos was the best women's team in Brazil, in all of South America, and with Érika, Cristiane, and Marta in their lineup, they were one of the best women's teams in the world. During one press conference, Marta said, "Santos is a club that has been very big in developing women's *futebol* in Brazil and we're very proud of that."

On the men's side, when Neymar was courted by European clubs in 2010, it was Pelé who urged Neymar to stay in Brazil. And Santos management did whatever it had to in order to pay Neymar a salary that could compete with the European sides.

Including cutting the entire women's team in January 2012.

In a press conference, when a reporter asked Neymar if he felt bad that his high salary had resulted in the dissolution of the women's team, Coach Álvaro grabbed the mic before Neymar could respond. "I didn't say that Neymar was guilty for the end of women's football," he said. "What I said is that the goal of Santos is to have professional football that can last for hundreds of years. Other side activities [like the women's team] are possible when possible. As we're champions, wages are higher, the players are more expensive and we have to readjust."

The women's team operating budget was 1.5 million reais a

year ($826,000 in 2012); the club was then paying Neymar 1 million reais ($558,000) a month.

Later Neymar would say, "Of course I was sad. If it's possible to help, I'll help. Not just me, I think all the players could help just a little bit so that the *futebol feminino* can return. The women have won titles for us too." His anguish sounded sincere, as did his admiration for the women.

One of the women's players tweeted directly to Neymar. "How about you help us? We also have dreams, and many of them are just like yours."

According to the newspaper *Folha de S. Paulo*, Érika, a national team player who had spent six seasons playing for Santos, called up the club – she asked directly, "Will you bring back *futebol feminino* if we can raise the money?" They told her yes.[27]

The whole thing seems like a movie – the protagonist faced with the task of finding huge sums of money. Érika is not someone who's easily dissuaded. As she once told a local newscaster: "The rocks in my path, I stack them up and make a staircase. It's the only way I know in my life."[28] As a kid, she had no money for the bus she needed to take to get to training but she boarded it anyway; she kept her head down and the bus driver looked the other way as she got on, each day saving a place for her. Always, she has found a way to play. With women's *futebol* in Brazil, nothing had ever come easy.

So she sought out Neymar – took him at his word and asked him to help her. And he did. Together, they found 1.5 million reais in sponsorship.

When Érika came back and told management she had their money, Santos still refused to bring back the women's team. I can only imagine what it feels like to pull off the impossible – to find 1.5 million reais so that you can continue to play – and still be told no.

In the press conference announcing the dissolution of the team, Érika cried. "We play because we like to play," she said. "We *love* to play."[29]

• • •

IT'S WORTH NOTING that 2011 was Santos's 100th anniversary; to commemorate the occasion they produced a calendar featuring the Santos women's team in bikinis.[30] Marta was not in the shoot but national team players Cristiane and Érika were. Not long after the photo shoot, when a news anchor interviewing Érika asked her about it, Érika kind of shrugged. "The calendar was fun," she said. "It wasn't our idea. Some girls like it – but me, I just prefer to put on my cleats and play here."

The Santos team is not, of course, the first example of women's soccer players taking off their clothes for publicity. Brandi Chastain posed in nothing but cleats for *Gear* magazine in 1999, saying, "Hey, I ran my ass off for this body. I'm proud of it." In 2000, no one came to the Icelandic women's national team games. So, in 2001, Icelandic captain Ásthildur Helgadóttir organized an unsanctioned bikini calendar, her thinking being: *use sex appeal to get them there, our skill to keep them there*. That year they sold out every game. In 2011 several German professional players posed nude for the German *Playboy*. Ahead of the 2011 World Cup, three French stars posed topless in an ad meant to rebuke at the same time as tantalize, their portrait above the caption: "Is this how we should show up before you come to our games?"[31] American players have regularly posed nude in ESPN's annual "Body" issue; composed of both male and female portraits, the issue sells itself as a celebration of strength and athleticism in all its forms.

But there's an altogether different tone when you're asked to walk down a catwalk in a bikini and then your team is cut at the end of the season.

• • •

NEYMAR DIDN'T STAY with Santos. Barcelona paid a transfer fee of more than €57 million to acquire him in May 2013. Marta, on the other hand, has struggled to find a league that can support her. Of the eight professional teams she's played for in the past, seven have folded, unable to stay financially afloat.

Her first squad, the women's side at Vasco de Gama, shut down after two seasons; her next team, a club in Minas Gerais, did the same a season later. In 2009 Marta went to play for the second attempt at a US women's professional league, Women's Professional Soccer. As MVP, she led the Los Angeles Sol to a first-place regular season finish. At the end of the season, the Sol ceased operations. In 2010, Marta, again league MVP, led the FC Gold Pride to another league championship. At the end of the season, FC Gold Pride ceased operations. In 2011, she led the Western New York Flash to one more championship. At the end of that season, the entire league folded. In 2012, she returned to Sweden, where she had played for Umeå from 2004–08 – it seemed to be the one league she could rely on. She signed with Tyresö FF, who then won their regular season championship. In June, Tyresö FF announced their withdrawal from the 2014 league, citing a financial meltdown.

On the field, always, she delivered, but FC Gold Pride – who, like Tyresö FF, found sponsors to cover her controversial six-digit salary – had banked on the power of her *ginga* to bring in revenue. "We weren't selling out stadiums, and Marta jerseys weren't being sold off the racks," FC Gold Pride general manager Ilisa Kessler told *The Equalizer*. "It was a bit of an experiment for us to see if there was any considerable incremental revenue that could be driven by a player like Marta. And that just did not happen."[32]

Marta, five-time World Player of the Year, struggled to find teams that remained financially solvent. After Tyresö went under, Marta approached Sweden's FC Rosengård, who said they were "flattered" but didn't have the budget for her wages.[33] She agreed to play for less, signing an initial six-month contract that she extended. In interviews, she bemoans the absence of a professional league in Brazil. There is no option of making a decent living in her own country.

• • •

WHEN I PLAYED for Santos in 2005, our leading scorer Nenê had already given up *futebol* twice because she could make more money to support her family by working at a toy factory outside of São Paulo. But both times she came back, unable to stay away from the game.

We trained six to seven hours a day on the worst field I've ever played on, more cow pasture than pitch – and then at the end of the second practice, no one left. Everyone continued to play, to juggle, to tinker – often in the rain of the Brazilian winter. No one ever got sick of it.

Once, my coach, Kleiton Lima (the man who pretty much single-handedly made our team possible, coaching the team, his father housing the players in the dormitory-style hostel in Itanhaém), took me to a men's game. Not just any game – a Copa Libertadores match, the South American version of the Champions League. All season, via charades, emotion, Portuguese and a touch of English, he had kept saying to me, "You *have* to see." Blue smoke bombs whizzed down the alley as we raced to the stadium alongside thousands of others. When we first stepped into our section, Kleiton watched me as I took it in. Firecrackers whistled and smoked; shirtless, hairy men sweated and sang, their arms around each other's shoulders; kids in number ten replica jerseys stared ever so seriously at the field, at Robinho, the resident magician. He was months away from leaving for Europe and a multi-million-dollar contract. *Fica Robinho*, *Fica Robinho*, the whole stadium sang. Stay, Robinho.

Sometimes at Santos practice, after my fifth hour on the field, I didn't feel like being out there anymore. I was tired of it. And I didn't understand how my teammates could still be absorbed. But inside the stadium, inside that throb of national passion, I understood – all I wanted was to play.

Our team was on the outside looking in. Maybe that makes you want it all the more.

• • •

"WE HAVE NO FANS," Érika told a local news station not long before the team folded. "The future of women's soccer depends on the fans." It's hard to get fans when no one knows you exist. Most games aren't televised or covered in local media. According to one study, between 2007 and 2011, in the three leading national news magazines, *Época*, *Isto*, and *Veja*, and the leading sports magazine, *Placar*, there were only eleven articles featuring women's soccer.[34] *Futebol feminino* was not a part of the national conversation.

"It's a vicious circle," Fernando Ferreira, who heads Pluri, Brazil's leading sports-development consultancy firm, told *The Globe and Mail*. "There is no interest from fans, so there is no interest from TV, so there is no interest from sponsors. It's hard to say which comes first. Maybe the fan comes first, because male football has a monopoly over the fan."[35]

How do you change it? In the United States, NBA star Kobe Bryant raved about Marta in 2009: "My daughter plays AYSO soccer, right. The first time, she really didn't know what she was doing. I tried to work with her and stuff. Then we go home and I bring up Marta on YouTube and said, 'Watch this.' She sat there for like fifteen minutes just watching. She's only six, but she [recognizes] what's amazing. What [Marta] does is phenomenal. It's incredible. Marta's gifted, man. The things that she does on the pitch, I've just never seen anybody do, male or female."[36]

Does this kind of vocal, genuine admiration from cultural icons with huge followings have an impact? If Brazil saw their heroes – Neymar and the rest of the Brazilian squad – keenly following the women, tweeting, attending their games, would the country follow suit?

Could a collaboration between male and female players in advertising help? The Mia Hamm vs Michael Jordan Gatorade TV commercial that ran in the States comes to mind. A garish song plays in the background – "I can do anything better than you" – as Mia throws Jordan to the ground. It's fun to imagine a Neymar vs Marta commercial, or, say, a recast of the 1998 Nike ad of the Brazilian men's team juggling through the airport, but this time featuring Marta rainbowing the ball to Phillipe Coutinho who then lobs it on toward Cristiane. The Brazilian federation has the same sponsors for the men's team as the women's, which makes a collaboration between the two teams seem logical.

In the United States, the Mia vs Michael ad is one of many commercials featuring players from the US women's team. The support of marketing heavyweights – including Nike, Adidas, Budweiser, and Barbie – helped propel the American women's team into the national consciousness and onto magazine covers. This surely influenced the level of attention the 1999 US women's team enjoyed, selling out the Rose Bowl, and setting an all-time record for a women's sporting event with 90,185 attendees. That public frenzy then fostered even greater participation at the youth level: 48 per cent of the 3 million registered US Youth Soccer players are female.[37] This is in sharp contrast to Brazil, where according to FIFA's 2006 global study on football, only 1 per cent of Brazil's 2 million registered players were female.[38]

In 2015, Jonas Urias, a Brazilian club coach, estimated that there were only around ten elite soccer clubs for girls under the age of seventeen nationwide.

The players themselves fight for change at the grassroots level: Aline Pellegrino, former captain of the Brazilian women's national team, co-founded the Guerreiras Project, where professional female football players host workshops and visit neighborhoods, play with the kids, and show them that *meninas* can play *futebol*. Even without the support of the media, of clubs, of marketing heavyweights, they push for a groundswell: in São Paulo, a former player named Bibi Martins started Pelado Real FC, a group of about 500 girls who play *futebol* every day. In the favelas, on the streets, on the beaches, more and more girls play alongside the boys. And when she is good, they call her *Mart-inha*. Little Marta.

• • •

TO MARTA, THERE HAS always been only one answer: if she could bring home the World Cup, or an Olympic gold medal, surely then her country would care. In the award ceremonies for her "Best Player" awards, she has said that those awards have done nothing to advance the women's game in her country. In the 2015 World Cup, when she scored her fifteenth World Cup goal – that's three more than Pelé himself and the most in women's World Cup history – *O Globo*, the national newspaper, did not cover it. While her *ginga* had been appreciated by her country in flashes, that gift had not ultimately been enough to create any changes. If individual achievements could not do it, maybe a world championship could. Going into the 2016 Olympics – on home soil – a gold medal was her last great hope.

Of course, with the absence of youth teams, professional teams, funding, national interest, and infrastructure, they would be the ultimate magicians if they managed to win a title. While the men's *ginga* was nurtured and groomed, the women's *ginga* rose out of nothing.

For Neymar and the men's side, the stakes felt nearly as high. There would be no undoing the horror of losing 7–1 to the Germans in the World Cup. That will be a scar in the national psyche until the end of the time. But Brazil had never won an Olympic football gold medal, and a return to the top would go a long way in restoring the faith of the nation.

Marta and Neymar both entered the 2016 Olympics with everything to prove.

• • •

FROM THE OPENING match, the women's side dazzles the country, scoring a shower of goals against traditional powerhouses in the women's game: a 3–0 victory over China, a 5–1 drubbing of Sweden. For once, they are all over the media – on the highlight reels, in the Olympic promos, on the newspaper covers. While Marta is the best player in history, fans have the chance to discover the other women's magicians – such as Cristiane, who has scored more Olympic goals (fourteen) than any other player, man or woman, in the world, including Marta.

When the team lands in Manaus – a city surrounded by a huge rainforest and accessible only by boat or plane – a throng of fans await their arrival, shouting and holding signs that say, "We are with you." At 1am, hundreds of girls stand outside the stadium, waiting for Marta, screaming her name as she boards the team bus. *The New York Times* publishes an article with the headline "In Brazil, Where Men's Soccer Once Was King, the Women's Game Rules." Finally, the *futebol* fervor has spilled over to the women. The country falls not just for Marta but for the entire team.

The men are not faring as well. Their first two games are scoreless draws against Iraq and South Africa. Failing to score on home soil against traditionally weak teams is seen as an act of heresy in Brazil. The team is booed off the pitch and faces an early exit from The Games. Fans chant "Marta, Marta, Marta." Kids cross out NEYMAR and scrawl MARTA in magic marker across their backs.

The homemade Marta jerseys are not just meant to make a statement. If you want a shirt with MARTA on the back, this is the only way to do it. The sports stores, t-shirt shops, Nike stores and street vendors who walk up and down Copacabana carry endless NEYMARs but no one has a single MARTA. They are nearly impossible to find – Brazilian TV star Alexandre Nero vents on social media: "I cannot have a Brazilian soccer team shirt named after one of the best soccer players in the world simply because of some medieval market thinking that no man would wear a shirt with the name MARTA." His indignation spreads across the media.

On the field, the wind of fortune changes directions. The women's well runs dry – now they are the ones who produce two 0–0 results. Meanwhile, the men find the scoring touch. Yet, when they beat Denmark 4–0, the Brazilian newspaper *Folha de S. Paulo* headline declares, "THEY PLAYED LIKE MARTA."

In the final, in dramatic fashion, the men face none other than Germany. Neymar is again the hero – he scores a swerving, swooping incredible free kick to put Brazil up 1–0, and after Germany equalizes and both teams head to the shootout, it is Neymar who scores the final penalty to win. He drops to his knees and sobs as the stadium explodes in sound.

The women's side scrapes through to the semi-finals, again facing Sweden – who are looking to undo the 5–1 trouncing. The team Brazil just walloped is now able to hold them at zero. Marta cannot score. After 120 minutes of playing, they find themselves plunging toward a shootout. Marta, like Neymar, buries her penalty. But a teammate misses. They lose the match. Like Neymar, Marta falls to her knees and sobs; in her tears, you feel the disappointment of more than a decade of efforts falling short.

After the game, she talks to the reporters: "I ask the Brazilian people now, keep on supporting us, keep on supporting Brazilian women's football," she pleaded. "We need you so much."

• • •

MARTA'S FEAR WAS that without a win, women's *futebol* would continue to be ignored. Yes, the whole country had followed the women like never before. The media had declared them "the sweethearts of Brazil." But who could say whether this would be a sustained shift in public perception or just a fleeting moment in time that lead to nothing?

Ferreira, of the sports consultancy firm Pluri, had told *The Globe and Mail*, "The [Brazilian Football Confederation] doesn't give a damn. They say there are going to do this, they are going to do that, that they are going to change women's football. But CBF never did anything for women's football." But in January 2017, something rather extraordinary happens – what may feel, to Marta, like the most incredible achievement of all: The South American Football Confederation (Conmebol) announces new regulations: in order to compete in the cherished Copa Libertadores, by 2019 each men's professional team must also have a women's side.

In Europe, many of the most successful women's teams are paired with a men's professional team (Paris Saint-Germain, Olympic Lyonnais, Manchester City, Liverpool, Arsenal, and FC Bayern among others) that provides backing and allocates money for their women's club. And in the US's third attempt at a professional league, the Portland Thorns, the Orlando Pride, and the Houston Dash share ownership groups and benefit from the marketing staff, stadium, and fan base of the men's side. But South America – a continent that has historically ignored the women's game – is the first to *mandate* equal playing opportunity for all at a professional level.

The United States knows firsthand that the fervor generated from an Olympics or World Cup is hard to sustain in the off years, in the pro game where not every team has a star. (And considering that most of the Brazilian women's national players currently play abroad, this will be a definite issue.) But Brazil is the most *futebol*-mad country in the world. Fourth division teams and youth teams generate thousands of fans. Is it crazy to think that Brazil – the country that banned women from playing altogether less than 40 years ago – could actually be better poised than any other country to find a fan base and a niche for the women?

At the national team level, Brazil is also making changes. Instead of a national residency – which was ideal when there wasn't a national league for the women to play in – there will now be separate playing camps targeting each geographical area, pulling players from the wide-reaching country, from undiscovered stretches of Amazonian rainforest and savannah and mountain. It will be a unique format – suited to the vast, diverse country – and a smart one: who knows where *ginga* will once again rise out of nowhere, as it once did in Dois Riachos. There, on a white cinder block wall, the graffiti now reads: *Aqui Nasceu A Melhor do Mundo*. The best in the world was born here.

The Comeback Moms

GOALKEEPER MELISSA BARBIERI had been on the Australian national team since she was 21 years old. She had played in three World Cups and two Olympic Games. She captained the team in 2010. In 2013, aged 33, she gave birth to her daughter – and suddenly, after more than a decade representing her country and playing for Australia's W-League, there was no place for her.

The Australian W-League has one-year contracts. If you get pregnant, that just means you get no contract for a season. There's no maternity leave. So Barbieri sat out the 2013 season. At the national level, probably, she thinks, long-time coach Tom Sermanni would have kept her in mind – but when Australia named a new women's national coach, Barbieri found herself off the radar. "I think they just thought women who have babies don't really come back afterwards," says Barbieri.

Everybody else may've thought she was done but she didn't. Six weeks after birth, she was training again; five weeks after that she was back on the field. But she had no team. She emailed every club in the W-League. No one wanted her. Some said, "Sorry, we've already got our keeper; wish we could help you but we can't." Some just said, "No thanks." In order to be in contention for the national team, you've got to be on a professional team – and she didn't have one. Barbieri's normally even-toned voice wavers: "It felt like they were forcing me out of the game."

• • •

IN 2010, AFTER winning everything there was to win with Arsenal, English national team player Katie Chapman packed up her husband and two small sons and headed to the United States for a new challenge – playing for American professional team the Chicago Red Stars. It didn't go well. Emma Hayes, the coach that signed her, got sacked. "And then we were just on our own," she says. Her husband couldn't find work. So less than a season after it began, the American experiment was over.

They returned to England. Only they'd rented out their house, which meant the family of four had to move into Chapman's mother's small two-bedroom flat. She was trying to get everyone settled and get her boys back in school and she was questioning the upheaval she'd put her family through. Then there was national team duty. Having just hauled her family across the pond and back, she didn't want to take off for national camp and leave them. While the US provides nannies at training camps so that players can bring along their kids, England has no such policy. So, ahead of a friendly against the Americans, Chapman had a ten-minute conversation with Hope Powell, the team manager. "I asked for a short break while I sorted out my family," says Chapman.

Three hours later, Powell terminated her contract with the English Football Association. Powell sent her a short email: "It basically said, 'You've served your country well. It's a shame to see you leave.' Even though I had never said I was leaving."

The influential playmaker had been on the team since she was seventeen years old. The previous year, she had won FA International Player of the Year for the second time. She had no intention of retiring from international football; she had no idea her request for family time ahead of a friendly would cost her a spot on the national team she had anchored for the past decade.

For the rest of Powell's tenure – four more years – she was never invited back to the team.

• • •

AMY RODRIGUEZ had just won an Olympic gold medal when she discovered she was pregnant. Rodriguez, a 28-year-old forward for the US women's soccer team, says her son, Ryan, is the "biggest blessing in her life," but initially, she panicked. She had no idea how her body would react or how willing she'd be to leave her son to go to training camps and tournaments. "I had no idea how I would do it," she says. "I just knew I wasn't ready to be done."

Having signed with the Seattle Reign in the third iteration of the US women's pro league, she was expected to be their star forward. Instead, she spent the 2013 season watching the team play without her. In September of that year, a month after giving birth, Rodriguez went to breakfast with the Reign coaches. They told her they were eager to get her back on the field and gave her a tiny baby onesie with the team's logo. "I was like, okay, they *are* excited about me," says Rodriguez. "It meant a lot to me."

One month later the team traded her to FC Kansas City.

While her husband Adam had family in Seattle whom the couple had been counting on to help with their newborn, in Kansas City their closest family members would be 1,700 miles away. Adam couldn't leave his job to go with her. For the six-month long season, they would be forced to live "like a divorced household," as she put it, taking turns spending time with their son.

Rodriguez had been traded before; she understood that it was a business decision. "I interpreted it as, 'Oh, they don't have faith in me, they don't think I can come back.' I was definitely motivated to prove to them, that, 'Hey, you probably should've kept me.'"

• • •

JESSICA MCDONALD KNOWS what it's like to be traded. In four years, she had played with five different NWSL teams, which isn't that unusual – in the NWSL, many players ping from team to team as coaches navigate tight salary caps. That's one thing when you're single; it's another when you have a husband and a baby. But no matter how many times she had to uproot her life, McDonald was determined to keep playing. "I want to be able to tell my son I went for it," she says. "I want him to be proud of his mom." In each new city, she figured it out: in Portland (NWSL team number three) there was a "players only policy" at the team's apartment complex – no spouses or significant others allowed. McDonald was unfazed – she talked with management and her two-year-old was allowed to stay. On the field, she set out to prove herself: she scored eleven goals – the most on the team, second most in the league. She figured this meant she wasn't going anywhere. Her husband Courtney enrolled in firefighter school and finally they planned on living together and setting up a life.

In the offseason, she was on a bus in Germany – where she and her son moved so she could play until the NWSL season started up again – when she heard the news via her agent: she'd been traded to Houston. "We had worked so hard to get things set up, to get [my husband's] career kicked off," she says. "He's been supporting me for so long and once again, because of my career, he had to put his own on hold. You don't know where you're going to be tomorrow. It's kind of hard to plan a future."

In Houston, the team helped her husband find a job, and put her family up in an apartment. That season, she was again her team's leading scorer. At the end of the season, she was again traded – this time to the Western New York Flash. Once again she had to start from scratch. But each time she was traded, the more motivated she became to prove she was worth hanging on to.

• • •

IN 1999, WHEN the US women's soccer team burst into the public conscience, motherhood and soccer seemed to go hand in hand: in *Sports Illustrated*, Rick Reilly wrote about the "diaper bags" in the same breath he wrote about the dominance. *The New York Times* article's subheading ran "Bags of Soccer Balls, Bags of Diapers." Magazine spreads featured both Joy Fawcett and Carla Overbeck, medals around their necks, kids in their arms. And it's true that the US national pool has included a fairly steady stream of mothers since then. The 2015 US World Cup team included three mothers – Christie Rampone, Amy Rodriguez, and Shannon Boxx. But that isn't the global norm. Take a look at the women's game around the world and mothers are few and far between. Of the 24 teams and 552 women who competed at the World Cup, there were only eleven known mothers. The majority of national teams have none.[39]

At the professional level, women's leagues are marked by low salaries and instability. It's difficult to make it in the leagues in the first place; throw in motherhood and for most, the balance is tipped toward retirement. Take Jenny Anderson, a player for New Jersey's Sky Blue FC: she lived in an extended-stay hotel, saw her new husband once a month, and worked a second job as a coach, battling rush hour to make it back to practice in time. While those weren't easy circumstances, she thought it was worth it to continue to play the game she loved. But when she found out she was pregnant, she stopped chasing the soccer dream. "I had a family to support now, I couldn't do it financially," she says. "I had to make a bigger contribution. I'd seen Christie [Rampone] and other players do it so I knew it was possible – but I don't know how."

At a national team level, countries have ever-deepening talent pools; it's harder and harder to hold onto your spot. England's Casey Stoney and Sweden's Hedvig Lindahl, two of the eleven mothers at the World Cup, both opted to have their female partners carry the baby. Stoney told the *Telegraph*, "I will want to have children myself one day in terms of going through the whole birth process. I have watched Megs and it is so magical." But for now, with talented replacements ready to step in at any moment, she says, "Taking nine months out of football was not doable."

The mothers who do go for it often face a climate of doubt: there's the perception that it's too dicey to take a chance on a player undergoing both a gigantic physical transformation and a shift in priorities. But for most athletes, there's nothing more motivating than proving someone wrong. In women's athletics, there seems to be an emerging phenomenon: mothers who stay in the game come back faster and stronger than they were pre-pregnancy, and the shift in mental landscape makes a mother more of a player, not less.

• • •

DURING AMY RODRIGUEZ'S pregnancy, she gained 35 pounds – "I weighed almost more than my husband. It was embarrassing," she says. "And my muscles got *gooey*." Her first day back in the gym, six weeks after giving birth, she was lightheaded and nauseated. "I thought, if I'm getting blurred vision and losing my footing just from lifting weights, what was going to happen when I hit the field?"

When she first got back out there, she played with teenage boys' club teams and national youth teams and felt incredibly awkward. She had no strength. Her balance was off. Every day, the US fitness coach Dawn Scott sent her exercise regimes. Her parents watched the baby while she trained. She'd drop him off in the mornings, go work out, shower, come back, and be a mom. "I'd be breastfeeding and pumping, not sleeping, but I was so determined," says Rodriguez. "I'd missed the sport for months and months. Soccer is what I love to do. And then all of a sudden, when I got pregnant, it was like, *errrrkk, you gotta stop*. And I wasn't ready to stop. I couldn't wait to get back."

In January 2014, Rodriguez was invited to her first US training camp since giving birth – her son in tow. Because her son wasn't a good sleeper, she'd sleep in three-hour stretches at night before waking up the next morning to train. "And not just train, but train with the best players in the world. And have to stand out," she says.

Four months after getting back on the field, she lined up for one of the US speed tests, a 40-meter dash, and to her shock registered the fastest time on the team.

• • •

SHE ISN'T THE only one to experience a surge in speed. Katie Chapman told the *Guardian*, "After my second baby I felt the fittest I'd ever felt. I came back in preseason and was flying." Jessica McDonald also says her body got stronger and faster post-pregnancy. When she ran 120-yard sprints, a standard test, she clocked times that were two to three seconds faster than her pre-pregnancy times. Barbieri too noticed a physical difference: "I felt faster and stronger. I was quicker off the mark and off the ground." She thinks part of this can be attributed to the labor experience: "Whatever you go through in training is so minimal compared to giving birth. You see how much your body is capable of and you realize you've underestimated it the whole time you've been an athlete."

In the world of long-distance running, where improvements are easiest to track, there has been chatter for decades that having a baby can actually make you faster. In 1984, the 27-year-old Norwegian runner Ingrid Kristiansen became one of the first post-pregnancy runners to cause a stir: she won the Houston Marathon five months after having her first child, then set the course record at the London Marathon four months later. Since then, there's been a continuous stream of runners with small babies – Colleen De Reuck, Liz McColgan, Paula Radcliffe, Kara Goucher, Mary Keitany – who win races, shatter records, and run faster than they ever have before.

Could "super mom strength" be more than just a myth? There have been very few concrete studies examining how changes in the body during pregnancy can affect performance. With so many variables – how the pregnancy went, how the birth went, whether there was a C-section – it's difficult to have a controlled study. Researchers generally agree that certain changes in the body – such as a 60 per cent increase in blood volume and a strengthened musculoskeletal system – can benefit athletic performance in post-partum runners. But Jim Pivarnik, director of the Human Energy Research Laboratory, also says that if there's any physiological advantage, it most likely ends after the first two months. While most mother-athletes he interviewed reported personal heights in physical performance, Pivarnik believes this is less physiological and more mental – stemming from an *I'll show them* mentality.[40]

• • •

DURING THE FIRST game of the 2014 season, Amy Rodriguez scored. And that, she says, felt incredible: "There have been seasons when I only scored one goal in a whole season. So, it's like, *wahoo, already tied that record, got that one under my belt*. And I was just super ecstatic, I knew all this hard work coming back from having a baby was worth it," says Rodriguez. With that goal, the floodgates were opened: she became the second-leading scorer in the league. Her team, FC Kansas City, made it to the final, where she faced none other than the Seattle Reign, the team that traded her. Rodriguez scored both goals to give Kansas City the 2–1 championship win.

US national team coach Jill Ellis was in the stands watching, and Rodriguez was eventually selected to the 2015 US World Cup roster. On July 5, like Fawcett and Overbeck, the US mothers who came before her, she stood in a shower of confetti, a gold medal around her neck and her son in her arms.

The *I'll show them* mentality was a large factor in her comeback, but she also credits motherhood in general. Kicking a ball is no longer her number one priority, and that, somewhat counter-intuitively, helped her career: "As a forward, you're required to be composed in front of the net. I think the reason why I scored so many goals this year is because I was more relaxed. I know now that my son is what's important in my life. Soccer, I just play for enjoyment."

Long-time US super mom, Christie Rampone, mother of two, also notes the shift in thinking: "Before kids, as a player, you have a tendency to over-think. You've got too much time on your hands – you sit there in the hotel room stressing out, imagining things. As a mom you can't do that – you're focused on real problems. And that really helped my game."

For moms trying to make it back, there is both the hunger to prove you can do it, and the calm of knowing it's only a game. That may be the psychological sweet spot.

• • •

THOUGH EVERY SINGLE team in the Australian W-League had passed on her, Melissa Barbieri kept training anyway. With every "no thank you," she grew more determined. And then she got the chance she needed: Adelaide United, the bottom team in the league, had hired a new coach, Ross Aloisi. Aloisi knew Barbieri, knew how much she wanted to play. His first order of business was getting her on the roster. In the W-League, there is no league minimum wage; some players make $10,000, some make zero. The Adelaide front office told her directly, "Look, if you come, we can't pay you much." She said, "That's fine, I just want to play."

So, for $2,000, she packed up her daughter, left her husband behind, and went to live with her sister-in-law in Adelaide. To make it work financially, she auctioned off her Australian national team gear. She's not a sentimental person but giving away the World Cup jerseys and the gloves got to her – "Only because those are things I could've given my daughter," she says. Players from the Australian men's team got wind of what she was doing and donated gear to help out, and she raised $10,000, twice as much money as she had hoped. She gave half of it to her teammates, who were also struggling to make ends meet.

Adelaide United wasn't just bottom of the table: from the middle of 2008 to the middle of 2012, they had not won a single game – 34 games without a win, the longest losing streak in league history. When Barbieri arrived in 2013, they won three games, drew four and lost three. The previous season they'd had 40 goals scored against them; in 2013, Barbieri cut that to fifteen.

At the end of the season, she was named W-League Keeper of the Year.

This coincided with another change in the national team coaching staff. Barbieri was called back into camp to compete for a roster spot. She didn't have much of a shot. The coach told her directly that he didn't envision taking her to Canada in June; he just wanted her there in camp as a good example for the younger players. Which meant Barbieri was again looking at a nothing-to-lose, everything-to-prove scenario. "I don't know what it is about me. But the more difficult it is, the more appealing I find it," says Barbieri. In each training session, she denied goal after goal and performed so well they couldn't ignore it. To the shock of the soccer community, probably to the shock of the coach himself, he named Barbieri in the 2015 World Cup roster. In Australia's opening match against the United States, Barbieri was starting in goal.

It wasn't all triumphant jubilation; playing in the World Cup also meant leaving her daughter behind. Men's players make large enough salaries to fly over their families should they so desire; most mothers playing in the 2015 World Cup – including Cameroon's Madeleine Ngono Mani, Ecuador's Erica Vasquez, England's Casey Stoney, as well as Barbieri – couldn't swing it financially. Though Barbieri was on the World Cup roster, she wasn't a contracted player and was only making a casual daily rate. Her husband was the sole bread winner and couldn't take off work. "It was the first time I had been away from my daughter for more than four days ... it was a big jump to six weeks." She only let herself video-chat with her once a week – "Otherwise, I would've been too overcome with sadness."

But her daughter is part of why she went for it. This World Cup jersey and this set of gloves she will not auction off. She's proud of what they represent, what she wants to teach her daughter: that no one can tell you what you can or cannot do.

• • •

JESSICA MCDONALD HAD the unhappy distinction of being the only mother in the US professional league who had not been called up to the national team. She had hoped her eleven goals in Portland would earn her a call-up ahead of the 2015 World Cup.

Though she was her team's leading scorer in the next NWSL season too, the phone call still didn't come. With each passing year, a national team call-up seemed more unlikely.

When she packed up and headed to the Western New York Flash, she was 28 years old, the second oldest player on the team. Courtney, her husband, couldn't immediately relocate to Buffalo. The general manager helped her find a good daycare for her son. And sure, you could look at the trades and the constant uprooting as difficult – but you could also look at it as an adventure. Her son can speak a few words of German, hangs out with professional female athletes, and watches thousands of fans cheer for his mom. And while many parents aren't able to pick up their kids until 5 or 6pm, she's able to pick up Jeremiah as soon as the two-hour training is over.[41]

In New York, she scored ten goals, second in the league only to teammate Lynn Williams (who scored eleven). With the two of them up front, they were the surprise 2016 NWSL Champions. After five seasons, McDonald has scored more goals than any other American in the league. And on November 2, 2016, she earned her first call-up to the national team.

Thanks to Fawcett and Overbeck, who helped put the policy in place, the US Soccer Federation pays for a nanny, which means McDonald didn't have to leave her son behind. After reporting to her first camp, she posted pictures of herself and now four-year-old Jeremiah making faces to the camera – "Made it to LA for USWNT camp with my travel buddy!! Taking over hotels like uuuhhh!!!"

McDonald's victories did not mean that she finally got to stay put in one place for longer than a season. The NWSL announced that the entire Western New York Flash team would relocate to North Carolina for the 2017 season ... bringing McDonald's count to six US cities in five years. As she reported to preseason, she posted on Facebook: "Whaatt Upp North Carolina? #FeelingRightAtHome."

• • •

FOR FOUR YEARS, while Hope Powell was manager, Chapman watched her England team play without her. The 2012 London Olympics was probably the hardest to watch – "It was a once-in-a-lifetime opportunity twice over. Playing in the Olympics, and playing them in your own country. It would have been a dream come true for me," Chapman told *Bea Magazine*. "I was quite hurt, really. I think I'm still performing at my best."[42]

In 2013 Powell was fired and England got a new manager, Mark Sampson. Eventually, Chapman got a phone call: Sampson said, "I was wondering if you'd be interested in coming back to the team."

"Oh God yeah," she responded. "Of course. I've never wanted to not play for England."

The team environment is much different this time around. "It has really come full circle," says Chapman. "Mark is much more understanding of [the family] side of it." The FA contract now includes a player-approved maternity policy. And in response to Chapman's experience, the FA issued the following statement to the *Guardian*: "The FA will fully support any England women's player should they wish to take maternity leave or spend time concentrating on their family life." Chapman hopes that the next generation will not think they have to choose between football and family.

Chapman made the 2015 World Cup roster. Playing in a World Cup still meant leaving her three boys for six full weeks. "We didn't even talk about having them come out – with finances, with school, I thought it was impossible," says Chapman. In a sentimental moment, she wondered aloud whether she could do it. Her oldest son, Harvey, said, "*What*? It's a World Cup! You have to go!" She laughed, and thought, *You're right – I have to do it. I have to do it for you.*

Several weeks later, she was in her hotel room in Canada. Her teammate told her there were new boots from Nike waiting for her at the front desk. She headed downstairs, not thinking anything of it. She walked around the corner and there they were: her family. Her husband had decided this was something they could not miss – that they'd find a way to make it work so that her sons could witness their mother play in a World Cup.

"I just stood there and cried. I didn't even move. I didn't even run to cuddle them or anything, I just froze, stood there crying like a big baby," says Chapman. Her boys were in the stands, witnessing their mother run the center of the midfield for England. She helped lead the team toward their historic third place finish.

Back in England, when Katie Chapman drops her kids off at school, everybody recognizes her. She poses for pictures and signs autographs. "And," she adds, "apparently I've been amazing on FIFA." Since the arrival of women's teams in the video game, kids run up with their hands on their backpack straps and shout, "I played you on FIFA last night! You scored loads of goals!"

The entire Chapman family goes on the *Good Morning Britain* talk show.[43] (Her youngest, Zachary, is on the move the whole time, playing with the French press and the fruit bowl and babbling happily – Chapman is entirely unfazed.) The interviewer asks her oldest, "And what do your mates at school say about having such a success of a mother?"

"They say, 'It must be lucky to have a mum who's a footballer'. And that they'd like to have one – that I'm the lucky one."

The Indomitable Lioness

ESKILSTUNA, SWEDEN, JULY 2014. Cameroonian Gaëlle Enganamouit walks into her shared apartment, holding a fourteen-inch frozen fish by the tail. "Tonight we cook," she announces in English to her American roommate, Kim DeCesare.

She throws the fish in the sink, grabs the largest knife in the kitchen, and begins to hack at it, fish scales flying all over the linoleum. She is here in Scandinavia, thousands of miles away from home, in order to play professional football for Eskilstuna United DFF, newly promoted to the Women's Premier Division. She is the only African on the team. She speaks zero Swedish and, so far, maybe a few hundred words of English – the words Kim has taught her over the past month as they sat together in their apartment between practices. "Kitchen," says Kim. "Kitchen," repeats Gaëlle.

There are times when she needs to say things – in French – and there is no one for her to say them to. When she finds herself longing to be back in her home city of Yaoundé, this is what she does: she heads to the tiny African market she found on one of her walks and comes back with enough food to prepare a Cameroonian feast – crepes, beignets, fish stew. She stands there at the stove, listening to upbeat French-African music, singing and dancing and grooving as she cooks – bringing her country into her kitchen in Sweden.

On this night, at the table, Gaëlle, Kim, and Elena (a team-mate who is half-Albanian, half-Swedish) eat with their hands, the way you would in Cameroon. "Now," Gaëlle announces, "is time to try the – what you call it? – the eye?"

Kim, an outgoing 22-year-old Long Island girl with a contagious laugh, just looks at her. "The eye? As in the eyeball?"

"You try."

"Gaëlle, I'm not eating that eyeball."

But Gaëlle explains that in Cameroon, they eat *all* of the fish; so, before they know it, Kim and Elena are holding one eyeball each. *One, two, three!* It squirts and crunches in their mouths as they squeal and grimace, and Gaëlle rocks with laughter.

A little less than a year from now, during the 2015 World Cup, the irrepressible Enganamouit will skyrocket to Cameroonian fame – but right now, at this moment, she is just one more player trying to make it far away from her home.

• • •

GAËLLE'S MOTHER HAS a hard time believing that her daughter cooks. Every time her phone rings and Gaëlle is on the other end, asking about yams or cocoyam or coriander, Mama Enganamouit has to take a second to collect herself before she relays instruction. As a kid in Yaoundé, Gaëlle – the youngest of nine – wanted no part in any cooking, steering clear of the kitchen until food was on the table and ready to eat. While her six sisters helped with meals, Gaëlle was invariably three blocks away – on a wide dirt lane beneath a large tree, the impromptu gathering spot where she, her brothers and the other boys met to play football. While neither parent was enthusiastic about their daughter playing football, there were eight other kids to worry about. Every so often they stopped and took note that Gaëlle was once again out, once again playing with boys. "Wait a minute," they'd say to her. "You should be learning from your mother how to run a household. You should not be out there with the boys." But she had her big brother Assambo to help fend them off – "Mom, Dad, she's fine; she's with us" – and it was never long before she was back out on the street.

When she was twelve years old, she watched the 2004 Africa Women Cup of Nations on television in her home. It was her first time seeing women play. The Cameroonian team, the Indomitable Lionesses, made it to the final against Nigeria, the continental powerhouse, and all of a sudden her whole country was paying attention to women's soccer. In the cafes and bars – in any place where there was a TV – everyone watched as their Lionesses were annihilated in a 5–0 loss, one goal after another raining down upon them. Gaëlle burned. "I felt so, so hungry to be out there," she says. "I told myself, *One day I will play for my country, and we will take our revenge*."

Three years later, she watched the 2007 Women's World Cup, which ratcheted up her dream. Sweden's Caroline Seger was her favorite; the 22-year-old white-blonde midfielder was everywhere. "All the good action she was in the middle of," says Enganamouit. She took in the Swedes' intricate football and orchestrated passes, and started dreaming: *One day I will play football in Sweden*.

• • •

FIVE YEARS LATER she headed to Serbia. It wasn't Sweden, and she had never heard of it before, but it was still Europe, the continent of Manchester United and Barcelona and Caroline Seger. She had never been on a plane before and now she was taking three. She spent one night in the airport, lying on the floor with her head on her suitcase, trying to sleep but wide awake, trying to imagine what lay ahead.

One thing she had not imagined was the cold. When she stepped out of the airport the following morning, wearing her one windbreaker, it was waiting for her: bone-chilling, below-zero-Celsius cold. Nothing in her duffel bag was warm enough to deal with it.

On the ride from the airport to the coat shop – her first stop in Serbia – she stared out the window, feeling the first pangs of culture shock. She had never before seen snow and now it coated everything: the ornate, 20th-century art nouveau buildings that were as pretty as the Europe she recognized from TV; and the concrete buildings that were not pretty, not at all like the Europe from TV. She stared at the gray slush in the street. Her home, a temperate green city sprawled out across seven rolling hills, with Mont Fébé looming above, felt like another universe.

Her Serbian teammates at ŽFK Spartak Subotica were friendly smilers but they spoke no French and she spoke no Serbian. There was no team translator. There was one other African, a Guinean who did speak French, as well as a tiny bit of English. The Serbs, too, knew a limited amount of English; so Gaëlle's only means of verbal communication was a multilingual relay – each message passed along between three people and in three languages. All her life Gaëlle had been unabashed and exuberant, a high-wattage goofball, but when you can't communicate, it's hard to be anything at all. There was football – "the universal language" – but every time she stepped onto the field in arctic conditions, Gaëlle felt disbelief: *How am I supposed to play football when I cannot feel either foot?* After a few days of training, she called home, in a small voice, and told her mother, "I can't do this. I want to come home." Mama Enganamouit was firm: "This is the decision you've made. You must stand by it."

So she listened to her mom. And right away – from almost the first second of her first game – she produced: she stepped onto the wet, cold grass with feet she could not feel and scored the fastest goal in women's football history. You can watch the clip on YouTube: you see the stadium, storm clouds and trees up above, SPARTAK bannered across empty bleacher seats. The whistle blows, her teammate ever so slightly touches the ball, and Gaëlle hits a drive that sails straight into the top corner.[44] The other team stands there dumbfounded as Spartak players pile on top of Gaëlle.

Off the field, she developed a routine to combat loneliness: she went on long walks through the city – because in Cameroon, everyone was always out on the clay streets, always ambling here or there, saying hello to neighbors, just checking out whatever was going on. The walks in Serbia weren't the same: "In Cameroon, when I wake up, I go somewhere, I see someone in the streets, I can say 'Good morning, how are you?' In Europe, no one cares about you, they just walk by like you don't exist," she says. But a few blocks away from the apartment she found a market that reminded her of home, merchants hawking all manner of goods – bananas, jars of stewed vegetables, gently used sneakers, bottles of hair spray. In place of batik print fabrics and plantains, there were rows of fur coats, knit Serbian slippers, and bottles of vodka. But the feeling, the atmosphere, was the same: it was the one part of the city where people called out to you.

On June 8, the day before her birthday, she scored the winning goal in the Serbian championship. Afterward, she went out to eat with her teammates, who had made her a cake. At the restaurant, another party was going on – a party full of old people. Eastern European women with big breasts and wide hips were moving and grooving, and Gaëlle – who loves to dance – started bobbing in place. One of the ladies beamed at her and walked over. "She said, 'Mama, you need to dance,' and she pulled me up out of my chair," says Gaëlle. Soon, the entire restaurant was dancing. They held hands, forming a giant circle, dancing a traditional Serbian dance. Gaëlle and the woman who pulled her up were in the centre of the circle, Gaëlle's hips swaying, her smile wide.[45]

• • •

AT THE END of the Serbian season, once she had returned home to Yaoundé, she tattooed her mother's face across her lower back. Because in Serbia, she missed her so much – enough to think, *I need my mother with me always*. "Now, wherever I go, she'll be with me," she says.

Her mother's face goes with her next to Sweden, the country of her childhood dreams. In her suitcase, she packs traditional Cameroonian clothing: a yellow, green, and red batik-print free-flowing blouse and matching pants. The outfit serves as a kind of security blanket, a connection to her country – she knows she won't see a single person wearing this in Sweden. And, she thinks, *I will wear this if there is any kind of official ceremony – to represent my country*. Some days when the nostalgia is strong, she puts it on in the apartment and walks into the living room to show American Kim. "This is what we wear in my country," she says. At some point, Kim tries it on: the blouse won't fit, but she gets into the pants, and the roommates stand together in front of the mirror and laugh.

Kim and Gaëlle spend long stretches of time together, killing all those hours after practice, sitting at the kitchen table or lounging on the futon, Kim teaching Gaëlle English. They pass back and forth a phone with Google Translate, constantly teasing each other. While Kim was willing to eat even eyeballs, to Kim's disbelief, Gaëlle refuses to try the pizzas Kim makes. "What the hell, Gaëlle?" demands Kim. Gaëlle, who calls Kim "Americana," tells Kim to call her "Choco" on the field. "Gaëlle, I am not calling you 'Chocolate' on the field," Kim says. So then Gaëlle wants Kim to call her "Nico Chico", Nico referring to the stylish French forward Nicolas Anelka, because, Gaëlle says, she too is a goalscorer who likes to dress well. However, when Gaëlle walks in wearing fluorescent t-shirts with glittery text and white-washed denim jeans, Kim says, "Gaëlle, *what* are you wearing?" Gaëlle responds, "What? This is popular in my country. This is cool." Gaëlle, who has seen the American movie *Mean Girls*, asks Kim if that is what America is really like. Well, the school buses, the cafeterias, the high school scene – "Yes, I guess," says Kim. Gaëlle wants Kim to know that Africa is *not* naked people swinging from trees, which is what she sometimes believes is her teammates' impression of Africa.

They trade stories and life details: Kim talks about her middle-class life growing up in a 1,100-square-foot house in Massapequa Park, Long Island. The soccer guys always hung out at her place. (Before one high school playoff game, she bleached all their hair in the sink of her bathroom.) In summer, she and the guys played pickup games on the beach, thundering and splashing into the water afterwards, throwing jellyfish as they chased each other up the shore. Thanks to soccer, Kim became the first college graduate in her family, a scholarship player at Duke University. ("I'm so mediocre – how did I ever give birth to you?" her short, Italian mom would often say when she looked up at her 5'10", tall-drink-of-water daughter.)

Unlike the United States, in Cameroon, soccer and school are separate; choosing soccer means leaving school behind. You go play for a team instead of continuing your education. Gaëlle's parents wanted her to stay in school; for years they were against her football. "It wasn't until the coaches knocked on my door that they thought, okay, maybe this is serious," says Gaëlle. Her brother, Assambo, also dreamt of playing professionally, and they spent every day playing and training together. She tells Kim that his football is going well. He has just landed a tryout in Tunisia.

From the kitchen table, Gaëlle also helps run her family business, operating a taxi. "In Africa," she explains, "when you have something, it's not just for you, it's for all the family." The baby of the family, the one they all used to protect, has become the primary breadwinner – every week she sends home the majority of her €70 earnings. (This also factors into why she got the tattoo on her back. She tells Kim, "My mama carried me on her back – now I get to carry her on mine.") With her first paychecks from Serbia, she invested in *un moto*, the primary method of transportation in Yaoundé; everybody catches rides on motorcycles that whistle down clay streets. Soon, they made enough money off the moto and Gaëlle's Swedish paychecks to buy an official yellow taxi. She pays for insurance, hires someone to drive it, and now every week more money is coming in for her family. She knows football doesn't last forever, knows she needs to build a foundation that can sustain her family for the rest of their lives. "She is such a businesswoman," says Kim, "always on the phone, running the show."

• • •

ON SEPTEMBER 28, Gaëlle's world tilts. Assambo, her sister tells her, is dead. A day earlier in Tunisia for the tryout, he was killed in a car accident. She sits at the kitchen table and sobs.

It's a game day. They play Umeå at 4pm. Kim gets on the phone, tells the Eskilstuna coach Victor Eriksson what happened. He of course excuses Gaëlle from playing, but Gaëlle waves that talk away. "I need to play for him," she says.

Usually her pregame routine is all dancing celebration. With her headphones on, French-African beats playing, she dances from one end of the locker room to the other, trying to get everyone to dance with her. Earlier in the season, she taught her teammates a Cameroonian dance, instructing them how to move and what to say. When she was away for a national team game, the Eskilstuna team sent her a good luck video in which they proudly perform the dance: standing in a circle, as they wave their arms and lean in and out, they chant a call and response: "*Bungala, Bungala, Bungala! Bungala, Bungala, Bungala, eh!*"

But today there is no singing or dancing. She is silent as she puts on her socks and cleats.

Her coach tries again. "You don't have to play; you shouldn't play," he says.

She insists. Sixty-four minutes in, from just inside the eighteen, she scores. She's off-balance and falls over as her shot sails into the net. It is for Assambo. From the ground, she starts to cry as she looks up to the sky and points with both hands.

• • •

THAT NIGHT GAËLLE wakes up at 3 or 4am and her pillow is wet with blood. She put her hands up to her face and feels it gushing out of her. She is groggy and disoriented and doesn't understand what has happened. She only knows that her brother is dead and now blood is streaming down her face. She gets out of bed, runs through the living room to Kim's room, stands in the doorframe and shouts, "Kim! Kim! Wake up! What has happened to me? What has happened to me?"

"What, Gaëlle? What?" Kim shouts back, eyes blinking rapidly as she tries to process what's happening.

"What has happened to me?"

Kim looks at her roommate and diagnoses, "It's just a nose bleed. You're okay, Gaëlle."

Gaëlle's never had a bloody nose before. Why she would get one now of all times she doesn't know. She is spooked. As she leans over the sink and washes her nose, Kim stands at the bathroom door and tries to calm her down, "You're fine, Gaëlle, you're fine." Gaëlle keeps splashing the water in her face – unable to make sense of anything, unable to believe her brother is gone.

• • •

SHE BURIES HER grief in playing, which gets better with every game. In the 2015 season, she scores one goal after another, leading her Eskilstuna team – a newcomer to the Damallsvenskan division – to one unlikely victory after another. Tunavallen, the stadium where the team plays their home games, is in the heart of the city; locals are huge women's soccer fans and with each win the stadium is fuller and fuller. Against Gothenburg, they set the attendance record for the season with 6,312 fans.

Toward the end of the season, they face Rosengård, the top team in the league, maybe in the world. On the bus ride to Malmö, where Rosengård is based, Gaëlle scrolls through pictures of haircuts on her phone. She wants something drastically different, something bold. There's one picture that speaks to her: part Mohawk but with more swoosh to it – a reverse lion's mane. That, she decides, is the haircut for her. When they arrive in Malmö, she and teammate Elena head to the store and buy two kits of hair dye. In the hotel bathroom, she leans her head back into the sink as they triple-bleach it. They shave the sides and straighten the middle until they are staring at a torch of yellow hair in the mirror. Elena looks at her and says, "Let's see what that head can do."

The next day she scores. In every game after that for the rest of the season, she scores. It's because of the hair, they say; it is lucky hair. Eskilstuna will finish second in the league; Enganamouit, with eighteen goals, becomes the Swedish league's top scorer – the first African to even come close to doing so. Every game she plays with her brother in mind, carrying the weight of both his dream and hers.

• • •

IN JUNE, WHEN she suits up for the Cameroon national team in the 2015 World Cup, that hair is her signature. It is the first time the Indomitable Lionesses have qualified for the World Cup: it is a chance to permanently alter the course of women's football in her country.

When she finds out the date of their first game – June 8 – she lets out a small, happy whelp: it's the day before her birthday. On June 8, 2013, she scored to win the Serbian Championship. On June 8, 2014, she scored in an African Championship qualifier. "I *love* this day!" she says. "It is my lucky day."

On June 8, 2015, she steps onto the field for her first World Cup game.[46] She helps create the first goal (launching a driven shot that is parried by the keeper and finished by Madeline Ngono Mani); scores the second (a beautiful, confidently executed break-away); plays a hand in the third (she drives down field and sets up her teammate, who is fouled, leading to a penalty kick); scores the fifth (finishing a cross); and scores the sixth (after being taken down, she scores her penalty). Kim laughs harder and harder after each goal – so amazed, so proud. Enganamouit's three goals lead her team to a 6–0 victory that is as resounding as the defeat that motivated her back when she was twelve years old. At the end of the game, Enganamouit runs to the camera and tugs on the bottom of her jersey as she kisses the Cameroonian crest. She looks directly in the camera and blows a kiss – to her country, to her family, to her brother.

They lose their next game, 2–1 to Japan, the reigning world champions, but Enganamouit is still a force. At home, the fans start referring to her as a "freight train" because of the power with which she drives toward goal. By the third game, a must-win against the Swiss, Cameroon's supporters form a raucous sea of red, yellow, and green. Switzerland scores first and the cameras zoom in on one despondent Cameroonian fan clad in a balloon hat with dangling ribbons. Then Cameroon equalizes and the cameras return to the crowd – the fans go wild, jumping, screaming, blowing horns, banging on drums, everyone's hands up in the air. In the 62nd minute, the other colorfully haired Cameroonian player, magenta-braided Madeleine Ngono Mani, scores a diving header to complete a historic comeback. In their very first World Cup, they have made it out of group and reached the round of sixteen. When the whistle blows, the players run to their fans. Gaëlle, standing directly up against the boards, leads the crowd in song – shouting, exuberant, euphoric.

While there are no published TV ratings assessing how many Cameroonians tuned in, they themselves will tell you: *everybody* was watching.

• • •

WHEN THE INDOMITABLE Lionesses return to their country, they are met with hero worship. (Their loss to China in the round of sixteen does nothing to dampen the country's spirits.) Enganamouit is mobbed in the streets. A camera crew is sent to her town for her homecoming. Her neighborhood throws her a fete and it is all energy and color, a fusion of the traditional and the modern. Women wearing colorful batik head wraps and carrying straw baskets stand in front of wooden homes and look at Gaëlle. Others in loud t-shirts and denim shorts dance, hips moving. People snap pictures on neon-colored cell phones. A poster of her face with the words MERCI GAËLLE! is draped over the side of her house. Kids climb all over her. Dozens more – mainly boys, a few girls – gaze up at her, wowed. The street vendors, who watched her grow up, joyfully argue over whose stand will have the honor of feeding her today. She leans down beneath their colorful umbrellas and shakes hand after hand. The women hoot and holler as their local-girl-turned-superstar buys a Cameroonian specialty wrapped in shooting plantain leaves. When the cameras are turned on her mother, she says, *"Cette plus jeune fille nous a apporté l'oeil de la lune."* Which translates roughly to "This youngest daughter has brought us pride that can touch the moon."

When she is awarded 2015 African Footballer of the Year, Samuel Eto'o, one of the most famous Cameroonian footballers of all time, addresses Enganamouit directly:

> [I have] special emotion regarding my compatriot Gaëlle Enganamouit's sacred Player of the Year [award]. In a recent interview you said you wanted to look like me. Know today that I can see myself in you, little sister. You [and the women's team] have the spirit of champions, and you embody the rebirth of football in Cameroon. Thank you for continuing the hope and the dream.

• • •

ON FACEBOOK, SHE has over 43,000 followers. She has a Snapchat account on which she is constantly posting videos – dancing in the weight room, dancing as she cooks, always dancing. She features her mother prominently on social media: she has a giant photo of her mom's face as her background picture, and she frequently posts shots of her hugging her mom, along with the caption: "*Je t'aime, mère!*" (I love you, mom!)

In 2016, she tears her meniscus and goes quiet on the field. She recovers in time for Africa Cup of Nations, hosted by her country. Three and a half hours before the opening match, Cameroon v. Egypt, the 40,000 capacity stadium is nearly full. Cameroon makes it to the final, facing perennial champions Nigeria (to whom they will lose 1–0). This time the 40,000 capacity stadium is full more than five hours before kickoff. Thousands more gather right outside the stadium. In Cameroon, women's soccer appears to have tipped. The Federation has taken note – Enganamouit says everything is starting to change and that they are experiencing more support than ever before.

In February 2017, Enganamouit signs with Dalian Quanjian FC of the newly wealthy Chinese League for an undisclosed sum of money. Like Yaoundé, Dalian is a coastal, hilly city with lots of green; it sits on the tip of Liaodong Peninsula in Northern China, bordering the Yellow Sea. With her mom's face on her back, her traditional Cameroonian clothes in her duffel bag, and her brother's memory always in mind, Enganamouit heads to one more new continent, one more new adventure.

• • •

A CAMEROONIAN RAPPER, Anderson, writes a song in her honor:[47] in the music video, throngs of people pack the wide balconies and staircase of a three-storey building. Everyone wears multi-colored t-shirts with her number, seventeen. There's a choreographed dance in a dirt field cut with Anderson and his troupe chanting the chorus: *"Gaëlle Enganamouit, Engana Engana Engana mouit."* Toward the close of the song, they flash to an official FIFA photo in which she is roaring like a lion. Presumably, after she sat down for the traditional roster pic – muted smile, hands behind her back – she made one more face before she walked away from the camera, spontaneously morphing into her best "indomitable lion" impression: her blonde mane brushed forward, her mouth mid-roar, her hands out like claws swiping at air.

Beyond the Field

LEGENDARY AMERICAN SPORTSWRITER Gary Smith was once asked in an interview, "If you could trade places with any athlete, who would you choose?"

"I probably wouldn't," he responded. "For the most part, they've had to whittle down their lives so much to excel at something that their possibility for personal growth is greatly compromised."[48]

What fascinates me about the women's game is that this doesn't seem to hold true. Maybe it starts early. A twelve-year-old growing up in the eighties and nineties might have dreamt of playing, but she wouldn't have dreamt of *being* a soccer player. She couldn't. There wasn't a sustainable professional league. There was the national team – and in the United States, a kid watching the World Cup imagined wearing that jersey herself, but that aspiration had nothing to do with a salary or a career. Most kids, like me, probably didn't even know national team players made money. We just wanted to be as good as they were.

From early on, soccer was thought of not as a destination but as a route. Americans played soccer to land a college scholarship, to provide academic possibilities. As opposed to "whittling down" our lives, the game was a chance to open it up. The popular National Collegiate Athletic Association (NCAA) commercial told us that "nearly all NCAA athletes go professional in something else" – and we knew it was talking to us. From the beginning of our playing careers, we prepared for the end.

Male professional soccer players don't often go on to have second careers outside of the game. But women at the top of the game are in a constant state of hatching plans and pursuing alternate lives – ready at any moment to shape-shift and become someone else. In the United States, the women's professional league has folded twice – which meant that many players had no stateside playing option when they graduated from college. Those who did have an American league to play in still knew that it was tenuous, nothing to bank on. In 2016, the starting salary for a US professional player was $7,200 for a six-month season. That's $300 a week. If you convert that figure into a 40-hour work week, that's $7.50 an hour – right around minimum wage. To make it work, players often live in unconventional situations – from extended-stay hotels to retirement homes. On one side of the world for six months, on the other side for the next six months, they live out of the two checked suitcases permitted by the airlines. And this isn't the romantic chapter of the story – the lean years of hustling and scrimping that you can talk about affectionately after you've made it. This *is* making it. This is the top.

Meanwhile, with every passing year, more friends outside of the game are buying homes, having babies, and advancing up a career ladder. The basketball coach and commentator Al McGuire once said, "Thoroughbred athletes have an incredible need to succeed, a fear of failure"; somewhat ironically, that need to succeed drives many female soccer players at their athletic peak to cut their losses and chase down a new dream. Those who do keep playing through their prime have a strategy – they are hustlers, big-picture thinkers. Most have side jobs. Many go to school. Everybody's got a backup plan, an idea for what's next. This isn't just true for the American players of course – it's true for professional women players all over the world. Here's a glimpse into some of those players' pursuits beyond the field.

• • •

WHEN COCO GOODSON'S MOTHER signed her up for a dating
website, she protested: "You've got to be kidding mom." The
24-year-old's lifestyle as a professional soccer player for Sky Blue
FC made it difficult to have a relationship. She lived out of a bag
for six months in New Jersey, then spent six months back at home
in California. She was too busy training to have much of a social
life. But, her mother argued, she wasn't going to get any younger.
She made Coco a profile without her consent and when the floods
of responses started coming in, her mother kept bugging her until
she said, "Alright! I will do it."

On her very first date she met a sportsaholic from Sitka, Alaska,
a remote series of islands only accessible by boat or plane. They
were good together – both were "chill"; both loved sports. Before
long, they were engaged and she was introducing her fiancé to her
teammates. She bought a dress, picked out a ring, rented a venue. In
October, she flew to Alaska to spend the offseason with his family.
Three weeks into her stay, she was driving by herself, going around
a curve in the road, when she hit a patch of black ice. Another car
was coming straight at her and she panicked – did exactly what
you're not supposed to do and hit the brakes. The car flipped. She
hung upside down by her seatbelt in a ditch. She wasn't hurt but she
was rattled; she started questioning what her life would be like in
this place. Suddenly, the idea of life on Sitka – where there are only
fourteen miles of road from one end of the island to the other –
made her clammy. Because that was the plan, the compromise: he'd
follow her through her career and then, when it was over, they'd
live here. But after she flew home to see her family, she knew she
was never going back to Sitka. The engagement was off.

Now, aged 24, she was in the middle of a full-on tailspin –
maybe every decision she had made was bad. Maybe it was stupid

to still be playing soccer as an adult. Maybe she needed a job with a real salary. A friend of her parents offered to get her set up selling real estate in La Jolla, California – so she did it. She quit soccer, and spent two months wearing wedge heels and walking around cliff-side mansions, the wind wafting up from the ocean. But no number of ocean breezes or commissions could keep out the panic – she knew she had made another bad decision. She should never have left soccer. "It is what I love more than anything in the world, and it doesn't matter how little I make or how hard the lifestyle is – I'll do it for as long as I can," she said. She called up the coach and begged him to let her come back. One month later, she was once again the starting center back for Sky Blue FC.

In the offseason, she got a job at Starbucks to make ends meet. Her sister ratted her out to her co-workers: told them that when Coco wasn't Sharpie-ing names onto cups, she was a professional soccer player in New Jersey. They went home and Googled her. "Do you know you have a Wikipedia page?" they asked. Question two was whether or not she knew Mia Hamm. (*No*, she told them, Hamm hadn't played in ten plus years.) Question three was whether or not she knew Alex Morgan. (*Yes, I play against her.*) Then they all went back to scrawling out orders and foaming lattes. At 1pm, Goodson hung up her green apron and headed out to the field to train, so that come May, she'd be at her peak.

But the following season, she pulled her hamstring, which meant she wasn't playing. And playing was the only thing that made everything else – like weird housing situations – worth it. She and five other teammates lived with a 66-year-old man who griped about fridge space and made uncomfortable comments when they swam in his pool. "Dealing with the same stupid stuff every single year got old," says Goodson. Without being able to play, it was hard to remember what she was doing there.

She started thinking about a moment two years earlier when her friend, a pilot for the Coast Guard, let her climb into his helicopter. As the engine roared to life and the propellers started to spin, she had thought to herself, *I like the feel of this.* Now, in Jersey, as she rehabs her hamstring, she does a mental tally: she is composed under pressure; she has great eyesight; and she has always loved spikes of adrenaline. "As a kid, I loved roller coasters," she says. "Flying – it's like I'd get to control my own roller coaster." She starts studying for the pilot exam, which she passes. In March 2017, she applies to be an officer in the navy. On the phone, she laughs and pronounces: "I'm ready to fly."

• • •

THERE WERE 20,000 HENS on the rural farm where German national team player Tabea Kemme grew up. Every Saturday morning, amid the floating feathers and incredible cacophony of clucking hens, she spent two hours collecting eggs, moving up and down the rows of crates. Her home she describes as "part zoo" – the hens and the horses – and "part sea" – a little harbor not too far off from the farm, along with the river where she and her sisters liked to water-ski. Pictures on her social media feature not soccer but her adventures in nature: in one photo she is mid-sky, boulder behind her, water in front of her; in another she is mid-wave, her face emerging from the surf; next she is mid-stride, moving barefoot through a dry and dusty field, wearing a sarong-like dress, and passing by a crumbling monument. She is an adventurer who likes to roam, and you can see this even in the way she plays: as a defender and occasional midfielder, she streaks up and down the wing, comfortable in space, constantly going forward.

As a kid she was not allowed to focus just on soccer. Her parents wanted her to do everything and she did – an approach she has kept as an adult. One of the most popular players on the German national team, she is also training to become a police officer. Why? She sort of shrugs. "Because I thought it was interesting," she says. "After my career is over, it's important to have other work – to have a new life."

She is fresh out of police academy – where she studied proper handcuff technique, what to do with a shoplifter, how to calm someone down in a crisis situation. She'd have four-hour target practice with the shooting instructor. In April 2016, she started her internship with the criminal police, where she does detective work and investigates crime scenes. After ten-hour shifts, she heads to the field. "I can't just be a soccer player, I'd be bored," she says matter-of-factly.

• • •

ON THE WEEKENDS, during her sons' nap time, Casey McCluskey and her husband Greg run sprints in the driveway of their picturesque, two-storey home in Nashville, Tennessee. In the heat, wearing her old college t-shirt – DUKE SOCCER – she does her own specially concocted workout, a different exercise for every suit in a deck of playing cards. When she pulls a diamond, they do switch kicks and then sprint to the bottom of the driveway and back until she is gasping and sweating and "gross."

"Our neighbors think we are crazy. They'll see me sprinting away from the house, Greg behind me – and he *is* behind me I will note – and they'll ask, 'Is everything alright?'"

Casey and I played together at Duke University. As a freshman, she was the leading scorer on our team. We played in the Atlantic Coast Conference, the best in the country, and she was Rookie of the Year. As a senior, she was the leading scorer in the conference and was named ACC Offensive Player of the Year. In four years of practice, her side never lost a single drill. That's not hyperbole. Once, when I took out her ankles, she stood up and told me quietly, "I'll kill you." I have a memory of her passing the ball to where I should have been, to the part of the field I would have gotten myself to if I had her vision. She passed it to the space not because she thought I'd be there, but because she wanted to emphasize my absence. She couldn't help herself. She was the most competitive player – and the best – I ever stepped on the field with. While she would likely have been a first-round draft pick, the league folded the year before she graduated. At 22, her career was over.

So she went to law school because everyone had always told her she'd be good at it (due to an occasionally showcased ability to eviscerate anyone she disagreed with). She was in her second year at the College of William and Mary when the league came back. She considered putting everything on hold – spent a night in her apartment imagining herself going for it again. But then she reminded herself of the facts: on a women's professional soccer salary, she couldn't have supported herself. Living off her parents wasn't an option.

"If I could have made a suitable living – say a teacher's salary – I would have done it," she says. "But not being able to do that, it just wasn't viable. I wanted to be able to do with my life what I wanted to do and obviously, women's soccer wasn't going to do that."

Now she's a litigator. "And in a way, I'm glad my playing career got cut short," she says. She likes her life. She's happy. Two fantastic sons and husband, and a career she's good at. She likes writing briefs, defending clients, commanding a room. And she likes the professionalism that goes with it, enjoys straightening and curling her hair every morning, putting on a pencil skirt and high heels. In the courtroom, does she ever "get in the zone"? "No," she says, without hesitation. Sure, there are translatable skills: she credits her playing career with her "total focus," her ability to "grind out a brief until it is done." And there are definitely moments of adrenaline when she's arguing a case.

"But 'in the zone' when you're … untouchable, when you feel like you're floating," She gets embarrassed, "I don't know how to describe it, but no, no, I don't have that feeling any other time."

Greg, her husband, never saw her gift, which does kind of bum her out. "Everyone has a distinctive way they play," she says. "The fact that he never really got to see me play, it's like there's part of my personality that he doesn't know about, and there's no way to recreate it. It's just in the past." Other than one law firm tournament, she hasn't stepped back on the field. "Part of that, I think, is my personality – soccer is over, so soccer is completely over," she says. "I felt like I needed to figure out how to be me without playing. A clean break." And, she says, after a pause: "I didn't enjoy playing for the sake of it – I loved being good at it. I don't know that I ever loved it for what it was. And if I went out there now, I wouldn't be good. I wouldn't be fast. I haven't been practicing all the time." She doesn't want to play some watered down version of her old game. "I'm leaving the memory as it is."

But you can still find her out on the driveway, her skin splotchy and red, t-shirt soaked. Greg may never have seen her play, but he has observed her ability to "take it to another level." Because it will be humid, 90 degrees out, and he'll think about cranking it down a notch because, you know, why kill yourself? But not Casey. "I cannot let him beat me. It can't happen," she says. "Why do I care so much? I don't know why I'm like that. It doesn't matter. But it's like I'm still trying to be the best. Even though I'm not."

• • •

JAZMINE REEVES DOESN'T tell her Amazon co-workers that she

used to be a professional soccer player. Nobody knows that in her rookie season for the Boston Breakers, she'd scored a hat trick against the Portland Thorns – most of them don't even know what a hat trick is, which is fine. She has left that life behind. At the end of that rookie season, as a 23-year-old who hadn't hit the peak of her athletic potential, she retired. Like Casey, she doesn't play anymore, not even a little bit. Mainly because she's too busy but also, she admits, because it would be too hard. It would make her miss it and she doesn't want to miss it – she doesn't want to question her decision.

Because she *was* ready to move on with her life. One season had been enough. She got drafted and she went, because she had to – otherwise she would have always wondered, *What if? What if she played incredibly and the national team coach had told her to come try out?* But that hadn't happened. She'd done pretty well, but she didn't see the national team knocking on her door anytime soon. And her life as an NWSL player didn't feel like she was a "professional athlete." "Except for in Portland," she adds. "Playing in front of those fans, it was incredible. If all our games had been like that, who knows? It would be a whole different story." But all the games weren't like that. And she didn't like being dependent – were it not for the family hosting her, donating their basement, she wouldn't have been able to get by on $2,000 a month. The family was amazing, with three adorable kids; she ate family dinners, kicked the ball around with them in the backyard, went to their games. But she didn't feel like an adult. She wanted to be able to stand on her own two feet. And the job offers that she'd passed up when she graduated from college made her anxious. The Amazon job was the opportunity that seemed too good to let go, and she knew it wouldn't be around forever.

Maybe, she thought, she didn't truly love soccer. Not enough to hang around and work her ass off and make next to nothing while other job opportunities evaporated. She was grateful to the game – without it, maybe she would never have gone to college, maybe she would never have learned how to compete. Maybe *that's* the part she loved: the competing, trying as hard as she could. And she didn't need a field to compete. So she announced her retirement and went to work for one of the fastest growing companies in the world, where every day is a challenge.

Fast forward to July 2015: it's two weeks before "Prime Day," a huge sales event for the company, and Reeves is slammed. As area manager, she's running the entire warehouse in New Jersey, training 200 new hires to make sure they're ready to sort and scan 100,000 packages a day, constantly getting packages out to the surrounding area. It's grueling and crazy and normally she'd have another manager helping her, but unusual circumstances have led to it just being her; she's in charge and she's working ridiculously long hours and doesn't know if she can make it through. But three weeks later, after the storm has passed and they've gotten the numbers – after she's seen that their facility did *well* – she thinks, *I kinda dug that.* "I love that feeling – having the odds against me and performing; working hard, then seeing the payoff. That feels *good*," says Reeves. And familiar. It feels like soccer, reminds her of preseason, when you're gutting it out and killing yourself, but in the end, when it's over, you feel euphoric. She ends up winning Area Manager MVP for Prime Day. "And even though it's just a small, corny award, it means a lot. It's, you know, *accomplishment*," she says. "Like the old days."

Her co-workers eventually find out she's a former professional soccer player; an article about recent NWSL retirees gets sent around and then everyone comes up to her and says, "Wow! You're a superstar!"

"No," she says, "I'm not."

• • •

DURING MAMI YAMAGUCHI'S first camp with the Japanese national team, when she was twenty years old, she was roommates with Homare Sawa – the Mia Hamm of Japan, a revered celebrity. Sawa's signature had been pinned up on the wall of Yamaguchi's bedroom since she was twelve. And now, somehow, the superstar was lying on the hotel bed next to her own. Mami was silent, awe-struck, incredibly nervous, but Sawa was friendly and inquisitive. She kept asking Mami questions, kept putting her at ease, wanted to know all about her life. And they had things in common: both grew up in Tokyo; both played for Belleza, the top women's club in Japan; and both went to play in the United States.

One thing about Tokyo: there is no space. Which means there's a limited number of places to play. All fields are split and shared. Sometimes, for fun, Yamaguchi played on futsal courts on the rooftops of skyscrapers, neon lights of the city all around her. Most of the time, she traveled an hour and half each way to get to practice with Belleza. After school, still wearing her uniform, Yamaguchi squeezed onto the metro, caught a bus, then walked the rest of the way to the field, which her team shared with three other teams. They occupied a quarter of the pitch. Maybe this explains Japan's entire style of play: they are incredible in small spaces. After training, Yamaguchi would stay late, continuing to work on her touch, her turns, her shots, and on her way back home, around 11pm, the metro would no longer be packed. She would sit down, do her homework, and sleep.

Yamaguchi first dreamt of playing in the US after she went to a Women's United Soccer Association professional game while on vacation as a fourteen-year-old. Two years from then, the league would fold, but on that day, the league was at its peak and the game was sold out. When she entered the packed stadium at Nickerson Field, Yamaguchi looked around, dumbstruck, and told herself, *One day I will play in the United States.*

College, she realized, was her fastest route to getting there. When she was back in Japan, she bought college directories and looked up the top college programs in the USA. Three years later she signed with Florida State University. She was not there for the education. The school part – the classes, the books, the English – was just something she had to get through in order to play. "I hated it," she admits. It was too much, too hard because she couldn't really speak English. She walked around with a notepad and a pen and wrote down anything she wanted to say – and her teammates wrote down anything they wanted to tell her. It allowed her to get by, to generally know what was going on outside of the classroom. But inside the classroom, she had no clue.

On the field, she was incredible. In 2007, her junior season, she set the FSU record for goals and assists; led them to their first national championship game; and won college soccer's top individual honor, the Hermann Trophy. Umeå IK, the top team in Sweden, home to Marta herself, came knocking – they offered her a contract and she took it, foregoing her senior college season. "It was the chance to play with Marta," she says. "I could not pass it up – I took the risk."

For three years she was Umeå's holding mid, combining with Marta every practice and game. (Marta is as good as she had imagined – "on a different level than everyone else.") Playing in the Champions League and excelling for one of the top teams in the world, she was in contention for one of the 21 roster spots ahead of the 2011 World Cup. After the final Japanese national team camp, the coach called. "You are a wonderful player. But I am sorry – you are player 22." When she hung up the phone, she cried. She had to tell her parents and friends. "I felt like I let them down." (When I ask how her parents responded, if they hugged her, she says, "Oh no. We do not hug in Japan – we are not a hugging culture. They gave me space, which is what I wanted.")

Her parents had already booked a flight to Germany and bought tickets for the games. They watched the team without her. She watched the games on television. All of Japan watched as Sawa and her team won the World Cup. Mami was glad for her friends, glad for her country, but she cannot describe it as a good feeling to watch from home.

When she headed back to Sweden, she went out to the field by herself, so hungry to be better, to prove that she had belonged. On the empty field, she took shots at goal. She fired ball after ball, as hard as she possibly could – until she landed badly. She sat by herself in the grass, holding her torn-up knee. Three surgeries later, it was not better. The decision to retire was easy – she was in pain.

But three years of rehab later, as she jogged through a wing of the hospital, she noticed, to her disbelief, that her knee didn't hurt. A few months after that, she was unretired, playing with Belleza's professional team. Her very first game, she scored in extra time and her teammates dogpiled on top of her. "That's all I wanted – one more season to be playing with my friends, for fun. I was so, so happy."

At the end of the season, she retired, this time on her own terms. And she headed back to Florida State to see about that degree. In 2016, nearly ten years after she first arrived, she became a proud graduate in a maroon cap and gown. She doesn't know what exactly she wants to do with the rest of her life, but she knows that she likes being nervous – likes the shock of new beginnings, the adrenaline you experience when you go for it completely. Wherever she lands, she knows she wants the feeling of having to rise to the occasion. She hears about an agency that scouts Japanese players for American clubs. Back in Japan, they've just held a tryout in conjunction with the LA Galaxy. Five players have been selected to come over and try out for the feeder team. She calls up the agency and in a quiet, unsteady voice, explains that she wants to be a part of it. They hire her as the liaison, the coordinator, the on-the-ground problem solver, and a week after I talk with her, she heads to New York to start this new life – a new life informed by her old life. She will show the young players how to make it in this new country – "if," she adds, "they are good enough."

• • •

DURING THE SUMMER before her third season as an NWSL professional, Courtney Jones was on the start line, surrounded by 6′6″, 250-pound linebackers training for the NFL combine. Jones's father is a former NFL player and an old friend of his led the workouts: Olympic lifts, short sprints, cone work. The guys she sprinted with – the ones who make a team – would make a minimum of $450,000 in their rookie seasons. For her own season, she'd make around $10,000.

She spent a second summer in the gym with the NFL hopefuls – only this time she wasn't training for anything. At the end of her third season, as a 25-year-old, she retired. She is matter of fact in her explanation: "As a female athlete, you're always looking toward the end point. I wasn't making enough to support myself. I was fortunate enough to be able to have my parents supporting me. But I couldn't do that forever. I realized if I was going to succeed in life it wasn't going to be through soccer."

Jones can't tell you exactly why then she was still grinding out 40-yard dashes in a gym – other than that she loved it, and that she'd spent her whole life working hard. "That's what I know, and if my body could still do it, why should I give it up?" she says. She got married that summer – to an American football player – and at 7am on her honeymoon in Tahiti, they did sprint workouts on the hotel treadmills. He was in training; she was not. "I could've been on the beach, sipping mimosas," she says. But when her husband cranked up the incline or increased the speed and indicated that she didn't have to, she just looked at him, like, *yeah right*. "It's weird – I can't be beat. I don't want to be the one who turns down the speed," she says. "The athlete mentality never goes away."

Post-soccer, in her new professional life, she's not the only one with the athlete mentality: she launched a makeup company, Sweat Cosmetics, with four other soccer players. Emily Hines – the only one at Sweat not to have played professionally ("Call me crazy for peaking in college," she quips) – had the idea while she was playing at the University of Denver. Why, she wondered, was there no makeup designed specifically for athletes? Makeup you could play in, that could last a workout? Taryn Hemmings, a University of Denver teammate of Hines, went on to play professionally for the Boston Breakers, where she shared the makeup idea with her teammates – Courtney Jones, as well as Lindsey Tarpley and Leslie Osborne, former national team players and Olympians. In Boston, they had sleepovers and sketched out their visions for the future: they tracked down venture capitalists and top chemists, started tinkering with names and designs. They timed their big unveil to coincide with the start of the 2015 World Cup – to stay aligned to the game they'd played their whole lives.

The cosmetics industry, however, isn't exactly a jock hangout. When the five won't-take-no-for-an-answer athletes burst onto the scene, they were pretty astounded by certain differences – the pace, for example. Their first shipment was supposed to arrive in June but didn't actually arrive until July, which was hard to wrap their minds around. In soccer you are on time. There's no being late to a practice or game.

They dreamt, as all cosmetics companies do, of getting their products into Sephora, the multinational makeup store. When the email from Sephora came three months after their launch, they thought maybe it was a prank. But it was indeed real. They were upfront with Sephora about their newness – that Sweat Cosmetics was just starting out – but they also said that they were athletes who would do whatever it took to make the business successful. Sephora declined, saying, "We think that you guys are just too new – that you're not ready yet." And maybe Sephora was only suggesting that they needed more time, but that's not how the Sweat team took it. "It felt as though we had been benched," Osborne says.

Jones thought, *They must not know what it means to be an athlete. This is going to happen. We will make this happen. We will succeed.* She fired off a response, "We're going to take the makeup industry by storm with or without you," which made the rest of the team panic a bit, think *Oh geez*. But Jones's instincts were spot on: a week after she sent the email, they signed a contract with Sephora.

Do they miss their other lives? Two-time gold medal winner Lindsey Tarpley also works as an occasional broadcaster, and when she's interviewing the US national team the nostalgia will hit: "I miss competing on the big stage; I miss being nervous." Taryn misses the playing, the game itself. Leslie misses the friendships. Jones still has a ball in the back of her trunk. It's flat; she hasn't used it in a long time. But she can't bring herself to take it out. When she cleans out her car, it stays, rolling around with every turn.

• • •

THORA HELGADÓTTIR, the Icelandic national team goalkeeper and my college roommate at Duke, did so well on the math section of her SAT (the college admissions test) that she was admitted to Duke in spite of the fact that her English was still a work in progress. On the field, she had an extraordinary horizontal leap; she resembled a flying cat. She could punt the ball further than the Duke men's keeper. My freshman year, she carried our team on her back and did not let us lose, even though we were decidedly worse than many of the teams we played. She did this for Iceland too; once, when her national team played the US, even though Iceland was pretty much the US's punching bag – the shot tally something absurd like 33 shots to one – the final scoreline was 0–0. Thora was like a comic-book hero, punching, leaping, sprawling, sidekicking balls away – and we, her college teammates, watched on with pride.

When college ended, she did what we all did: began preparation for a new life. It didn't matter if she was, as we frequently told her, the best keeper in the world. She immediately landed a job as Iceland's CFO of DHL, the international shipping company – not exactly a tiny post. Then it was off to Brussels, Belgium, to work as a project manager for Deutsche Bank. But four years into the world of finance, she realized that post-business-hour football and periodic national team games weren't enough. She missed playing. So, when she got an offer in 2009 to play in Norway for Kolbotn, she took it. A desk job, a career in finance – she figured that would be there when she retired.

She played for seven more years. After being named the Norwegian League's Player of the Year, she moved over to Malmö/Rosengård, the best team in Sweden and maybe the world. Here she was named Goalkeeper of the Year in 2012 and 2013. All this was good and she was happy. But she was also, she admits, bored. She didn't want to just be a soccer player. So after practice, she pursued her Master's in sustainable development leadership. In 2014, as a 33-year-old, she retired this time for real. She got hired by Iceland's Central Bank as project manager; she is in charge of implementing a new payment system for the entire country. She likes "being nerdy on her computer with Excel." And she likes having constantly changing projects: "It's similar to a really long season. Lots of ups and downs, slow periods and hectic periods. I love that rhythm. You're always preparing for the peak." And as the one in charge of leading a team, her entire soccer experience feels relevant. "I learned as much from the bad coaches as the good ones. I make sure my employees are heard, that they feel like I trust them. I give them responsibility; I never doubt their work … unless there is a problem. And I make sure they know that if we fail, I'll be the one who takes responsibility."

Then the work day ends – and there is no practice, no workout to get in. "I seriously can't believe it that after work I can just go do whatever I want." She goes home. On the wall of her living room, there's a painting by Tolli, one of Iceland's most famous artists. The Icelandic Football Federation gave it to her when she earned her 100th cap for the national team. She sits across from it, puts her feet up, and drinks a glass of wine.

• • •

RACHEL BUEHLER VAN HOLLEBEKE was destined for medicine. As a seven-year-old, she would sit on the floor with her heart-surgeon father and watch footage of open-heart surgeries, mesmerized by the magical beating organ filling the TV screen. As a high school student, she tore her right ACL; then on her very first day after being cleared to run again, she tore her left ACL. Her surgeon did more than just mend her ligaments and reassure her that her soccer career was not over; he also picked up on her unusual level of interest in the minutiae of the surgeries. He took her under his wing and let the high schooler sit in on a few of his surgeries. She watched as he put people back together – reassembling knees, mending ligaments – and she was fascinated. "It's like carpentry work but with really little, sophisticated tools – your body has these levers," she gushes. "They're not gentle with your body – chiseling and drilling away at things, [it's] so weird and interesting."

At Stanford University, on a full soccer scholarship, she majored in human biology. She got some call-ups to the US national team but in 2007 she didn't make the final World Cup roster. So, she went into full medical mode: prepping for the Medical College Admission Test (MCAT), taking a biology class, writing application essays. Then, unexpectedly, there was a coaching change and she was back in with the team. There was no way she was passing that up. She took the medical show on the road with her. Every second of free time at national camp, she studied for the MCAT, prepping for physics. Abby Wambach would swing by her bus seat, take over her flash cards, and quiz her with the enthusiasm of someone playing at school. In July, she took the MCAT. A week later, she flew to Beijing for the Olympics where she won a gold medal.

When the medical school acceptance letters rolled in, she deferred – she wasn't stopping soccer now. But all the time she played professionally, for the next six years – two with San Francisco's FC Gold Pride, one with the Boston Breakers and three with the Portland Thorns – she shadowed the team doctors, "just to stay in it, to make sure it was still what I wanted to do."

In 2015 she announced her retirement and penned a letter: "If you've ever watched me during the national anthem, I take it very seriously and sing with all my heart. Wearing the red, white, and blue for over 100 games is the greatest honor of my life and playing in two Olympics has been the highlight of my career. I will never forget the feeling of standing on the podium, gold medal around my neck." But now, she wrote, she was going to medical school. She flung herself into one passion for 25 years and now she was ready to fling herself into the other. In her send-off game with the Thorns, hundreds of fans in the North End of the Portland stadium dressed in scrubs.

After she finished her first year at the University of San Diego, she posted a picture on her Instagram, standing in front of the medical building – "One year down!" Her fans posted comments, things like, "You Buehldozed it!" One fan, Tamara Hamilton, wrote a longer message; she explained that following a Thorns game, she was having a discussion with some of the girls who played for her daughter's club:

> I always like to talk to them about hard work, hopes, dreams, what they want to be ... Several of them mentioned they wanted to be a doctor and talked about you and that you were not only their favorite player, but how you'd played and then gone on to medical school and they were pretty impressed that maybe they too could have both someday ...

• • •

ERIN REGAN IS in the firehouse when the call comes in: a man has gotten his arm caught in the huge, heated rolling pins of a t-shirt press machine. It takes 45 minutes to disassemble the machine, and when they're done his arm looks cartoonish, pancake flat, like Wiley the Coyote after he is run over by a train. He's in incredible pain and will eventually lose the arm. As the medics put one arm in a sling and attach an IV to the other, and Erin is about to leave, he says, "Can I ask you one more thing?"

"Sure," she says. "Anything."

"Do you think you could scratch my nose?"

This is a day in the life of a firefighter for the LA County Fire Department. It's a life that involves simple acts of helping – like nose scratching, cat fetching, and car unlocking – as well as more extreme duties, like her main role wielding chainsaws on the roofs of burning buildings, when she has to be mindful of supporting beams while cutting through shingles to provide an outlet for billowing smoke.

In another life, she was a professional soccer player, a goal-keeper for WUSA's Washington Freedom. She was backup, second string, "bottom of the totem pole" in her words. But one day at the beginning of the season, the starting keeper Siri Mullinix was out with an injury, which meant that Erin, a 22-year-old nobody fresh out of college, was going to be Mia Hamm and Abby Wambach's last line of defense. She denied every shot and after the game, as she was standing at the Gatorade machine, Mia Hamm came up to her. *Mia Hamm* said, "You played well."

"I will remember that for the rest of my life," says Regan.

At the end of the season, the league folded. The league commissioners encouraged players to continue to play in the local semi-pro league in the hope that the league would eventually return, but Regan knew that was it for her. She wasn't going to hang around, keeping her fingers crossed that a league might one day come back so that she might make a roster. "It was a weird spot to be in. It was super cool to have gotten that far – it was what I'd always wanted to do ... but it wasn't going the way I planned. So, I thought, maybe I've got to give up on this."

It took exactly one day at a desk job, working as an insurance claim adjuster, before she thought, *This isn't going to work. I cannot die here at this cubicle.* After the stakes and pressure of being in goal, she could not just sit still in a desk chair. It felt a whole lot like settling. While one part of her brain did her job, the rest of her started growing a new dream. She came from a police family – her grandmother was the first woman in her department and carried a gun in her handbag. Putting yourself in the line of fire was appealing to her; it may be in her blood, may be what she loved so much about being a keeper, occupying the point on the field where you are the only one who can make a difference. A realization dawned on her as she filled out insurance forms at her desk. She likes dire situations. "All my life I wanted to be a hero," she says. "I wanted to be counted on."

Three years later, she is an LA County firefighter. Of the 4,000 firefighters in the county, 38 are women. She helps create a program called Girls' Fire Camp in which 50 girls aged 14–18 shadow Regan and her colleagues. It's not an attempt to recruit them – it's just an exercise in possibility. Because when she was a kid, being a firefighter was nowhere on her radar, and she wants to make sure that for these girls, it is. She also helps launch a program called Women's Fire Prep Academy, an eight-week program with classes twice a week that targets high school graduates. More than 100 women show up.

A youth coach once told her that an athlete who makes it to the top of the game has a duty to coach – to give back to the game that has given you so much. Regan has not stayed in soccer, but she has very much absorbed this lesson: she wants to do for this next generation what Mia Hamm and her cohort did for her, expanded her notion of what was possible. In the camps and academies, she stands in the middle of dozens of teenaged girls as they take turns trying on the 50 pounds of gear. They pull on the fireproof jacket, the pants that banana peel open at the bottom, and the heavy yellow fire boots, and they walk thoughtfully around the fire station, considering, imagining, trying this life on for size.

• • •

IN THAT SAME interview with Gary Smith, the one in which he describes the way life is often whittled down for elite athletes, he distinguishes Muhammad Ali from other athletes:

It felt like he was [boxing] to help the world. And, so, he had a much larger motivation in a way than people who were just on a singular quest for their own betterment or riches. What's been lost to a large degree is that sports is a vehicle through which you grow as an entire person. When it becomes an end in itself, imagination gets quashed.

However, for the stalwarts of the women's leagues, the players who stick around and stay in the game long after their teammates have left, soccer is in no way "an end in itself"; they are not just looking for money or personal glory. They're playing to leave the game better than they found it. It's a work in progress, a scene they are still fighting to create. Rebecca Moros – who has played in three different leagues, on two different continents and for nine different teams in eleven years – is one of the older players in the league at 31. She's upfront about the difficulty of the lifestyle: every year it gets harder to uproot herself, to live out of a suitcase, to keep pressing. But her hope is "to be remembered for more than just how little we make." She will play for as long as she can and, when her career ends, she'll stay in the game – because she wants this league to be the beginning, instead of yet another end.

Rose City 'til I Die

IN 2014, CERTAIN members of the Rose City Riveters – the supporters group for the Portland Thorns – sometimes fretted about Alex Morgan. They worried that she didn't feel loved. Across the United States, she is probably *the* most loved player – by twelve-year-old girls and their parents, by the entire male gender – but that, in some ways, made Morgan a poor fit for the city of Portland. Because Portland, as everyone knows, is the city of weirdos and beardos and lesbians and so on. They love the offbeat, the underappreciated. They *are* the offbeat, the underappreciated. And Alex Morgan, well, she isn't that. But that doesn't mean they didn't love her! They did!

In Portland, she didn't play her best soccer, suffering a string of injuries. And the Riveters worried that her "failure to thrive" was, in some deeply subliminal way, their fault – maybe they didn't nurture her properly, maybe she didn't feel fully embraced. No one knew if she actually felt this way, but once one Riveter floated the idea, the rest were horrified by the possibility. The next game they created a bed-sheet-sized banner in her honor: MOREGON emblazoned in giant letters over the Oregon map. In times of injury, the banner still hung; they just sewed on three-foot Band-Aids, a symbolic "Get Well Soon." (Band-Aids are surprisingly difficult artwork to get right – it took several tries before they succeeded in making the nude ovals resemble anything like a Band-Aid ... red polka dots turn out to be the answer.)

The MOREGON banner, the Band-Aids: it's their way of

saying, *We are with you.* Those four words – we are with you – are the essence of the Rose City Riveters, of the Thorns, of the entire city of Portland.

• • •

THE PORTLAND THORNS is the Promised Land of women's soccer: while the most well-established women's leagues all over the world only average an attendance of around 1,000 fans a game, a whopping 17,000 fans routinely come out to Thorns games. Back in September 2015, I wrote about this phenomenon for *Howler Magazine.* The piece was in part an homage to Portland goalkeeper Nadine Angerer, set to retire at the end of the season, and it also investigated the question everyone was asking (and is still asking now): *How do they do it?*

There are the most straightforward explanations: one, unlike many women's teams, their stadium, located in the center of a city, is easy to get to. Two, operated by the same organization that runs the men's team, the Timbers, they benefit from existing infrastructure and support. And three, Portland is a soccer city – thanks in part to the legendary coach Clive Charles and his iconic University of Portland teams. A large trove of fans were already in place. But I wrote about this scene from almost 1,000 miles away, and the bird's eye view made me hungry for the street level one. Every person I spoke with about Portland said something, well, *cool,* and the more I found out, the more I wanted to know. Pretty soon it became clear that I needed to get myself to Portland. I wanted to drink the KoolAid, or rather to smell the roses, bathe in the rosewater, etc. So a year after I wrote the piece, with my husband, three-month-old baby boy, and three-year-old son in tow, I headed to Portland to see it for myself; my plan was to go deep within the utopia of women's soccer, root around, and discover the secret to everlasting women's footballing happiness.

• • •

ACCORDING TO ONE saying, happiness is precisely what Portland is founded on: *San Francisco and Seattle were founded by settlers looking for gold*, goes the oft-repeated proverb, *while Portland was founded by those looking for happiness*. And right away, from my first step into the streets, I am indeed happy. The whole city is zestful and sure of itself. We rent a loft on 23rd Street above Marine Layer, a clothing store that sells "absurdly soft t-shirts." Behind the store there is not a park but a "parklette." Two buildings down is Salt and Straw, an ice cream shop with flavors like "almond brittle with salted ganache." Standing at the window of our loft, we can smell baking waffle cones (happiness in a smell) and hear buskers playing banjo. Further up the street, there is an "artisanal popcorn store," as well as something called Tender Loving Empire, which is both a record label and a storefront selling the wares of local artists. There are leather mason jar handles, earrings in the shape of honeycomb and paper airplanes, tarot cards that actually give cocktail recipes, pillows designed for easy tooth fairy access, and tiny glass jars intended for raindrop collecting: *Genuine Portland Rain/Curative powers/Extracted from the purest Oregon Clouds. Good for man and beast*, reads the label. The further we wander, the more magical the city feels – through Washington Park's 10,000 roses and meandering trails, back down to the city sidewalks and the legendary Powell's Books, where I sit with my son and read a book about a bear and a boy who love to explore. On a chair designed for a child, I feel outsized happiness.

• • •

THAT NIGHT AS the sky turns pink, the hunt for football answers begins. Books, as it happens, are my entry point because there happens to be a Portland soccer supporters' book club. It has a witty name: Booked! (On the club's bookmark, a referee flashes a red card.) And maybe because I am a fellow lover of books and football, Todd Diskin, the social chair of Booked!, helps me navigate his city, one of several football spirit guides during our stay. Todd – a tall fellow with crinkly eyes and cinnamon facial scruff, who is both Timbers Army and Riveter – picks us up in his Subaru and takes us to the southeast side of town. Todd, we learn as we drive, also runs The Children's Book Bank, a nonprofit that collects and delivers books to kids who might not otherwise have access to them. (His old job was equally noble, equally only-in-Portland sounding: he helped teenagers implement city policy and programs they designed and thought up themselves.) As we drive, he points out cool things: the cider breweries, the barbeque joints, the big school chimney around which people picnic, watching the swifts (these are birds, apparently) roost before continuing their southern migration. And then we arrive at Bazi's, the unofficial bar of the Riveters, and what may be, as one article declares, the only women's-soccer dedicated bar in the world.[49]

Walking in through the cranked-up garage door, you see jerseys mounted on the wall and a chalkboard listing 30-odd beers on tap. The Thorns 2013 NWSL Championship banner, signed by the team, hangs from the main rafter. The kid-friendly Belgian-style pub opened a week before the 2011 Women's World Cup and they've stayed aligned with the women's game ever since. Three-hundred-plus fans spilled through the outdoor beer garden for the 2015 WC semi-final – some of the Thorns themselves came here to watch. Run with trademark Portland gusto, bar owner Hilda hosts events ranging from the previous weekend's human foosball game, to Todd's book drives. For major women's international matches, they'll open at crazy times and serve breakfast. A Guatemalan whose father was a professional referee, Hilda is herself a soccer-lover and Thorns fan. For Thorns away games, she holds Game Watches. Only six NWSL games are televised each year – the league unable to land a more substantial TV contract for the leagues in their first four seasons. But at the little pub on 32nd Avenue, when Hilda broadcasts the internet feed on the projector, fan upon fan streams through the door. Here, at a bar that will one day go down in the annals of women's soccer history, as my baby-wearing husband chases my three-year-old as he darts through the crowd, I meet the folks who helped dream up this whole thing, this wild city of Thorns.

• • •

MO ATKINSON, NOW an eighteen-year-old with purple hair, may be square one. Back in 2012, she was a sandy blonde thirteen-year-old with pink cheeks and a shy smile. Her father Paul was a Timbers season-ticket holder and a member of their supporters group, the Timbers Army. When they heard Portland was getting a women's team, for Mo, it was just logical: we will do for the women the same thing we do for the men – a supporter's group, chants, giant billowing banners, smoke buckets, the whole shebang. Owner Merritt Paulson announced that the team would be named the Thorns, in keeping with Portland's nickname, Rose City; not long after that, the Atkinsons took a road trip. They spent four hours brainstorming, among other things, scarf and motto ideas – a process she continued the next day at school, doodling roses, stems, thorns, and ideas on the back of her math homework. She chewed on rose metaphors until she lit upon that line from *Romeo and Juliet*: "A rose by any other name would smell as sweet." Now she felt like she had something because those four words, "by any other name," captured what she felt, what she was sure everyone else would feel: no matter the name on the front of the jersey – Timbers or Thorns – we will support you.

Paul posted his daughter's scarf design on Facebook, which led to hundreds of responses, which led to 40 or 50 people sitting in his English Craftsman house in Irvington, a historical neighborhood in northeastern Portland. People filled the living room, the dining room and spilled into the kitchen and the nook beyond. There was thirteen-year-old Mo, there were fathers, there were 40- to 50-year-old women who had seen two other leagues fold. The buzz and energy was palpable, everyone ready to be part of a great beginning, to take the women's game where it had never gone before.

What, then, should the supporters call themselves? "Rose Guardian" was floated, but there's another group in town called the Royal Rosarians – a charity that runs the Rose Parade and performs ceremonial rose plantings. There was some concern that the name similarity would ruffle their feathers. (Hurting rose-tenders' feelings strikes me as a distinctly Portland problem.) "Briar Patch" was another idea that triggered initial excitement – but, wait, those Br'er Rabbit books are undoubtedly racist. "Red Tide" was a favorite; the brainstormers stood in the living room with their arms folded, whispering period jokes, delighting in quip after quip: *Super plus support! She flies with her own wings!*

And then someone said, "Rosie. What about Rosie the Riveter?" That iconic emblem representing the women who worked in the shipyards and factories during WWII. I imagine the room going silent as everyone engaged in their own private visions of Rosie the Riveter: red bandana tied in a knot around her hair, rolled up denim sleeves, flexed bicep, fierce face. *The Riveters*. They liked that it's tough – not silly, not girly. And Portland has a history of female laborers during WWII (they were ship welders, not riveters, but it's close). It would be exceedingly cool to pay homage to these heroes of the past while supporting the heroes of today. Plus, Rosie was a symbol of female economic muscle, so, with two leagues of women unable to sustain themselves, this image is a rallying call, a reminder of the slogan accompanying the original 1943 J. Howard Miller artwork: *We Can Do It!*

Name in place, then began creation, hammering out committees and traditions. How to give Timbers traditions a Thorns twist? *Instead of handing goal scorers a slice of log, we will hand out roses! Instead of the iconic tree trunk spewing green smoke, let that smoke billow red!* Who's in charge of what? They divvied out responsibilities: *You have set design experience – good, you help with the rigging. You're good with a jingle, enjoy a tune? You come up with the chants. Play the trumpet? Fantastic, we need another horn. Introverted? Fine, you paint!* Folks dispersed into different pockets of the house, everyone tinkering, thinking, creating, and working toward the same goal: filling a 20,000 capacity stadium not just with bodies but with color and sound, song and dance, flavor and art.

• • •

ART IS THE element that most captivates me. Because I hadn't really thought of a stadium as a place for art. (Sure, football is its own kind of art, but I'm referring to traditional, visual-image-with-emotional-impact-and-cultural-message kind of art.) I had never heard of the term "tifo." Originating from the Italian word for fanatic, *tifosi*, a tifo display is a kind of stadium performance art – a choreographed show of smoke and flags that surround the unfurling of a colossal, 40-odd-foot by 60-odd-foot banner created by the fans. (The word "banner" feels insufficient, too pedestrian to describe these sweeping, beautiful, and pointed paintings.) Tifo displays have been around for decades in Europe and South America, and have been embraced in the US by men's Major League Soccer (MLS) teams – but outside of Portland, Oregon, it's likely that no tifo display has ever honored a women's team.

On August 4, 2013, during the Thorns final home game of

their first season, the Riveters unveiled their first tifo. Thorns players looked on at the billboard-sized art and saw, beneath the giant yellow caption SUPERHEROES, their own image, drawn in bodysuits and capes, hovering over the city of Portland. For the season finale the following year, in 2014, the Riveters channeled famous artists for their tifo display: the main banner featured a Picasso bouquet of flowers, inscribed with his words: *TODO LO QUE PUEDAS IMAGINAR ES REAL*. (Everything you can imagine is real.) This message was flanked by 22 pieces of pastiche art, portraits of each player. *Nude Descending a Staircase* by Duchamp for Cristine Sinclair, a Warhol-style portrait for Allie Long, *Girl with a Pearl Earring* by Vermeer for Alex Morgan, and da Vinci's *Mona Lisa* for Mana Shim.

That incredible array of artwork was the first tifo display I had ever come across. I encountered it while writing a story during the 2015 World Cup on the fledgling NWSL. I stared at the photos of 17,109 fans and the re-imagined masterpieces, and my eyes kept going back to those words: *Todo lo que puedas imaginar es real*. Everything you can imagine is real. These words have so much power because – until Portland – this has never been true. Right before I graduated from college, the first women's pro league folded in 2003. And then in 2012 the second one did too. In the third iteration of the league, the NWSL, the 2016 starting salary is $7,200. Only six of the season's 103 games are televised. Some stadiums aren't stadiums; they're just fields with a set of bleachers. Some crowds are so small you can isolate individual shouts, individual sets of hands clapping. Your average citizen doesn't know the league exists. Beyond that one-month shimmer of time that is the women's World Cup, nobody cares about women's soccer. Everything we had imagined – everything we dreamt up as kids – had pretty much turned out *not* to be real.

So imagine what it's like to be a player – to walk through the tunnel at Providence Park and be hit by the wall of sound. To see a city on their feet, helicopter-waving football scarves above their heads. It must be profoundly disorienting to stand there in the center of the field – roar in your ears – as a note on a giant stretch of sailcloth – written to you, for you, in honor of you – appears in the sky and tells you, "Everything you can imagine is real."

I wanted to know *who* exactly is making it real, who is responsible for those magnificent billowing things? Who are the people that spend hours tinkering over words and ideas, sketching out designs, on their knees with a paintbrush, bringing to life everything they could imagine? At Bazi's, I sputter out these questions to Todd. With a tilt of his head, he indicates that I should follow, then leads me to a back table, around which three people stand. "I believe this is who you are looking for," he says with a sweep of his hand.

• • •

AT NOON THE following day, I get dropped off in front of a tan house with a rainbow flag hanging over the porch on the north side of Portland. As instructed, I open the back gate and head to the garage, otherwise known as "The Honeycomb Hideout." (The name comes from the 1970s cereal commercials that featured a ramshackle kids-only fort.) Ducking beneath the garage door, I enter a world of paint-filled cottage cheese containers and coffee cups. There are bundles of PVC pipes, folded sheets and sailcloth, rolls of masking tape, tongue depressors, and a crate filled with vinyl records. On the back wall of the garage, across from a projector, there are traces and remnants of old designs from where the paint has bled through the sheets – words and lines interlocking on top of each other like a street map.

Pottering about the edges of the garage is Holly. Maybe 45 years old, she has short hair currently streaked with stray white paint, retro eyeglasses, and a quiet, friendly-squirrel-like manner. She's got art school in her background and according to the others, she's the one who can turn everyone's hare-brained ideas into something that actually looks good. Her wife Lexi – a short woman with short black curly hair that is almost always under some kind of hat – drifts in and out of the scene, coffee mug in hand. In the center of the garage, on his elbows and knees, sponge brush in hand, is John – a 40-something-year-old with a canvas hat, a long brown ponytail, eyeglasses, flannel shirt, jeans and hiking boots. Something about him – whether the ponytail, the affinity for words, or the brooding-but-excited aura – gives off a distinct feeling of David Foster Wallace. Three or four days a week he walks the mile and half from his place to Holly and Lexi's, ready to paint, ready to plan.

I sit on an overturned pickle bucket, listening. A sea of lingo flies by me – supporters' terminology, geographical references, and allusions to memes, old children's books, cult movies, and Twitter and Instagram conversations – words they assume I understand which I can't quite bring myself to admit that I do not. I secretly jot down terms to look up later:

> *Cascadia* (unique coastal bioregion that defines the Pacific Northwest of the United States and Canada);
> *two-sticks* (smaller handheld signs attached to, well, two sticks);
> *Klingon* (a language used in *Star Trek*).

Holly is in the process of cataloguing the "rail banners" – banners of various sizes that are slung over the wall surrounding the field. One banner shows a refined gentleman reading the newspaper. With enthusiasm, they explain: at an away game, Chicago fans had chanted, "We all hate Allie Long, we all hate Allie Long." Which the

Riveters found appalling. Now, historically (a word used partly in jest, considering the league is still in its infancy), the Thorns fans have been the ones with the "bad boy" reputation. They may or may not have chanted "Fuck You, Se-at-tle" during that first season – a chant that stirred up an indignant outrage on the Seattle internet forums. "You shouldn't use foul language!" one mom typed. "Think of the children!" wrote another. That last one was the comment the Riveters found the most amusing. Their "Think of the Children" scarf is still one of the more popular designs. In other words, the Riveters weren't an ounce apologetic. They had no interest in toning things down. Because *that* – the notion of toning it down for a women's game – is what the Riveters found offensive.

So yes, they use profanity. And yes, they occasionally jeer a player ("Hope Solo loves Nickelback" comes to mind). But they are, John and Holly maintain, ultimately tasteful, and the chants directed at Allie were not. "There was nothing subtle or wry about them, they were just *mean*," complains John as he sits up on his knees, gesturing with his sponge brush. So, they explain, they decided to respond, to issue a coy banner-rebuke. They would make it clear that in Portland they are above that kind of behavior. To do this, they excitedly went "full-blown hoity-toity." They assemble clip art of top hat, eyeglasses, and moustache to give off the impression of both an old English chap and a Portland hipster. A newspaper in hand – pinky finger raised in the manner of a proper gentleman drinking tea – he observes the headline CHICAGO JEERS ALLIE LONG. His thoughts float above him: *Good Gracious … Ruffians*.

"The raised pinky was my favorite," says Holly. "I thought we should keep it going, put the pinky into everything." I too dig the pinky – in that raised finger, you can see the level of thought that goes into each of these.

There is a four-foot-high pile of banners in the garage and that's nowhere near all of them – some of them were lost along the way, some repainted, some given to the players, some hung up at Uno Mas and other Thorns haunts around town. One of their goals for this season is to honor every player, and it can't just be anything. It has to be clever. For Kat Reynolds, they made a sign featuring the Reynolds brand aluminum foil box (sharp teeth emphasized) and the text *Foiled!* – but John wasn't happy with it because she had probably, definitely, heard that one before. It wasn't *original* enough, he felt.

The sign they made for Allie Long was cheekier: after she finally, finally broke into the national team roster and made the Olympic team, they created a banner that indicated she took THE LOOOOONG WAY, interlocking Olympic Rings acting as the O's, with small thorns adorning the red Olympic ring. (They made one other sign in her honor, because they couldn't help themselves: WE KNEW IT ALL-IE LONG.)

For Meghan Klingenberg, they called upon the Klingons, the brutal, war-like alien race from the *Star Trek* series. They painted the Klingon emblem and a message inscribed entirely in the Klingon language. ("Because she seems a touch nerdy and we thought she'd be down for something like that," they explain.)

For Tobin Heath, they went with a candy theme – a Heath bar sign for one game, a Toblerone sign later on – and not just because her name so obviously lends itself to candy bar references, but also because she seems to be one of those flexible Michael-Jordan-like athletes, constructed out of malleable, nougat-like substances.

For defender Emily Menges, they go with Steinbeck: OF MICE AND MENGES. Holly replicated the cover of the first edition, a pastoral, green hilly scene with oak trees – but instead of two migrant farmers in the center of the dirt path, there were two female silhouettes playing soccer. And this wasn't just because "Menges" sounds like "Men" – it was also because in an interview Menges mentioned that she was working on a book, and her tone was sort of self-effacing, shy, which made John suspect that this would not be a "paint-by-number soccer book" or one detailing "how her particular mindset could benefit you too." John's hunch was that she was aiming to write a *real* book, one that "tried to get to the bottom of why the world feels like it does." So they honored that admirable literary goal by bestowing her with Steinbeck, literary giant.

And these aren't even the big, section-spanning tifos. The colossal tifo banners are created in a warehouse downtown large enough to accommodate their size. For those, it's not just three or four brains chewing on designs and wordplay. A whole committee battles it out, argues over which image will catch and resonate and mean the most to the players and their fans. The final game is always the tifo finale. It's got to be the crème de la crème. Last season was tricky because the Thorns were pretty much out of playoff contention. There was nothing on the line. And how do you make a good tifo display for that? Hours were spent agonizing, and then they got it: let's not hide from the fact that the game doesn't matter – let's embrace it. "*Let's Dance*" read the main banner. Like, ok, no hope of the playoffs? Well then, let's dance. Let's just enjoy ourselves anyway. "Belles of the Ball" another sign read.

And you can't talk about this tifo without talking about Richard, whom Holly describes as their "resident mad scientist." "Richard got it in his head that come hell or high water, he was going to make a giant spinning disco ball – it would hang and *spin* from the rafters, sunlight pinging from the square mirror tiles!" relays John. Working with a weather balloon and sheets of mylar, Richard spent hours creating a magnificent twelve-foot disco ball. He carried it inside the stadium for the test run. But it was windy outside. A giant, fairly heavy ball hovering over heads on a windy day – the front office vetoed it. "Poor Richard, he looked like a kid whose ice cream dropped off the cone when the stadium guy said no," says John. The ball wound up crumpled in the corner of the garage.

For a second, we are quiet, as if engaging in a moment of silence out of respect for Richard's loss. I mull over their commitment of time and thought – their many, many hours in the garage. I wonder specifically about John's fandom. Holly and Lexi, who are also long-time members of the Timbers Army, as well as females who support other females, make sense to me. But John's a bit more mysterious. He had not been a member of the Timbers Army – he'd only been to the occasional game. He wasn't a soccer player. He spent most of his time in libraries. So I float the questions I've been wondering, questions I worry sound vaguely insulting, "Why are you here? Why are you doing this?"

John props himself up on his knees and considers his answer, paintbrush now idle. "I've had the thought before that that sort of need for the team and league to succeed is part of the draw for me, the wayward straight male sports fan. There are zillions of sports teams people can choose to pick up and follow. But when you get right down to it, most of them really aren't all that special. You just kind of decide to think of them that way," he says.

"With a women's soccer team though, there is a need ... you can feel it radiating off everyone around you. It is actually important that your team wins. Even if that importance that you are picking up on has less to do with the sporting event than it does with some other lifelong struggle for which you haven't really been a frontline fighter, you feel it. You don't usually get that with Major League Baseball Team 'X.'"

Though he feels that importance, he also recognizes a distance between himself and some of the other Riveters. The Riveters' inner sanctum, he notes, can give off a gruff, intimidating impression. Wizened pirates with gimlet-eyes. "They seem older, unorthodox, kind of battle-scarred by life in a way that makes them seem less than friendly on first blush," says John. Later, in a Facebook chat with me, he'll describe a two-minute conversation he had with another male Riveter, a father. They rode in a truck, hauling stuff three blocks to the stadium, "both of us trying to get to the bottom of why, sometimes, we felt such ... intensity? anger? rudeness? We don't know exactly what it is – just *vapor* coming off of some of the old crocodiles of the Riveters. We basically decided that there is, on some level that we will probably never be able to fully appreciate [because of our gender], a thirst for the success of the team and league that comes right out of their very being."

And as for the banners, the signs, the hours spent tinkering with ideas, his thinking is basically: you have to do something with your free time, why not do this? Why not make beautiful things? Holly, Lexi, and John stay mum about tomorrow's design, as well as the design that will be the season finale. After hours and hours of deliberation, arguing, and painting, both tifos are freshly finished and currently drying on the floor of the warehouse. I'm not allowed to see them. They are top secret. Like everyone else, I'll just have to wait and see.

• • •

I WAKE UP EARLY the following morning: game day. On my first steps out of the apartment, to pick up coffee and doughnuts, I see a man in a Thorns jersey walking his dog, morning paper tucked beneath his arm. By this point I guess I should no longer be surprised by the city's enthusiasm for professional women's soccer, but all morning I still feel relatively stunned; as we traverse the surrounding neighborhoods with the double stroller, fans in red Thorns apparel are everywhere. Many are families like my own who have traveled to the city from somewhere else just for the chance to experience a Thorns game.

At noon, I leave the boys asleep three across the bed and head out two and half hours before kickoff. I'm on my way to meet Kristen, a quiet orchestrator behind the scenes and a wealth of NWSL and Thorns knowledge, whom I originally met at Bazi's. I walk through the Goose Hollow neighborhood, along gorgeous old streets with fallen apples on the sidewalks, until I arrive at Fanladen, though I'm not entirely sure what Fanladen is. The building in front of me is nondescript. I'm not sure at first that I have the right place, but then a salt-and-pepper-haired cyclist pulls up beside me. His t-shirt says: *Rated R for Riveter – Some material may not be suitable for children. Strong Language, Civic Pride, and Unwavering Support Throughout.* I notice a one-foot square of AstroTurf lining the bottom of his bicycle basket. I point and inquire. "Well, they were auctioning off the old stadium turf, raising funds for charity," he says. "And I thought, *OK, I think I'd like a piece of that.*"

I follow said cyclist, Huck, through the door and into what Kristen explains is Portland soccer headquarters, also known as the Land of 107: the nonprofit at the core of all things Timbers and Thorns. It takes its name from stadium section 107, where the core supporters sit. Here, at a giant table – a fifteen-foot slab of varnished blond wood with live edges that looks like it has been freshly "timbered" from a nearby forest – the board members gather round. (It is actually the third such table – the first two having collapsed and cracked under the pounding fists and zealotry of the board members.) On top of the table, fans en route to the game begin dropping off boxes of tampons, condoms, and diapers – goods that will later be donated to women's shelters around town. "I haven't bought any of this stuff in twenty years," one mustachioed man retorts as he dumps condoms and diapers onto the table. Small weekly drives and large, season-long efforts are very much a part of 107. Next week it will be school supplies

– calculators and colored pencils – for homeless kids in the area. Local organizations are brought into the sweep of Timbers-Thorns support. Operation Pitch Invasion, focused on creating safe places to play for neighborhoods in need, is one of the larger-scale efforts they're proudest of. There's a cheery, brisk, roll-up-your-sleeves-and-get-'er-done vibe to all of this. It's all nonchalant – like this is just an inherent part of what it means to be a supporter.

I sit with Kristen at the tree-table, drinking a can of local cider, chucked at me by a guy named Patch. Patch mans the merchandise table (proceeds supporting the Riveters) and runs the ticket swap, where season ticket holders unable to attend the match make their tickets available. Demand for Thorns games just keeps growing: while the upper seating sections of the stadium were initially tarped, the tarps have now come down. More than one family comes in to try to buy tickets, but today they're all sold out. Families head closer to the stadium to scalp them there. We see more and more people heading to the stadium and as game time gets closer, we join the stream. My husband and the boys will sit up with Todd's family – Todd's daughters able to help occupy my three-year-old – while I will head with Kristen to the illustrious 107 section itself, to take in the Riveters up close.

• • •

THE BOOKED! READING CLUB had read *Among the Thugs*, Bill Buford's famous account of English football hooligans, a few months before my Portland trip – one set of football devotees reading about a very different set of football devotees. As a college English instructor, I often teach a chapter, which includes the following:

> I felt weightless. I felt nothing would happen to me. I felt
> that anything might happen to me. I was looking straight

ahead, running, trying to keep up, and things were occur-
ring along the dark peripheries of my vision: there would
be a bright light and then darkness again and the sound,
constantly, of something else breaking, and of movement,
of objects being thrown and of people falling.[50]

And as I head to the stadium, one person in a steady stream,
that's what I'm thinking about – palpable energies, currents, erup-
tions. Buford's crowd can turn nasty, capable of bad behavior they
wouldn't exhibit on their own: "The crowd is not us. It never is."
Whereas in Portland, the irrepressible, live-wire feel tips in a different direction. There's nothing dark or sneering or violent about
the atmosphere in a Thorns' game – and part of me wants to
discard any thought of comparing Manchester hooligans to Rose
City Riveters – but there *is* very much the sense of something
alive, growing, rebellious. A Thorns game is more than football.
It's people fighting to keep something alive, fighting for rights.

Earlier this season, following the mass-killing at an Orlando
gay night club, the Riveters unfurled two enormous rainbow banners, along with the double entendre: UNDEFEATED. It spoke to
the Thorns' record; it spoke to the resilience of the LBGT community; and it spoke to a determination for the future – *We will
not be defeated.*

• • •

THE PORTLAND STADIUM, now called Providence Park, is a storied,
majestic ground. In a Timbers.com/*Howler Magazine* collaboration
piece, journalist Noah Davis chronicles the history: what began
as a 200-acre vegetable patch tended by Portland's Chinese population became a stadium with a 3,000-seat grandstand in 1926.
In its nearly 100-year history, this ground has hosted American
football, minor and major league baseball, newly elected President

Taft, the Royal-Rosarian-led Rose Festival and Floral Parade, a ski jump, open air concerts including one by a 45-piece orchestra, dog racing, Elvis, and Pelé's final game. In 2009 it became a soccer stadium and soccer alone. Beautifully renovated, with dark green trim and advertiser signs made out of slices of tree trunk, the current stadium preserved as much as it could – including the original grandstand. Old-timers can sit in the same seats they sat in as kids. Davis writes:

> [I]t's old school, with the type of eclectic charm that only comes after decades of use and dozens and dozens of different types of events. It's all part of the charisma that seeps out of the old growth wood and the ancient concourses that have been updated for the new era.[51]

The new era gives as much weight to the Thorns as it does the Timbers – as evidenced by the Thorns emblem right up beside the Timbers on the front of the stadium. We walk through the concourse and toward 107, where I intend to sit in the thick of it, but as I approach, I see fans jumping in time with their chants and generally frolicking from row to row, and my introverted side grabs hold of the wheel. I sit down on the fringe of this section and take in the visual feast: a rose tucked into a cowboy hat; a teenager with magenta bangs and a red and white polka-dot vintage dress; a toddler with pink noise-cancellation headphones and a red and black bandana tied around her neck cowboy-style. More than one set of fathers and daughters tilt their heads toward one another as they point at the players taking pregame shots at goal. Female couples drape their arms around each other's increasingly sunburned shoulders. The *Willamette Weekly* (which features the Thorns on the cover the week I am there and runs not one but two feature articles on the team) describes the scene as "mother-daughter bonding events, date nights for 30-somethings, and the city's largest outdoor LGBTQ cocktail party – a scene so thirsty that Providence Park has effectively replaced the lesbian bar in Portland's nightlife scene." Many love connections and more than one proposal have happened in these stands; Riveter Lora Brown made a scarf that read "Will you marry me?" and held it up toward her now wife. Twice that Kristen can remember, fans have chanted, "She said yes, She said yes."

As the eye pans the stadium: scarves. The neck décor of football fans since the early 1900s. Long before the days of replica jerseys, when British fans attended winter football games in black pea coats and top hats, a colored scarf showed your team support. The American soccer leagues – which happen in spring and summer months – can prompt some eye-rolling from the Europeans. But Portland don't care! It is one more medium in which to invest creativity – fans make small-batch editions themselves. SOCCER IS BORING reads one scarf. WE'VE GOT TOBIN FREAKING HEATH reads another. GET STUCK IN is a favorite. And there's the original scarf – the Shakespeare homage Mo sketched out on her math homework: BY ANY OTHER NAME.

The away team introduction begins, the Boston player pics flashing on the big board. Fans stand and shake their car keys, a metallic, tinkling shimmer of sound floating over the stadium, accompanying the cheerful jab: "Go home, ya bums/Go home, ya bums." It is the day's first chant. "Oh when the Thorns go marching in" and "Root for our girls in red/Until we're fucking dead" are two other staples that are accompanied by drums, trumpets, and trombones. Other chants are player-specific, spinoffs of pop songs: last season they sang not "Come on Eileen" but "Come on Nadine, you make saves for our team." This season, for Amandine Henry, they try out a song based on the first two lines of "La Marseilles": *"Allons, Amandine Hen-ry/La jour de gloire est arrivé!"*

One game, late in the second half, when Tobin headed to the corner flag to kill the clock by doing "Tobin-type-stuff" (which is pretty much an official Portland term, a reference to her sensational footwork) – several fans started heartily doo-wopping the Harlem Globetrotter theme song, "Sweet Georgia Brown."

Orchestrating most of the sound are the *capos*. The term originates from the Latin word *caput*, meaning "head." In the mafia, a capo is someone who heads a crew of soldiers. There's also a musical term – *da capo al fine* – meaning "go back to the beginning and play to the end." Both the mafia and the musical meanings seem relevant to the football variety of capo: the one who runs their swath of the stadium, the conductor who leads the crowd in song from beginning of the game to the end.

The most recognizable capo is Sunday White. (Even her name is glorious. It sounds – as a *Prost Amerika* Portland soccer writer put it – like it could be an "ice cream flavor or a brand of cocaine."[52]) Initially, in those first Thorns games, she donned her best Rosie the Riveter outfit – bandana and mechanic's jumpsuit. And people loved it. But Sunday's not the type to keep one outfit for too long. The first time I talked with her on the phone she was in the process of getting her hair done, mulling over which color to make her Mohawk that week. It often goes green for Timbers games, red for Thorns – but even that's too confining. One game it's combed and gelled into three purple spikes, and the next it's just a little dollop of hair on top of her head, like a peak on a meringue pie. At a Timbers game in 2014, after gay marriage became legal, she married her wife right here in these stands, surrounded by fans holding sunflowers and rainbow football scarves. She wore an elaborate, princess-style sage green wedding dress and rolled that Mohawk into platinum blonde, Marilyn Monroe curls gone vertical. The day I am there the Mohawk, she says, "just isn't working"; she bats it from side to side, shrugs and grins.

The one thing that is constant is her giant Jolly Roger pirate flag – a skull and crossed swords but with one of the swords subbed out for a rose ("Jolly Rosie" people call it). Already a Timbers capo, there was no question in Sunday's mind that she'd do the same for the Thorns, a team that "hit a little closer to home." She had watched two leagues fold and she wasn't going to watch another, not if she could help it. Grinning with her tongue out, tongue ring on full display, she charges up and down the stands – one tattooed arm waving that hulking pirate flag, the other holding her beer, while she leads the North End in song.

A few feet away is the other most recognizable capo: Hailey, a beauty queen, former Miss Preteen Oregon. Her first Thorns game she was thirteen years old. She sat there wondering why it was so quiet, why it didn't sound like a Timbers game. So she stood up on her seat and started shouting, trying to get everybody else to shout too. And certain Riveters saw that and thought, *Make that kid a capo*. And they did. Now the kid is eighteen, about to head off to college. She is beaming and unnervingly confident, but that wasn't always the case, no matter how many beauty crowns she has under her belt. Hailing from a suburb called Happy Valley, she didn't fit in – a black teenager who dreamt of the stage, of singing and acting. People would say, "Who do you think you are, Tyra Banks?" But then she fell in with Sunday and the other capos, a thirteen-year-old hanging out with 30- and 40-year-olds. They teased her affectionately, poking at her perfect elocution, her maturity. "Oh here comes Ms. Thirteen-going-on-thirty," Sunday would say. Once, when Hailey wore her hair in a faux hawk, Sunday did a *say-whaat* with her neck and put her hand on her hip. "*OH*, Beauty Queen's got her Mohawk on. You trying to be like me?" she chided. No, not quite – but watching Sunday be magnificently, unapologetically herself has taught Hailey how to be that way too.

These teenagers on the cusp of adulthood – they get to me. I keep spotting them in the crowd. It's the life-phase most burned into my memory. Beyond your standard insecurities and failures of instinct, what I remember most is earnestness: how hard I tried and how much I wanted. Looking around now, I keep recognizing that earnestness on the faces of fifteen-year-olds. Girls with their knees curled up to their chests, fingernails in their teeth as they study the field. When the games start, each will carefully watch the player occupying her position, maybe choosing a favorite, someone who reminds her of herself and her own strengths, be that tackling (Menges), orchestrating (Long), or foot-fireworks (Heath). It's a process I remember. There was no women's pro league, and there was no soccer channel, but I recorded every women's national team game, saved the *People*, *Newsweek*, and *Sports Illustrated* articles from the 1999 World Cup, read the auto-biographies three and four times. Mia was my favorite – and not because she was the fastest, the most famous, or scored the most goals, but because she was, like me, shy. Knowing that *Mia Hamm* was shy made me feel okay about being shy too.

All over the stadium, I imagine these little inner narrators, processing, processing, processing. And it's not just girls taking in the sweep of the game. In the discourse around women's sports, young girls tend to be the focus – *Let's give the little girls someone to look up to* – which is of course important, but Portland has also figured out the next step: little boys can want to be like them too. We don't have to categorically divide our role models along gender lines: brother and sister can share hero worship for both Tobin Heath and Diego Valeri; for both Timber and Thorn.

• • •

AFTER THE NATIONAL anthem, out comes the tifo display: a spinoff of a retro Captain Crunch ad. START YOUR DAY OUT

RIGHT is bannered across the top, accompanied by a panorama of a full breakfast table spread: a morning paper with the September 4, 2016 date and the headline SPORTS RACE CLOSE; a coffee cup with the latte foam swirled into the shape of a rose; a big bowl of Captain Crunch, next to the cereal box – CRUNCH TIME emblazoned across the top, above a mustached Captain depicted in all his blue-hatted, fist-waiving glory. (And the Captain bears more than a passing resemblance to Thorns coach Mark Parsons.) Last but not least sits a piece of toast with the Boston Breakers emblem etched into the bread, the message clear: *Breakers, you are toast*.

Then the banner comes down – all that effort for one minute, one flutter of magic, then gone forever. A week from now, Riveters will be in the warehouse painting over it. But even that speaks to the ephemeral nature of what we are all watching: in football, seasons end, players retire, leagues fold; who you see on the field today may not be there tomorrow.

Today on the pitch – you've got Australian star Hayley Raso, Icelandic star Dagný Brynjarsdottir, Danish star Nadia Nadim, six-time World Player of the Year nominee Canadian Christine Sinclair, World Cup Silver Ball winner Amandine Henry of France, and five US national team players – more than any other pro team in the country. It is without question the most star-studded women's team in the world.

It's important to note that the fans don't come because the stars are there; the stars come because the fans are there. I keep thinking of the film *Field of Dreams* and its takeaway message: "If you build it, they will come." I'd venture to say that every professional player in every women's league in every country has heard of the Portland Thorns. Playing in the stadium is on each player's things-to-do-before-I-die list; it's the pie in the sky. Some athletes can have a reputation as being *too cool*, like all their life force and passion got funneled into the game, leaving none to show out-wardly. But that's not the case when it comes to Portland: players pretty much shout their love back to the rafters. Post-game, they charge into the stands to find out who made which sign and do leaping bear hugs. In the 2013 NWSL Championship in Rochester, New York, when Sinclair scored in the 90th minute, she ran to the group of 40 Riveters who had traveled to New York and saluted them. Karina LeBlanc, the 2013 goalkeeper, once shaved a rose in the side of her head. Sinead Farrelly wore the Riveters ban-dana Rosie-style in her team pic – a clear shout out to the fans. "Every time they flash her picture up on that big screen, when I see her wearing that wrap on her head – that's not a team-issued bandana, that is a fan bandana – every time I see it, it gets me," says Sunday.

Sinead Farrelly and Mana Shim have talked about how they feed off the city – their pregame ritual was to drive around down-town Portland with the windows open, blaring music and singing as loud as they could. When Shim posted on Twitter that she really needed to learn how to cook, a local fan responded – *I'll teach you* – and for the next six months, Mana headed to that fan's house for a weekly cooking lesson. (This kind of fan–player interaction isn't exclusive to the women's side either: star Timbers center mid-fielder Diego Valeri emailed Todd about his book drive and said he would like to come with his daughter and help clean the used, donated books. "What was I going to say, no?" said Todd.) After games, Thorns players wander across the street to Uno Mas, a taco bar where they eat alongside fans and engage in candid post-game discussion. It has nothing to do with being courteous or gracious – they hang out with the fans because they *want* to, because they respect the fans as much as the fans respect the players. "They're a rad group of humans and I feel them," Shim said matter-of-factly in an interview with Christian Brookes for *Beats and Rhymes FC*.[53]

After her first season, Shim got traded to Houston. But after a time-out in the draft, she was mysteriously un-traded – and the rumor amongst the Riveters is that she refused to go – that she would rather retire than play anywhere but Portland.

That's not to say that Portland is the only NWSL team with devoted fans. Each team has a tribe behind them. New Jersey's Sky Blue FC has the worst attendance record in the league. But Sky Blue FC has Cloud 9, its own supporters group. Sure, in 2013, there were only five members – but they're proud to tell you that their ranks have now grown to about 60. They've developed a ride share scheme to pull in more fans. They've got a scarf or two – JERSEY PROUD and JERSEY GIRLS AIN'T NUTHING TA MESS WIT. And they too have unscripted, special interactions with their players. Ahead of one away game, injured Kim DeCesare posted on Twitter that she was looking to hitch a ride to the game. Cloud 9 member Erin Corbin saw that and did a double take. *Is she serious?* She thought, *Heck, we're a supporters group – no way we're going to leave a man behind*. She tweeted back "I can pick you up in fifteen minutes" and before you knew it, DeCesare was in a Prius with three Cloud 9 members, on a four-hour car ride, player and fan side by side.

Cloud 9 has never done a tifo display but they've been playing around with cloud and sky puns and they've got ideas. They are optimistic about the future; they figure "the sky is the limit."

• • •

IN PROVIDENCE PARK, the whistle blows, the game begins, and the whole stadium fixes their attention on the field. They are not the kind of fans who just "stand up and clap whenever you touch the ball," Christine Sinclair wants to make clear. "They know when they're witnessing a good play and when they're not." The Thorns lost their last match, in Seattle, 2–1. It was their first post-Olympics game, their first game with all of their international superstars back in action. It didn't work. They are all the take-your-team-on-your-back type and now they've got to make room for each other. Today they have figured it out, and the football is flowing. The players seem to channel the crowd – rhythm, art, and expression spilling onto the field. It's a shower of goals: the first three are all simple and effortless and matter-of-fact. The fourth goal is more highlight-reel-worthy – Allie Long tears out of the back, slipping the ball through a trio of defenders to Nadim, who jags left at the perfect moment. The small ball causes a stadium-wide air intake as we wait to see if the beautiful build-up will evaporate or produce. Nadim does a little boomerang touch around the approaching keeper and puts it home. Red smoke billows in the North End. The fifth goal comes in the 90th minute – Long chipping the ball to Heath, who streaks down the sideline, beats her defender and rips off a shot that the keeper deflects, a deflection that Nadim pounces on, launching herself over her defender, airborne, hungry, unstoppable.

David Foster Wallace once wrote that "TV tennis is to live tennis pretty much as video porn is to the felt reality of human love." It's an apt analogy for the difference between watching a Thorns game over the internet feed and watching a game in person. Just the fact that you've got to watch the game via the internet – because it is not being televised – already makes it feel small. And then, of course, the camera makes the field and the players still smaller. Not to mention that in the first season of the NWSL, there was no league standard for broadcasting and some teams' coverage looked like they had just stuck someone's uncle up in the announcer's box with a camcorder. Portland coverage is more professional – three cameras and an announcer – but an animated voice and multiple camera angles still can't capture the crackle of the live experience.

With cider-soaked thoughts, I look out upon Portland, where a beauty queen screams alongside a mohawked lesbian waving a giant pirate flag. Where thirteen-year-olds borrow from Shakespeare and sketch out daydreams in the margins of math tests, daydreams that become social progress. Where little boys rock Mana Shim jerseys and shave NADINE into the sides of their heads and where my three-year-old son shouts, "Go, Allie Long!" Where every play is met with a stadium-wide current, a reaction. Where 50-year-old librarians cycle around the city with chunks of Astroturf in their basket, where people will spend hours on their hands and knees painting pastiche art – because, why not? Portland is a place where everyone offers up everything, whatever it is they've got to offer – because it feels good to do so, because they've all decided to care. And then, at last, at game time, you honor the players on the field as well as the entire city behind them, and you chant the words you believe: *Rose City 'til I Die, Rose City 'til I Die.*

• • •

THAT FINAL TIFO display? At first, John had only been on the hunt for an idea for a rail banner to honor center-midfielder Amandine Henry. So he played around with anything French. "Holly put the kibosh on my idea of a sexy-eyed Pepe LePew looking over his shoulder saying, *'Ello Amandine* ... as being too creepy-stalker-like," he jokes. Eventually his mental wanderings landed on a classic French children's book, *The Little Prince* by Antoine de Saint-Exupéry. He reread the story and one line "bellowed, howled" at him – the line destined to become the final tifo for the 2016 season.

On September 11, 2016, it unfurls – a white backdrop dotted with small yellow stars and a slightly larger, four-pointed red star – the asteroid from both the Thorns crest as well as the Portland flag. One red rose grows out of the side of the moon, and the Little Prince, red and black Thorns scarf tied around his neck, hovers over it. The inscription reads: "It is the time you have wasted for your rose that makes your rose so important."

Then comes the moment when the Riveters watch the players take it in. For each Thorn and each Western New York Flash player it strikes a chord – because they've all spent much of their lives trying, "wasting" time, perhaps, playing in the shadows, just because they love it, and not for any other reason.

The words also speak to every fan in the stand who has devoted time to something they found beautiful, whether that be a football team, a giant weather balloon disco ball, or an actual rose garden. And to John, who observes the billowing tifo that was once just a tiny bloom of an idea, the words also speak of the league itself: "Perhaps it's not right to keep looking at the league as something that people will only come to love after its grown a little more," says John. "There's already a whole mess of us who care about the league – it's already important."

Notes

1. "WikiLeaks cables: Russian government 'using mafia for its dirty work,'" Luke Harding, the *Guardian*, December 1, 2010, theguardian.com/world/2010/dec/01/wikileaks-cable-spain-russian-mafia

2. "Russian nightmares: four former WPS players leave clubs abroad following contract disputes," Jeff Kassouf, *The Equalizer*, May 2, 2012, equalizersoccer.com/2012/05/02/russian-nightmares-four-former-wps-players-leave-clubs-abroad-following-contract-disputes

3. You can find more stories from Dani on her blog, *A Bottle from a Glass*, including "Another sauna story": dfoxhoven.blogspot.com/2012/03/another-sauna-story.html

4. For a profile of Nadezhda Bosikova in Russian, see this piece from 2005 in *Komsomolskaya Pravda*: vrn.kp.ru/daily/23453/165473. For a brief English-language profile, see *Alchetron*: alchetron.com/Nadezhda-Bosikova-189099-W

5. Valery Meshkov at *Women Soccer* interviewed Elena Danilova, July 11, 2006 [Russian], womenfootball.ru/news/2006/0035.html

6. Fara Williams: "I had football. A lot of homeless girls have nothing," Donald McRae, the *Guardian*, November 17, 2013, theguardian.com/football/2014/nov/17/fara-williams-football-homeless

7. For more information on the Street Football Association, check out homelessworldcup.org/team/england

8. "Women's World Cup 2015: England success a 'tipping point,'" Alistair Magowan, *BBC Sport*, June 29, 2015, bbc.com/sport/football/33308114

9. "France: fear, faith and football," James Gheerbrant, *BBC News*, June 8, 2016, bbc.co.uk/news/resources/idt-be776de1-2c1e-4dac-a67b-86571d02d67d

10. "Aimeacute Jacquet: We respect England, says Frenchman who conquered the world," Brian Viner, the *Independent*, June 11, 2004, independent.co.uk/sport/football/international/aimeacute-jacquet-we-respect-england-says-frenchman-who-conquered-the-world-731896.html

11. "Louisa Necib: 'Je n'ai pas choisi le foot,'" *Le Progres*, July 18, 2013 [French], leprogres.fr/football/2013/07/18/je-n-ai-pas-choisi-le-foot

12. "Playmaker Necib on glory trail," Kevin Ashby, *UEFA.com*, July 31, 2005, uefa.com/womensunder19/news/newsid=322294.html

13. Feature on Zinedine Zidane: "ZZ top," Andrew Hussey, the *Observer*, April 4, 2004, theguardian.com/football/2004/apr/04/sport.features

14. "Louisa Necib: Je n'ai pas choisi le foot," *Le Progres*, July 18, 2013 [French], leprogres.fr/football/2013/07/18/je-n-ai-pas-choisi-le-foot

15. "World Cup 2010: Raymond Domenech rounds on France's player revolution," David Hytner, the *Guardian*, June 21, 2010, theguardian.com/football/2010/jun/21/world-cup-2010-raymond-domenech-france

16. "Divided we stand: How France's race quota row ignites old tensions," Paul Gittings, *CNN*, May 20, 2011, edition.cnn.com/2011/SPORT/football/05/20/football.france.racism.history/

17. "French women take on US 'Goliath' at World Cup," Joseph Bamat, *France 24*, July 14, 2011, france24.com/en/20110713-usa-france-world-cup-womens-football-semi-finals-bussaglia-wambach-nike/

18. "Louisa Necib, Algeria, and the redemption of French football," *Soccer Politics*, Duke, July 1, 2011, sites.duke.edu/soccerpolitics/2011/07/01/louisa-necib-algeria-and-the-redemption-of-french-football

19. Gheerbrant, "France: fear, faith and football."

20. "Women's World Cup: flamboyant Nigeria plays exuberantly," Jere Longman, *The New York Times*, June 23, 1999, nytimes.com/1999/06/23/sports/women-s-world-cup-flamboyant-nigeria-plays-exuberantly.html

21. Copyright © 2012 by Wendell Berry, from *New Collected Poems*. Reprinted by permission of Counterpoint.

22. "Vanderbilt Divinity School Faculty Handbook," Vanderbilt Divinity School, Spring 2013, divinity.vanderbilt.edu/portal/Faculty%20Handbook%202013%20-%20FINAL%20with%20app1.pdf. See page 1 for the School's commitments and pages 6–7 for discussion of sexual and gender identity.

23. "Flourishing league kicks off again," *BBC Sport*, March 17, 2001, news.bbc.co.uk/sport2/hi/football/africa/1226860.stm

24. According to figures published in 2012: "Nigerians living in poverty rise to nearly 61%," *BBC News*, February 13, 2012, bbc.com/news/world-africa-17015873

25. Watch the pre-game dance here: "Josephine Chuckwunonye No 15 against

Korea," kazeem lawal, *YouTube*, posted January 10, 2014 (of a match on August, 19 2012), youtu.be/MTR1M-K0y5I

26. Ahead of the 2015 World Cup, I first looked at the succession of Brazilian magicians for *The Atlantic*. That piece was used as a starting point for this chapter.

27. "Considerado amador, futebol feminine leva atletas da seleção a jogar sem salário," Clara Velasco and Heloisa Brenha, *Folha de S.Paulo*, June 19, 2013 [Portuguese], www1.folha.uol.com.br/treinamento/2013/06/ 1294068-considerado-amador-futebol-feminino-leva-atletas-da-selecao -a-jogar-sem-salario.shtml

28. "Futsaia: A Historia das Sereias Da Vila o Time Feminino do Santos FC 2011," Futebol Feminino, *YouTube*, December 26, 2011 [Portuguese], youtube.com/watch?v=xBu8VoxugWw

29. "Entrevista Coletiva Érika e Laor – Anuncio do Fim do Futebol Feminino do Santos em 2012," SereiasdaVila, *YouTube*, January 3, 2012 [Portuguese], youtube.com/watch?v=wKiE2xfWU1Q

30. There is a video clip of the catwalk: "Jogadoras do Santos Desfilam de Biquinis," SereiasdaVila, *YouTube*, April 15, 2011 [Portuguese], youtube .com/watch?v=Wiz7GMrxALE

31. "Les joueuses de l'équipe de France de football se mettent à nu," *La Depeche*, February 20, 2013 [French, mainly a photo-story], ladepeche.fr/ diaporama/joueuses-equipe-france-football-mettent-nu/trio.html

32. "The Marta experiment: can WPS be the world's best league without the world's best player?," Jeff Kassouf, *The Equalizer*, November 18, 2010, equalizersoccer.com/2010/11/18/the-marta-experiment-can-wps -be-the-world%E2%80%99s-best-league-without-the-world%E2 %80%99s-best-player

33. "Tyresö won't finish season; players released immediately," Jeff Kassouf, *The Equalizer*, June 5, 2014, equalizersoccer.com/2014/06/05/tyreso -folds-players-free-agents-wont-play-2014-damallsvenskan/

34. "Women's soccer in Brazil," Carmen Rial, *ReVista: Harvard Review of Latin America*, Spring 2012, revista.drclas.harvard.edu/book/womens -soccer-brazil

35. "A 'vicious circle' plaguing the world of women's soccer in Brazil," Stephanie Nolen, *The Globe and Mail*, June 14, 2015, theglobeandmail .com/sports/soccer/a-vicious-circle-plagues-the-world-of-womens -soccer-in-brazil/article24954058

36. "Kobe Bryant welcomes Marta to town," Grahame L. Jones, *Los Angeles*

Times, March 6, 2009, articles.latimes.com/2009/mar/06/sports/sp
-kobe-marta-soccer6

37. Information about US Youth Soccer: usyouthsoccer.org/media_kit/
ataglance

38. "In Brazil, girls are still left on the sidelines in soccer," Patricia Kowsmann,
the *Wall Street Journal*, June 18, 2014, wsj.com/articles/in-brazil-girls-are
-still-left-on-the-sidelines-in-soccer-1403131630

39. During the 2015 World Cup, I looked at the mothers on the US soccer
team for *The Atlantic*; a few passages from that piece were reincorporated
here.

40. "Can Women Come Back Faster After Pregnancy?" Kelly O'Mara, *Competitor
.com*, May 10, 2014, running.competitor.com/2013/10/training/can
-women-come-back-faster-after-pregnancy_61244

41. "Jessica Mcdonald's Long, Unusual Journey to NWSL Stardom," Richard
Farley, *FouFourTwo*, October 7, 2016, fourfourtwo.com/us/features/jessica
-mcdonald-nwsl-championship-star-journey-wny-flash

42. "Interview: Arsenal's Katie Chapman talks about the Olympics, England, and
motherhood," *Bea*, August 14, 2012, beamagazine.wordpress.com/2012/
08/14/interview-arsenals-katie-chapman-talks-about-the-olympics
-england-and-motherhood

43. You can see the *Good Morning Britain* interview with Katie Chapman
and her family here: "Katie Chapman on Laura Bassett's Own Goal,"
Good Morning Britain, *YouTube*, August 5, 2015, youtube.com/watch?v
=bSHSR2MS35s

44. "Fastest goal in women's football history: WFC Spartak Serbia," ŽFK
Spartak, *YouTube*, June 1, 2013, youtu.be/mI9hUYPlyxg

45. To see the party and the dance, go to: "Enganamouit Gaelle U
Narodnom Kolu," ŽFK Spartak, *YouTube*, June 10, 2013, youtube.com/
watch?v=NPMcRAhPLJ4

46. You can watch the game highlights at: "Highlights: Cameroon v. Ecuador –
FIFA Women's World Cup 2015," FIFATV, *YouTube*, June 8, 2015, youtube
.com/watch?v=CPdY_CchYH4

47. You can listen to the song at: "Anderson 'Gaelle Enganamouit' (clip officiel
prod by K-Johnson)," Johnson Fofie, *YouTube*, June 4, 2016, youtube
.com/watch?v=oZZa4TkTbNo

48. "The Daily goes one-on-one with Sports Illustrated's Gary Smith,"
Sports Business Daily, Issue 91, January 29, 2009, sportsbusinessdaily.
com/Daily/Issues/2009/01/Issue-91/Sports-Industrialists/THE-DAILY

-Goes-One-On-One-With-Sports-Illustrateds-Gary-Smith.aspx?hl=
gary%20Smith%20kavanagh&sc=0

49. "This might be the only bar in the world devoted to women's soccer," Kirsten Schlewitz, *Fusion TV*, May 7, 2015, tv.fusion.net/story/161382/ women-soccer-bar-bazi-portland

50. Bill Buford, *Among the Thugs*, Martin Secker & Warburg, 1991. The edition referenced was published by Arrow Books, 2011; page 92.

51. "Howler X Timbers | A Beloved Creation: At the heart of Soccer City, USA, historic Providence Park shines as a home for soccer," Noah Davis, *Timbers .com* and *Howler*, June 18, 2015, timbers.com/post/2015/06/18/howler -x-timbers-beloved-creation-heart-soccer-city-usa-historic-providence -park

52. "Portland profiles: Sunday White, taking a stand just by living her life," *ProstAmerika*, December 2, 2015, prostamerika.com/2015/12/02/portland -profiles-sunday-white-taking-a-stand/132009

53. "Meleana Shim interview: Home in the islands, pride and purpose in Portland – Thorns' kama'āina burning bright again," Christian Brookes, *Beats and Rhymes FC*, May 6, 2015, beatsandrhymesfc.com/meleana -shim-interview-home-in-the-islands-pride-and-purpose-in-portland -thorns-kamaaina-burning-bright-again

Acknowledgments

I feel enormous awe and gratitude for the incredible women who shared their stories and their time. I also want to thank the friends and family members who made this book possible: Thank you to Luke, for being a super-dad; a thoughtful, patient sounding-board; and a supportive, encouraging husband. Thank you to my incredible aunts, Marjo, Mary, and Beth, and my mom, for showering my boys with fun and love while I wrote. Thank you to Aaron Heifetz, Rebecca Moros, and Kim DeCesare for helping connect me to players around the world. Thank you to all those who read and weighed in – Alex Katona-Carroll, Gary Hawkins, Luke Howitt, John McNair Clarke, Holly Duthie, Karen Parr, Casey McCluskey Parker, and Shelly Marshall. Thank you to my editor, Kiera Jamison, for her careful attention and on-point instincts. Thank you to Leonardo Rodrigo Carvalho, for helping me with all things Brazilian. Thank you to my Portland football spirit-guides – including John, Holly, Todd Diskin, Kristen Gehrke, Lexi Stern, and Mo and Paul Atkinson – for showing me around your fine city. Thank you to my dad – for making me love to read. Thank you to my coach – for making me love to play. And thank you to my teachers – Tom Rankin, Christina Askounis, Donna Lisker, Tom Ferraro, William O'Rourke, and Valerie Sayers – for opening my whole world.

Image Credits

1. Allie Long, playing for the Portland Thorns
   © Corri Goates

2. Rail banner created by the Rose City Riveters in honor of Allie Long's Olympic journey
   Courtesy of the author

3. "Baby" (Asaya), Augustine, Njoya, and Dani, on the flight from preseason in Turkey to Russia, to begin their season playing for FC Voronezh
   Courtesy of Dani Foxhoven

4. Liverpool Homeless Football Club
   Courtesy of Becca Mushrow

5. Becca (second from right) and Emily (center) coaching with the Street Football Association
   Joana Freitas and the Street Football Association

6. Nadia Nadim, celebrating a goal for the Danish national team
   © Anders Kjærbye – fodboldbilleder.dk

7. The wedding ceremony of Heather and Kelsey; Heather's teammate and best friend, Ashleigh Gunning, to the couple's left
   © Ryan Green, 30 Miles West Photography

8. Alinco's niece and mother in front of the home Alinco built for them
   Courtesy of Christina Onye

9. Alinco (right) with her Nigerian teammates for the Washington Spirit, Ngozi Okobi (left) and Francisca Ordega (center)
   Courtesy of Josephine Chukwunonye

10. Marta playing for Santos FC in the Copa do Brasil 2009
    © Ueslei Marcelino/Agif/Gazeta Press

11. Melissa Barbieri, holding her daughter following an Adelaide match.
    © Adam Butler

12. Gaëlle, cooking dinner in Eskilstuna, Sweden
    Courtesy of Kim DeCesare

13. Gaëlle, wearing her traditional Cameroonian clothing
    Courtesy of Kim DeCesare

14. Erin Regan, former goalkeeper for the Washington Freedom, is one of 38 female firefighters among 4,000 firefighters with the County of Los Angeles Fire Department
    © Kate T. Parker

15. The tifo created for the Portland Thorns' 2016 season finale
    © Craig Mitchelldyer

16. Hailey, a capo, leading the supporters at a Portland Thorns game on June 7, 2014
    © Corri Goates